What is criticism?

What Is Criticism?

What Is Criticism?

Edited with an Introduction by

PAUL HERNADI

INDIANA UNIVERSITY PRESS
Bloomington

Manufactured in the United States of America

Library of Congress Cataloging in Publication Data
Main entry under title:

What is criticism?

Bibliography: p.
Includes index.
1. Criticism—Addresses, essays, lectures.
I. Hernadi, Paul, 1936-
PN85.W47 801'.95 80-8096
ISBN 0-253-37733-1 1 2 3 4 5 85 84 83 82 81

CONTENTS

Preface vii

Introduction: Criticism as Re-presentation, Evaluation, and Communication *Paul Hernadi* ix

1. WHY DEFINE CRITICISM AND HOW?

The Problem of the Problem of Criticism *Francis Sparshott* 3

The Logic of the Question "What Is Criticism?" *John M. Ellis* 15

Demonstration versus Persuasion: Two Models of Critical Activity *Stanley Fish* 30

Three Notions about Criticism *Morse Peckham* 38

Criticism, Pleasure, and Truth: A Typology of Critical Statements *Marie-Laure Ryan* 52

2. CRITICISM AS RE-PRESENTATION

What Can Structuralism Do for Us? *Susan Rubin Suleiman* 67

Critical Truth as Necessary Error *Wallace Martin* 83

Viva Voce: Criticism and the Teaching of Literature *Roger Shattuck* 96

Criticism, Indeterminacy, Irony *Geoffrey Hartman* 113

A Functional View of Criticism *Mario Valdés* 126

Literature and Hermeneutics *Hans Robert Jauss* 134

3. CRITICISM AS EVALUATION

The Name and Nature of Criticism *Monroe Beardsley* 151

Criticulture: Or, Why We Need at Least Three Criticisms at the Present Time *Wayne C. Booth* 162

Art without Critics and Critics without Readers *Mary Pratt* 177

The Social Relations of Criticism *Richard Ohmann* 189

A Search for Subjective Truth *Martin Esslin* 199

4. CRITICISM AS COMMUNICATION

Criticism and Its Institutional Situations *Herbert Lindenberger* 215

On Feminist Criticism *Catharine Stimpson* 230

Criticism as Transaction *Norman Holland* 242

On Whether Criticism Is Literature *Cary Nelson* 253

Criticism Is the (Dis)closure of Meaning *Michael McCanles* 268

Criticism as a Secondary Art *Murray Krieger* 280

Appendix: A Historical Perspective

Literary Criticism *René Wellek* 297

Suggestions for Further Reading 322

Index 325

PREFACE

As I was preparing the predecessor of this collection of essays for publication it became clear to me that most answers to the question raised in its title, "What is literature?" imply answers to a no less intriguing question, namely, "What is criticism?" The plan for a follow-up volume that should spell out those and some other implications quickly began to crystalize. But that plan could turn into the present reality only through the generous cooperation of twenty-three articulate critics.

I trust that most readers of *What Is Literature?* (Indiana University Press, 1978) will find the related inquiry into criticism no less illuminating. Coming from several countries and many different intellectual climates, the contributors to this volume represent an unusually broad spectrum of current critical opinion. As respected authors of well over a hundred books and several thousand articles about literature, they should be able to tell us a great deal about criticism as well. And it can be assumed that they still mean what their essays say: all contributions were expressly written, revised, or updated for this volume even if some contain previously published material.

Once again, I wish to acknowledge the University of Iowa's support: I have received congenial teaching and administrative assignments, ample research assistance, expert secretarial help, and adequate funds for correspondence and duplication. Particular thanks are due to Jeanne Bogle for prompt and careful typing and to Lisa Nicholas for reading proof and preparing the index. Daniel Campion showed extraordinary dedication and expertise as we were preparing the typescripts of two dozen authors for the printer.

INTRODUCTION

Criticism as Re-presentation, Evaluation, and Communication

Paul Hernadi

This collection of twenty-three responses to the question "What is criticism?" follows an earlier volume in which eighteen critics addressed another deceptively simple question "What is literature?"[1] Such basic queries usually signal widespread disagreement. Yet the ensuing essays should appeal to readers who prefer facing troublesome problems to giving up fundamental inquiries.

Part One titled "Why Define Criticism and How?" offers some arguments for and against attempting to say what criticism is, as well as ample illustration that the attempt can be made successfully; indeed, cogent arguments even against defining criticism will tell us a great deal about their not-to-be-defined subject matter. The next three groups of essays highlight criticism as re-presentation, evaluation, and communication. Without ignoring other aspects of writing about the occasions of one's reading experience, Part Two stresses understanding; Part Three, value; Part Four, the motives and rhetoric of the critic's discourse. Most instances of public criticism communicate, of course, a particular critic's perceptions and standards against the horizon of earlier communications of perceptions and standards. Hence a historical sketch of the major trends in the self-understanding of critics since the emergence of the modern term "criticism" seemed indicated and is provided in the Appendix.

The twenty-three contributions to the volume exemplify just about as many critical approaches. At the same time, most authors show sympathetic awareness of several alternatives to their own positions. Thus my grouping of the essays according to their major themes had to be somewhat Procrustean, and the following rapid survey of the book's contents is merely intended to serve for the reader's initial orientation amidst polyphonic arguments. The Introduction concludes with a brief statement of some of the views I have acquired or learned to trust in the course of editing the volume.

Part One opens on a polemical note. Speaking of "The Problem of the Problem of Criticism," Francis Sparshott acknowledges the existence of a number of distinct critical goals and practices, yet concludes that most reasons for defining criticism are bad reasons because they are potentially restrictive. It is against such a charge that the rest of the book generates various kinds of explicit or tacit defense. John M. Ellis considers "The Logic of the Question 'What Is Criticism?'" and proposes not a "definition" or a "statement of fact" but a "normative recommendation" to be validated by the particular needs of the moment: critics today should reject the "conceptual pyrotechniques" of their overly abstract or "narcissistic" colleagues and "let the text speak for itself, through close attention to *its* emphases." In "Demonstration versus Persuasion: Two Models of Critical Activity," Stanley Fish opts for the second model on the grounds that "prejudicial and perspectival perception is all there is, and the question is from which of a number of equally interested perspectives will the text be constituted." Presenting "Three Notions about Criticism," Morse Peckham first distinguishes "interpretational statements" and "judgments of competence" from "ascriptions of value" where value is ascribed not so much to texts as to the person who does the ascribing; next he argues that all criticism presupposes a distinction between action and role-governed performance as two aspects of human behavior; finally he attributes the "very unsatisfactory" present state of literary criticism to our quasi-religious, canonizing attitude toward literature and to the economic pressure forcing university and even college teachers to publish. In "Criticism, Pleasure, and Truth: A Typology of Critical Statements," Marie-Laure Ryan classifies utterances according to whether their primary motive is to prompt action, to provide information, or to yield pleasure, and subdivides informative critical discourse about pleasurable literary works into three categories with decreasingly rigorous truth conditions: descriptions (including summary and paraphrase but also linguistic analysis), interpretations (aiming at a work's fictive world, its message for the actual world, or its characteristics as a verbal entity), and judgments (which can be more or less sincere as well as more or less persuasive).

The essays in Part Two focus on combinable modes of a critic's re-presentation of literary works: structural analysis, theoretical synthesis, interpretive performance, hermeneutic exegesis, to name a few. Susan Suleiman's response to the question "What Can Structuralism Do for Us?" yields the recognition that "structuralism and hermeneutics are coming to be perceived as potential collaborators, each one providing the other with a dimension it lacks." Wallace Martin insists on the unavoidable deficiency of any conceptual framework; he views "Critical Truth as Necessary Error" but argues that even "unsatisfactory theory serves a positive function because without the articulation it creates contrary insights cannot be perceived." Roger Shattuck warns against both the "analytical dismantling of a work" and excessive theorizing; in "Viva Voce: Criticism and the Teaching of Literature" he recommends oral interpretation—the "actual reading aloud of a sizeable passage"—as the best way of demonstrably validating critical opinion. In "Criticism, Indeterminacy, Irony," Geoffrey Hartman distinguishes the critic's "suspensive discourse" from scholarly propaedeutics and "the positivity of applied teacherly interpretation"; the humanistic critic should realize that "to keep a poem in mind is to keep it there, not to resolve it into available meanings." Mario Valdés's "Functional

View of Criticism" demands that the critic help other readers to enter into intersubjective dialogue about their reading experience and to develop their self-awareness of being imaginative "coproducers" of an experienced world. In "Literature and Hermeneutics," Hans Robert Jauss joins Hans-Georg Gadamer in seeing the "understanding," "explication," and "application" of a text as three integral phases of a single hermeneutic process; he further argues that the initial aesthetic experience of "perceptual understanding" should lead through philological exegesis to the historically conscious reader's appropriation of his or her place within a tradition.

The essays in Part Three discuss some of the ways in which critics generate, suppress, present, disguise, and/or revise value judgments. Monroe C. Beardsley's view of "The Name and Nature of Criticism" prompts him to consider the "analytical appraisal" of esthetically desirable and undesirable features as the primary responsibility of literary critics. In "Criticulture: Or, Why We Need at Least Three Criticisms at the Present Time," Wayne Booth pleads for ethical and political criticism as well as for a "higher journalism" which can provide the general public with carefully reasoned judgments as to "what is good for souls and what is good for societies." Considering "Art without Critics and Critics without Readers," Mary Pratt deplores the contemporary gap between (mainly academic) criticism and (largely untutored) mass culture; she suggests to both camps that "the Incredible Hulk and Pantagruel, put in the same room, will not devour each other. They will simply compare notes." Richard Ohmann stresses "The Social Relations of Criticism" as he argues that "to posit standards is always to engage in ideological maneuver, to generalize the interests and values of one class or group and present them as the interests and values of all." Martin Esslin in turn sees criticism as "A Search for Subjective Truth" leading, through the "dialectic of opinions within a period and in historical progress," to the establishment of a temporarily valid literary canon: "If the poets are the unacknowledged legislators of the world, the critics are the electoral college that puts them into power."

The essays in Part Four examine the critic's discourse as personal response, communicative self-expression, textual transcoding, or the creation of works of a secondary art. Citing several instances in which "Criticism and Its Institutional Situations" are inextricably fused, Herbert Lindenberger observes that "every critical statement can be described as a response to certain pressures and demands the critic feels obliged to meet." Relatively recent responses to an enduring set of pressures and demands are discussed by Catharine Stimpson whose essay "On Feminist Criticism" surveys "not a corpus of work but a corps of workers." Viewing "Criticism as Transaction," Norman Holland discerns a "deliberate blending of the personal into the transpersonal" throughout the often simultaneous phases of having the experience of reading a text, of analyzing the experience of having that experience, of having the experience of analyzing *that* experience, and so forth. While dissatisfied with a concept of criticism as nonliterary discourse *about* literature, Cary Nelson stops short of answering the question "Whether Criticism Is Literature" in the affirmative; instead, he calls criticism a "special form of discourse simultaneously preoccupied with and distanced from its own literary status." Michael McCanles goes further in following Jacques Derrida and others when he describes all texts as "creatively metaphorizing"; in "Criticism Is the (Dis)closure of Meaning," he argues that no text dwells "at the top" of an absolute Newtonian space and that each should acknowledge "its own motion as it were relative to the motion of the text it interprets." Murray Krieger offers to guide us back to a less uncanny cultural universe, where critical satellites, brilliant as they may be, revolve around literary planets; discussing "Criticism as a Secondary Art," he points out that "the interpretive act assumes that the poem is of greater interest and is less self-explanatory than the criticism of it is."

The Appendix comprises an updated version of René Wellek's survey of post-Renaissance "Literary Criticism," first published in *The Dictionary of the History of Ideas* (1968). Like any other history, this survey represents a particular observer's view of the past. Yet most readers will agree with its concluding observation: "There appears to be a tug of war between the main trends—judicial, personal, scientific, historical—a tension which was still continuing unabated in the 1970s."

As products of the last year of that decade, the essays collected here strongly suggest that the same tension will animate the pertinent debates of the 1980s as well. What else can we predict for the immediate future? Rather than engage in elaborate soothsaying, I prefer to outline what I hope some of us will—but what I fear many of us will not—do in the years ahead.

1. *Write for larger audiences.* Advance of knowledge in any field entails the development and refinement of a relatively esoteric terminology. But the literary critic should try to remain close, or should at least occasionally return, to a style of thinking and writing that allows professional and nonprofessional readers to share their literary experience.

2. *Beware of excess in specializing as well as generalizing.* The critical re-presentation of a text, whether explicitly evaluative or not, cannot help but presuppose certain theoretical and historical generalizations. All histories and theories of literature in turn presuppose a great deal of more or less explicit description, analysis, interpretation, and evaluation of individual texts by individual readers. We should thus be suspicious of any discussion of a single text, group of texts, or literature at large if that discussion appears to neglect, or even claims to renounce, either the generalizing or the specializing thrust of human understanding.

3. *Pay attention to what authors say, what texts conceal, what readings disclose.* Critical understanding of literary works seems to me to rely on three axioms of interpretation: authors communicate; texts conceal; readings disclose. These axioms necessitate three kinds of hermeneutic endeavor: we should try to explicate what is said and how; we should try to explain what is concealed and why; and we should try to explore what is disclosed and through whom. For the first project, texts are communicative signals; for the second, informative symptoms; for the third, experienced disclosures fusing one horizon with

another. Needless to say, all explorations of disclosures, once formulated, await further explications as signals and further explanations as symptoms in the course of subsequent readings. This is why neither the hermeneutic circle of reciprocally illuminating textual parts and wholes, nor the hermeneutic shuttle oscillating between a particular text and a particular reader, is an adequate spatial metaphor for the ever increasing penetration of critical understanding. But the ongoing interaction of words and minds could well be described as a hermeneutic spiral: progress through repeated recourse to the reconstructive explication, deconstructive explanation, and participatory exploration of authorial signals, textual symptoms, and experienced disclosures.[2]

4. *Estimate rather than judge literary value.* Literature has served many different functions and has been found "good" or "bad" according to radically different types of standards. In view of this, the concepts of "judgment" and "evaluation" imply an unwarranted sense of finality. We should prefer to speak or at least to think of "appraisal" or "estimate"; after all, no one is entitled to the judge's robe in the grand jury investigations of all men's and women's values. While it is the duty and privilege of critics to cast their individual votes, they should chiefly act as expert witnesses who combine professional acumen with personal opinion about the case being considered. The more articulate their testimony, the more likely that it will promote the truth-finding endeavor of the Readers' Courts continually in session.[3]

5. *Promote the exchange of insights between different types of humanistic inquiry.* Literature is, among other things, communication, art, sign system, symbolic action, privately or publicly motivated concealment and disclosure of significant meanings. It can thus be studied from the varied points of view of rhetoric, esthetics, semiotics, speech act theory, psychology, sociology, hermeneutics, phenomenology, cultural anthropology, and a variety of other "disciplines" or "approaches" as well. Faced with such complexity, we should attempt to correlate several perspectives rather than privilege one and ignore all the others. In so doing, we might even

adopt the role of multilingual interpreters, so to speak, between users of different conceptual idioms. If critics and other humanists agree to exert this kind of mediatory effort, the edifice of the human sciences—that ambitious tower under permanent construction, deconstruction, reconstruction—may yet escape deserving the name of a second Babel.

NOTES

1. Paul Hernadi, ed., *What Is Literature?* (Bloomington: Indiana University Press, 1978).

2. I consider explication, explanation, and exploration three interactive phases of textual interpretation. The importance of each phase has been emphasized by eloquent current spokesmen who appeal or could appeal to influential precursors. Emilio Betti and E. D. Hirsch, following Friedrich Schleiermacher, favor what I call explication—the reconstruction of authorial meaning through "objective interpretation." The deconstructive explanation of texts as symptoms has been advocated for vastly different reasons by Karl Marx, Friedrich Nietzsche, and Sigmund Freud or, if you prefer *soufflé* to *Sauerbraten*, by Louis Althusser, Jacques Derrida, and Jacques Lacan and their respective disciples. Hans-Georg Gadamer's concept of the "fusion of horizons"—the reader's merging into a tradition from which alone the present meaning of past disclosures can emerge—draws upon a long tradition of its own with Wilhelm von Humboldt and Martin Heidegger as relatively recent dignitaries. Let me add that Ludwig Wittgenstein's model of language games, in which use determines meaning, and the pursuant approach to texts and utterances as speech acts offer closer parallels to Gadamer's and Paul Ricoeur's participatory hermeneutics of exploration than is generally supposed. (I hope to complete a less schematic comparative study of recent theories of interpretation and to provide a selective bibliography of pertinent statements in the foreseeable future.)

3. On more than one occasion, Northrop Frye has described evaluative criticism in terms far harsher than mine; cf. esp. his essay, "Contexts of Literary Evaluation," in *Yearbook of Comparative Criticism*, volume 2: *Problems of Literary Evaluation*, ed. Joseph Strelka (University Park and London: The Pennsylvania State University Press, 1969), p. 16: "When a critic interprets, he is talking about his poet; when he evaluates, he is talking about himself, or, at most, about himself as a representative of his age."

What Is Criticism?

1

Why Define Criticism and How?

The Problem of the Problem of Criticism

Francis Sparshott

1

If I meet an unfamiliar word (say, *himax*) and ask what a himax is, I may be appropriately answered by being shown a himax. If you show me a himax and I ask you what it is, I may be appropriately answered first by its name (himax, of course) and then by an account of the himax's place in the most appropriate classification and categorial scheme—most appropriate, that is, from the point of view of contemporary science, or social utility, or whatever you think is uppermost in the part himaxes play in people's lives, or whatever you conjecture to be my predominant interest and level of education. But if I ask what criticism is, what kind of answer would be appropriate? I may be presumed acquainted with the word and its application: all readers of this book must be familiar with both to the point of boredom. Is it then as if I were to ask of a piece of writing I showed you, "What's *this*?" It is hard to imagine any circumstances in which I would ask that, and perhaps harder to imagine any in which the answer "It's criticism" would be suitable. Perhaps I might ask the question in protest at an unusually irrelevant, irresponsible, unjust or bizarre review of something I had written, and your reply might be sardonic or (if you thought I was being silly or oversensitive) bracingly brusque; but such complex language games have little in common with finding out what a himax is. If I can read the piece of writing, I can see what it is because I can see what it says, and a piece of writing is what it says. My question makes sense only if there can be presumed to be some genre of writing to which the specimen before me must belong. But, although there might be civilizations in which that presumption holds, ours is not one of them, and to ask of such a specimen "What is this?" has no obvious point.

Although the question "What is this?," asked of any piece of writing, has no one inevitably clear point, the context might give it a point. Nor is a context always necessary: if I were asking about a verse stanza with a complex rhyme scheme you might conjecture, even without sustaining context, that I wanted to know the name (and rules if any) of the verse form. If I were asking about a piece of prose, the answer "criticism" or "a critique" might well be true, even if unlikely to tell me whatever it was I wanted to know. Does that possibility guarantee that there is a literary kind or genre called *criticism*, with its own rules and history? There certainly are histories of criticism, and criticism is presumably what histories of criticism are about. Roughly, a history of literary criticism (or of art criticism) consists of a description of all the kinds of things that have been written about books (or works of art) at various periods; accounts of how and why different standards of evaluation, different modes of description and choices of emphasis, different choices of books (or works of art) to write about, and different methods of interpretation have succeeded one another; some account of the media (such as newspaper articles, pamphlets, scholarly treatises) that have been preferred from time to time; and, most conspicuously, descriptions of the opinions and writings of those who have won and retained most fame by writing about books (or works of art) at various times. The history of literary criticism, in fact, is the history of all and only what has been written about literature, subject only to such principles of exclusion and emphasis as all historians share. No kind of writing about literature is excluded. Therefore, literary criticism is identical with writing about books. It really is almost as simple as that, and unless what I have written above is grossly misleading, any account that makes criticism out to be anything more complex or more restricted than that must itself be grossly misleading. As to why people should write about books, the obviously true answer is so simple it looks like a joke: anyone who reads a book is obviously somewhat interested in books, and writing about books caters to that interest. Some people want to know a little, some want to know a lot, some want to know all about them, and in the variety of their self-images different people like their interests to be represented as mundane, or exalted, or esoteric, or advanced. Writers have to make a living, and pander to all these tastes—and, being themselves as polymorphously perverted in their humanity as their clients are, do so in sincerity and good conscience.

The account of criticism we get from looking at histories of criticism, I said, is *almost* as simple as that. I put the restriction in because another kind of history of criticism can be written, in which the centers of interest are not the great critics but the great criticized. A history of what has been written about books is at the same time a history of how books have been read and received. But the complication this threatens to introduce seems harmless. That a book about a book that interests us may have a double interest calls for no more comment than that an ill-written biography of a great man may interest us no less than a well-written biography of a nonentity.

2

To ask "What is criticism?" makes no sense unless the word *criticism* stands for a single identifiable body of practice; to discuss what criticism is makes sense only if that body of practice is in some way problematic. A body of practice is problematic if it has no obvious purpose to define it, or if diverse "obvious purposes" are ascribed to it in such a way that one must choose between them, or if the purpose ascribed to it is at variance with the aims implicit in what is actually done—or something like that. It is far from clear that any of these conditions are fulfilled in the present case; and, if they are not, the reason for posing the question "What is criticism?" is the only problem that confronts us.

That the word *criticism* is not reserved to a single body of practice is sufficiently clear from René Wellek's essay on "The Term and Concept of Literary Criticism."[1] The term and its cognates have been and still are used in a variety of ways that are only loosely linked. Without retracing Wellek's steps, we may distinguish four such ways. An early use of the vocabulary pertains to *textual criticism*, the practice of establishing what the author of a literary (or other written) text actually wrote. That is a necessary task if literature is equated with those texts that a society has decided are to be preserved verbatim, and if earlier conditions of transmission have jeopardized that preservation. The text of Homer was the first to be seen to need this service, and it was probably in Homeric studies that the first critics got their name. Second, *critic* was at one time used as we use *connoisseur*, to mean a person expert in the stylistics of works of fine art and other objects of refined and recondite excellence. Third, *criticism* as an abbreviation for *literary criticism* is applied, as we have seen, to any sort of writing about literary texts, and as an abbreviation for *art criticism* is applied to any sort of writing about works of fine art.[2] And fourth, *criticism* is generally used to mean any commentary on how well or how badly things of any sort are done or made—with emphasis on how badly, because if something has been done properly there is no need to talk about it.[3]

The four uses of the word *criticism* clearly answer to four quite different concepts, and there is no prospect of reducing them to one. The sum of the four sets of practices they pick out would be uninterestingly heterogeneous, and their product a mere curiosity. No one of the four seems problematic in any interesting way. To get something to discuss, one would have to pick out some part of the total range and insist that it alone was really criticism, or that it alone was worthy of the title "criticism." But why would anyone want to do that? The only likely reason would be that the term *criticism* carried some prestige that one wished to reserve for a preferred candidate, or if there were some professional body of critics whose collective exercise of their business one wished to influence in some way. But the word *criticism* carries little prestige, and there is no such profession as criticism. There are indeed the trades of reviewing art and literature, and of teaching literature and "art appreciation," but no one seriously maintains that reviewing is a profession or that a professional teacher of literature is properly called a "critic." There are individuals who have won fame by writing about books and who are called "critics," but (as one would expect from the opening paragraphs of this essay) there is no one sort of thing they discuss in the books they write about and no common methodology they employ. It seems to follow that no general answer to the question "What is criticism?" can be given and none should be sought.

Perhaps if we lean on our four concepts we can make them converge. First, is there anything about literature and the fine arts that makes them especially suitable targets for evaluation, or for discourse apt to ground evaluation? There certainly is. If a work of literary or other art is to yield aesthetic satisfaction, to yield up its primary value in the act of looking or listening or reading, it must be worth looking at (or whatever); and what would make it worth looking at, if not that it was one of a kind, something special? But if it is something special, there is bound to be a problem as to what exactly it is, what has been done in which the artist might have succeeded or failed. At least until a work and its relation to other works have become familiar, divining what an artist has done will require special study and sensitivity: to be a critic (sense four) one will have to be a connoisseur (critic, sense two), and to make the fruits of this special study and sensitivity available will require a highly developed and specialized literary tact appropriate to writers about books and art (critics, sense three). Second, is there anything about literature that makes it more suitable than the other fine arts for critical exegesis? It is noteworthy that Plato's dialogues (*Ion, Protagoras,* and *Hippias Major* as well as *Republic*) contain examples and discussions of literary criticism in various modes, but neither they nor any earlier text in our western tradition does anything comparable for any of the other arts. One wonders whether that is a mere historical accident, or a reflection of Plato's own predominantly literary culture, or whether there may not be some reason for it. The obvious answers seem to be, first, that every good writer of criticism must know enough writing to criticize that, but may not know enough about music or painting; and that, after all, an author is saying something, and it is a common experience to wonder just what someone means by what he has said, so that literary works lend themselves immediately to exegetical criticism of a fairly elaborate sort (such as that satirized in the *Protagoras*) in a way that even paintings do not.[4] At this point, too, we may adduce the first of our senses of criticism, textual criticism: establishing the text of an author returns us to the original work itself as the restoration of a visual work can never really do, and this condition of perfect transmittability that generates textual criticism gives literary criticism an immediate point that art criticism generally lacks—the literary work can always be present at its discussion, as a visual work can seldom be. A musical work can also be summoned to immediate presence, given a satisfactory notation or tradition of performance, but in music nothing is shown, let alone said, so that exegesis becomes either highly esoteric or ludicrously anecdotal and irrelevant. There are thus three things about literature that make it the fairest game for criticism. Thirdly and lastly, we may ask: how much that is written about books as such (criticism, sense three) is, if not itself evaluative, apt to ground evaluation (criticism, sense four)? Here the blunt answer must be: all of it. A book as such is not a naturally given or found object, but something made or done, and all talk about things made or done is apt to ground evaluation because makings and doings are identified and defined by the purposes of their makers and doers and by the ways they fit into the purposive structures of other individuals and societies.

It follows from what we have said that the common practice of using the word *criticism* to mean everything that is written about books and yet supposing that criticism could have some further common character is less foolish than it looks. There seem in fact to be at least three possible problems that might arise in the further determination of what (literary) criticism is. First, is there any kind of discourse that might be confused with criticism but is not criticism—that seems to be about books but is not really, or is "about them" in what we might want to decide is the wrong way? Second, is there any kind of discourse about books that can be singled out as uniquely appropriate, so that everything else is improper criticism or pseudocriticism? And third, since a literary work is criticizable as something done or made, and criticism rests on establishing just what has been done or made, and the definitions of things made and done may involve the purposes of persons other than their makers, we may wonder whether there are proper and improper ways of determining what has been done in a literary work, so that criticism proper could be identified with the proper use of the proper methods.

The first of these three questions need not occupy us long. Literary criticism is not biography—talking about an author as a person is not talking about a book. One may indeed talk about a book by talking about its author as the author of that book; but that is not biography. So no one will confuse criticism with biography, and we need not labour to distinguish them. One may also distinguish between literary criticism, which discusses and evaluates texts, and literary theory, which discusses the principles on which that discussion should proceed, or literary history, which discusses not texts but the relations between texts. These distinctions again are perfectly clear, simple, and familiar, and no one is confused or puzzled by them.[5] Some authors like to use the word *criticism* broadly enough to include literary theory, but nothing of any consequence depends on this verbal quirk. In practice, a sharp separation of literary criticism from history and theory is neither possible nor desirable; but, since no sensible person supposes that it is, nothing of any interest follows from that either. So I would say that I know of no kind of discourse that is not criticism but is in serious danger of being confused with it.

The second question is more troublesome, but I will venture a blunt answer. Every literary work is something constructed out of the words of a language, and as such can have all the levels of organization that Ingarden distinguished,[6] and any others that industrious analysts can identify, and critics and readers may find interest in any or all of them. But there is no reason why a work should be interesting on all levels, or why the interest it has on any level should be interestingly related to the interest it has on any other level; and there is no reason why any critic or reader should take every interest in a work that could be taken, or why any critic or reader should observe any hierarchy among the interests he takes. Moreover, no less certainly than it is a verbal artefact, every literary work is the utterance of a real person—"Speake that I may see thee"—and the expression of a real place and time. It is both of these *as a literary work* and not as something else, because it fulfills both functions in a way that only literary works can. Language articulates humanity, and the valuable uses of language are coextensive with the values we find in and give to our lives. It is thus inevitable that a literary work, as verbal artefact, and as personal utterance, and as social expression, should be indefinitely complex, and should have this indefinite complexity as a literary work and not as something else. Appropriate discussion of it therefore is susceptible of the same indefinite complexity; and if any part of such discussion is not to be called "criticism" we have no other name for it. Nor is there anything in the past or present of the concept of criticism to make it more suitable to any part of its possible domain than to any other. One may choose to restrict one's own interest, as I have said, to some one aspect or set of aspects of a work, but to identify that restriction with the purification of criticism is merely silly. Interests do not cease to exist because one affects to ignore them, and it is useless to expel them from the domains of literature and literary criticism if one cannot find any other domain in which they would be more properly domiciled.

Why would one wish to restrict criticism or its proper target to a part of its domain, now to be deemed its only proper part? One reason may be found in the awkward fact that the thrust of my third question goes against what I have been saying. If criticism is necessarily of something done or made, and rests on establishing what has been done or made, so that my third question could be whether there were any methods of establishing that, it looks as if a literary work cannot be so inherently indeterminate as I made out, so that if criticism is to be possible one must after all restrict one's notion of what a literary work is by laying down some principles as to how its structure shall be construed. But that reasoning is specious. In the first place, enough determinacy is introduced by establishing the text itself: all that my argument ruled out is a complete and determinate account of everything that has been done in the writing of that text. But what is thus ruled out is a critique that said everything that could be said, in such a way as to make any subsequent criticism of the work in question otiose; and no one in his senses supposes that such a critique is possible, much less desirable. There need be nothing indeterminate in how a given question is to be answered, or in what can be seen from a given viewpoint; it is just that no antecedent limit can be set to the questions that can be asked and the viewpoints that can be taken. And if that is the case the answer to my third question is clear: there can be no method of establishing all and only what has been done in a given work, because no restriction can be set on questions and viewpoints: the critic may have to call on the full range of his sensitivity and experience in the affairs of life as well as in the world of books and the resources of linguistic skill. His limitations will be his limits of skill and personality, or limits he has chosen, not limits imposed by the nature of critical interpretation.

It is the merest commonplace of critical theory that a literary text combines a determinate verbal identity with the capacity to articulate over new experiences in successive readings and for successive generations of readers; and there is a supplementary commonplace to the effect that the greatest works are those within which we can live, those that contrive to combine the most definite structure with the richest ambiguity. And what is wrong with that? Nothing is wrong with it, except for pedagogical purposes. It is easier to make literature a teachable and markable subject if one can lay down rules for *explications de texte,* and easier to establish such rules if one can justify them. Besides, a teacher of literature must say something about his text, and say it with authority: and where can his authority come from, if not from his mastery of a method that enables him to say the right things? He could, of course, rely on his evidently superior knowledge of life and literature, his superior wisdom and intelligence, and the fact that he has read the book before; but then why is he *in a classroom?* Yearning for a unity in interpretation that is relevant to the concerns of teachers and students but not at all to that of writers and readers seems to breathe from Northrop Frye's *Anatomy of Criticism* and E. D. Hirsch's *Validity in Interpretation,*[7] to name two of the most notable vindications of unifying method. Frye's plea that the study of literature must be scientific if it is to be respectable makes no sense unless the respectability sought is to be wielded in curriculum committees and other battlegrounds of academe; Hirsch's insistence on the priority of authorial meaning rests on the necessity of establishing one meaning for a text, a necessity that obtains nowhere outside the examination hall and its purlieus.

It is against the background of pedagogic totalitarianism that the strategies of Roland Barthes's *S/Z* and *Plaisir du texte* are to be understood, though the narrow dogmatism which Barthes assumes to be the academic norm is surely nowhere exemplified in democratic anglosaxonry.[8] In place of Frye's and Ingarden's hierarchies of levels, Barthes teaches us to regard any text as the locus of intersection of as many cultural "codes" of reference as our ingenuity may suggest, to define the codes in any way compatible with such evidence as we elect to adduce, and to interpret in any way that pleases us the interweavings of what we thus find encoded. Why not? The author is our entertainer and enlightener, not our boss: the text is no more his than ours, for (as Jacques Derrida was reminding us at about the same time)[9] the author comes too late to language to bring it under control, and in any case his conscious will in its deployment cannot match in amplitude and force the lifetime of unconscious skill he brings to its use.

In sum: we all spend much of our lives, and use disproportionately big bits of our brains, in talking and understanding talk. If literary uses of language were less in range, power, and subtlety than other uses, there would be no point in bothering with them. In consequence, the understanding we bring to our literature must involve no less of our powers than that which we bring to other talk; but that means the whole of our capacity to interpret and sympathize, for the lives of others as revealed in their talk must be as full as our own lives, which we would sometimes gladly put into words if we could. No reason can be given why criticism should fall shorter than it has to of embodying our full understanding of literature. If there is nothing that has to be left out, there can be nothing that has to be put in, for we do not all have all the time we would like, and if we must all make the same beginning there will be ends that no one ever reaches. There can be methods of criticism, as many as you please; but no one of them is the one method of criticism, and there is no set of methods that comprises the methods of criticism. It is not hard to say what criticism is; but most of the reasons for saying it are bad reasons, and on the whole it is better not said.

NOTES

1. René Wellek, *Concepts of Criticism* (New Haven: Yale University Press, 1963), pp. 21–36.

2. The passages assembled in Liddell and Scott's *Greek-English Lexicon* (Oxford: Clarendon Press, 1968) to illustrate the Greek word *kritikos* seem to identify him as someone fully informed about, and able to teach, all aspects of literature—approximately the sense recovered for the word by Northrop Frye in *Anatomy of Criticism* (Princeton: Princeton University Press, 1957).

3. I have devoted a book, *The Concept of Criticism* (Oxford: Clarendon Press, 1967), to this fourth sense, supposing it to be logically and

etymologically the primary sense. To my surprise and chagrin, the publisher listed it under the heading of "Literature," so that most of those who read it were not those for whom it was written, and many of them were properly enraged.

4. One should not, however, forget that Homer has many more descriptions of visual works of art than of poetic performances. While few of the descriptions do more than list materials and costs, adding a brief encomium, the description of the shield of Achilles in the *Iliad* was eloquent and powerful enough to establish a whole genre of shield-descriptions. But none of these descriptions pertains to art criticism in the way that the critiques in the *Protagoras* pertain to literary criticism, because we are not persuaded either that the "works" described existed or that Homer and his followers knew what they would look like if they did exist.

5. Any residual confusion could be removed by reading Wellek's "Literary Theory, Criticism, and History," in *Concepts of Criticism*, pp. 1–20.

6. Roman Ingarden, *The Literary Work of Art* (Evanston: Northwestern University Press, 1973).

7. E. D. Hirsch, Jr., *Validity in Interpretation* (New Haven and London: Yale University Press, 1967).

8. Roland Barthes, *S/Z* (New York: Hill and Wang, 1974) and *The Pleasure of the Text* (New York: Hill and Wang, 1975).

9. Jacques Derrida, *Of Grammatology* (Baltimore: Johns Hopkins University Press, 1976).

The Logic of the Question "What Is Criticism?"

John M. Ellis

It seems that only the humanistic disciplines constantly brood over and search for their own nature and goals. Philosophers continaully debate the scope and purpose of philosophy, and it is not uncommon for historians to produce volumes with titles analogous to the present volume (E. H. Carr's *What Is History?* comes to mind).[1] But criticism is the most extreme case: literary critics hold and debate widely differing views as to what criticism is or should be. And in their case, the question is complicated by analogous debate and uncertainty as to what literature is—the subject of the volume which preceded this one. A compendium similar to the present volume appeared fifteen years ago: *The Critical Moment: Literary Criticism in the 1960s,* which included seventeen essays by prominent critics on the role of the critic, each a kind of capsule manifesto of the writer concerned.[2] Another group of practicing critics and theorists is now asked to provide another series of statements on the nature of criticism. It is natural to consider, first of all, what kind of progress there has been in the debate during those years: is there now any greater degree of agreement on the nature and methodology of criticism? Or has there been any significant clarification of the issues concerned, so that even where no greater agreement exists, there might be at least a greater degree of understanding of the fundamental differences on which the disputes between different schools of thought turn? Or have there arisen during that time any significant new positions which could at last command the assent of a majority of critics?

I doubt that anyone would answer the first of these questions affirmatively; the critical scene is more fragmented than ever it was. Not only is there an increase in the number of subvarieties of each major kind of critical position, but the variety of basic critical positions itself keeps increasing too. To the literary historians and biographers, Marxists, Freudians, myth critics, social critics, formalists, textually oriented critics, etc., are now added, therefore, not only new shades of opinion within each, but also structuralists, students of reception-aesthetics and implied readers, literary sociologists, and so on. Structuralism itself is already so fragmented that it would be hard to treat it as one school of thought, or even as a series of groups with a common core of thinking. The best we can do to define structuralist criticism, so it seems to me, is to refer to a series of critical and theoretical writings arising recently in France, initially as a revolt against a very conservative form of literary history and biography; a more analytic definition would be doubtful.

To take next the third of these questions: new positions in the last fifteen years have not been of a character which might at last provide a basis for a common opinion. We have not seen the emergence of a position both central to the issues of literary criticism and able by the power of its argument to convince a majority of critics. New positions of recent years have been of a different character: generally partial or peripheral rather than central, often speculative, even eccentric.

Opinions might be divided as to whether we have seen progress on the second question—greater clarification of the issues on which the debate turns. My belief is that recent theory has not been especially successful on this score: there seems to me to have been more of what René Wellek recently termed "apocalyptic irrationalism"[3] than truly analytical clarification of issues in critical theory.

To be sure, some would argue that the criticism and theory of a currently fashionable group of American critics influenced by recent continental trends was richly suggestive;[4] but even if one were to accept this judgment, it would still be hard to accept that such writing had made any real contribution to the kind of patient, rational, careful analysis which results in clarification of concepts and points of method in criticism. Striking new attitudes is not the same kind of activity as penetrating deeper into an already complex analytical argument. Some years ago, I wrote that the best *analytic* work was becoming more and more neglected, and I think that that is still more true today.[5]

The continued pursuit of questions like "What is criticism?" is in fact indicative of an uncertainty and confusion as to the nature and goals of our field of inquiry which has recently become more, not less, pervasive. It is not simply our own obsessive self-analysis that makes the question surface over and over again. Our academic colleagues in other fields of inquiry are evidently also impressed by our lack of clarity as to what we are about. "Now I shall find out what literary criticism really is," writes back a friend in another department to whom I had sent a copy of a book. I took the implication to be that he was rather puzzled by what he had seen of modern criticism, and could not see what it was trying to achieve. Another friend told me that criticism was his favorite reading, but only the kind of solid critical biographies from the nineteenth century tradition, because modern critics seemed to him to have quite lost the art of writing; by contrast with the fluently written, intelligible older works of criticism, modern criticism seemed poorly formulated, often full of meaningless jargon and pretentious nonsense. It was not difficult for him to point to some examples—prominent ones—which justified his contrast between the two, even though they could not, as a whole, do anything like justice to the real advances made by the best modern criticism over older work.

It is impossible to avoid the question: Why are we in such a perpetual state of confusion and disarray in criticism? There is, I wish to argue, something inherent in the very question "What is criticism?" which is symptomatic of our confusion, and something about its assumptions which guarantees that it will continue to puzzle us—at least until we see that the form of the question is part of our problem. Before any question can intelligently be asked—before the question itself becomes an intelligent one—we must be able to conceive of the *kind* of answer we should consider adequate. It will be one that would immediately strike us as the answer to the puzzle, an intuitively satisfying remedy to a feeling that we lacked a piece of mental equipment needed to deal with the situation facing us. Take a simple example of a question with an analogous form. A child reading a book finds an unfamiliar word and asks: "What is a unicorn?" The purpose of the question, and the kind of answer that is required, are both clear. And the answer, "A mythical, one-horned horse," gives the child the intuitive feeling that it clears the matter up—it fits perfectly into his expectation of the kind of answer he wanted. An intuitively satisfying answer is like a piece of a jigsaw puzzle—once found, it is obvious that it is the right one.

By contrast, no answers to "What is criticism?" ever achieve such a status. There are available plenty of sentences of the form "criticism is . . ." ("criticism is a social activity," "criticism is reflective reading," and so on) but no one of them fits into a preexisting sense of a kind of answer that would be intuitively satisfying as the thing we needed to solve the puzzle. And that in turn means that we have no clear idea of what our question is trying to do.

The truth is that questions of the form "What is X?" are logically very slippery questions; if we wish to make any progress with them, we must first give some attention to their logical status. One fundamental point is crucial to any further analysis: while they are all superficially similar, questions of the form "What is X?" may be fundamentally dissimilar in character and have at least three logically distinct kinds of answers. Some answers will provide a definition which explains the literal meaning of a word or concept; others will provide statements of fact which give information about a concept or thing whose definition is already assumed; and still others will be normative statements which recommend a desired or preferred state of affairs for the thing under discussion. But normative statements can also focus on many different kinds of issues: how the thing should be regarded, how it should be conceived, what its most essential features are, what is most valuable about it, and so on. Examples of these three types of statements might be: (a) literary criticism is the interpretation and evaluation of literary texts; (b) criticism is an ancient mode of discourse going back at least to the Greeks; (c) criticism is essentially evaluative. (I choose these as examples only, without endorsing any of them.) It is an important part of our confusion in criticism that when we ask the question "What is criticism?" we are not even sure what kind of answer we are asking for: definition, facts, or normative recommendations.

An important distinction must be made before we can proceed. Some forms of answer to the question are exclusive in character, but some are not. By this I mean that some kinds of answer make a legitimate claim to exclude others, and are correct or incorrect to the extent that they constitute the exclusively appropriate answer, while others do not necessarily exclude all other answers or derive their validity from being superior to all others. What this means is that if we conceive of the question "What is criticism?" in one way, it requires a single answer, and all attempts to provide it will compete with each other, but that if we conceive of it in another way, there may be many different answers in which the validity of one is quite independent of the validity of the others.

Let me explain how this is so. Of the three kinds of statements I have set out, only definitions always call for a single answer, so that attempts at definition always compete with each other. Factual statements about criticism, on the other hand, do not compete with each other to meet a particular need best. They may compete with their opposite ("criticism is in decline" and "criticism is becoming more interesting") but not with other factual statements of differing content. Normative statements are in this respect of mixed character. They are assertive by their very nature, and generally recommend that we should see criticism or pursue criticism in this way rather than that. To that extent they are exclusive—they attempt to take precedence over other possible statements. But though their thrust can be as exclusive as a definition, they can also be almost as nonexclusive as factual statements. For example, the normative statement: "criticism is evaluative" is directed largely at its opposite ("criticism is descriptive rather than evaluative") and need not seek to take precedence over a wide variety of other normative statements which address other aspects of criticism. But normative statements can easily be made far more exclusive than this simply by explicitly expanding the scope of the recommendation. They then begin with phrases such as: "above all else, criticism is . . . ," or "criticism is essentially. . . ." These phrases add exclusiveness to statements whose content was otherwise not necessarily exclusive. It will be important to focus on the logical character of this added kind of exclusivity, and on its derivation and justification, precisely because such statements are the ones which generate most attention and interest: they represent attempts to set criticism on the right path.

The question "What is a unicorn?" has an intuitively satisfying answer that is exclusive of others only because it is clearly a demand for a definition. Questions of the same grammatical form which are not really of the same type do not necessarily have answers of such a character. But there is nevertheless an instinctive carry-over of expectations from definition questions to other kinds of questions which look superficially similar, so that, even when we ask the question "What is criticism?" without any sense of asking for a definition, we still tend to want an intuitively satisfying, puzzle-solving answer which will take precedence over others. And this seems to me the most likely source of the tendency to add exclusivity to normative statements even in cases where their content does not automatically require such exclusivity.

Exclusivity and an intuitively satisfying character are provided by answers to questions which are inherently demands for definitions because those answers flow from—indeed are elucidations of—the concept which is the subject of the "what is" question. But though normative statements can in some cases be justified by reference to concepts and definitions,[6] the kind of added exclusivity that I have been talking about (the attempt to make one normative statement take precedence over others whose content is not comparable with its) is rarely justified in this way. Where then can this justification come from? A logical or conceptual justification is not possible; it therefore seems likely that the best that can be available is a pragmatic one. In other words, statements of this particular type are probably justified, if at all, only by the local circumstances in which they are made. If criticism today shows certain overwhelming defects, it will make sense to recommend that we pay more attention to those than to anything else, at least at the moment, and until the situation changes.

When we make exclusive normative recommendations for criticism, then, we must be clear about their limits: they may not reflect the essential nature of criticism, and are more likely to be no more than a needed corrective to a given local situation. Practitioners of different competing schools of criticism urge us to make criticism above all else psychologically informed, or politically conscious, or historically aware, or structurally formulated—but these competing recommendations, if I am correct, compete only for the status of the most important corrective to the current situation; they could not possibly give us the essential nature of criticism, regardless of the current critical context.[7] If criticism is generally failing at the moment in one particularly important respect, it may well be more important to recommend change in that respect than to make any other recommendation. At another time, in other circumstances, that recommendation might be unnecessary.

My argument may be now seem to have taken a pessimistic direction: though we really wish for an answer to "What is criticism?" of the intuitively satisfying, exclusive kind that is given in definitions, we shall not get it because we also want normative recommendations, not simply definitions; but norms are not inherently exclusive, and can only be made so by reference to the purely local features of a given situation. Thus in the absence of a single, exclusive kind of normative statement, we are left with a plurality of possible recommendations, and so with no clear, definite singular answer to the question "What is criticism?"—an inherently unsatisfying conclusion, since only singular, exclusive answers seem to provide solutions, and solutions certainly seem needed in so confused a field as literary criticism. In a situation where the question is unusually pressing, the answers would seem unusually limited. But this is not an inherently unlikely juxtaposition. Why is this frustration *not* found in a field such as physics? For the physicists seem to be able to find an exclusive, intuitively satisfying answer to the question "What is physics?" But the difference between their situation and ours goes to the heart of the problem. We can illuminate this difference by looking at the answers to the two questions ("What is criticism?" and "What is physics?") which are strictly definitions. We shall have little trouble in defining physics as the study of the physical basis of the world. As to criticism, if we look at the range of activities which go under that label, we shall only be able to define it as the discussion of literary texts, for we in practice allow any statements made about literary texts to be so called. In the one case, a kind of inquiry is defined, but in the other case, an object of inquiry is referred to. I have argued elsewhere that the definition of criticism implicit in the actual practice of critics is a hopelessly incoherent one.[8] Space does not allow me to repeat that argument here. It suffices to state my conclusion that a field of inquiry cannot intelligently be defined as "statements about X," but must instead focus on a kind and scope of inquiry. Physics, chemistry, and biology can all deal with the same phenomena, but the unique focus and aim of investigation of each are what make them relatively distinct fields of inquiry. Similarly, history, philosophy and criticism can all deal with literary texts, but each has—or should have—its own unique focus and aim in dealing with them.

And here is the source of our problem: the definition of our field, unlike the definitions of other fields, contains no unique focus for our activities. When other fields seek a definition of their scope, the result is an exclusive statement that is intuitively satisfying; but we get no such result from a definition, and so look elsewhere for the kind of answer which *only* a definition could provide. We then generally ask the question "What is criticism?" hoping in a rather vague way that some kind of statement which might derive from the concept of criticism will deliver a formula for a coherent discipline, but we simply come up against the fact that the concept of criticism is an inherently confused one, and conceptual analysis will only expose, not resolve the confusion.

The second kind of statement beginning "criticism is . . ." (descriptive statements or statements of fact) is clearly not any more helpful; there is evidently a great variety of such statements, and that variety indicates again how unfocused our field of inquiry is. And so we tend therefore to shift gears, to go beyond conceptual analysis or factual and descriptive observation to seek normative statements in order to introduce some coherence into the situation. But normative recommendations are crucially unlike definitions in character; they represent an attempt to *impose* an order on a field which is not present in its concept, and so to change a confused situation and improve upon it. And since such suggestions are not derived from the concept of criticism, but attempt to change it, there may be an infinite number of different normative recommendations for such a change. What this means is that the third kind of statement beginning "criticism is . . ." will necessarily involve us in a great many different kinds of prescriptions relating to many different kinds of aspects of the enterprise of criticism. None of them will have unique, exclusive status, and so constitute the single central answer to the question "What is criticism?" which the question always seems to seek.

Normative assertions that are currently prominent in critical theory can concern the character of the endeavor (descriptive or evaluative? more like the arts, or more like science?), the information relevant to the endeavor (knowledge of the author? the historical background? literary traditions?), matters of technique that must be understood (metrics, stylistics, etc.), the ultimate goals of the inquiry (period generalizations and concepts, or characterizations of authors, or just interpretations of great works), the mental operations which are most important (especially the role of judgment and interpretation), the use of the results (do they have the character of knowledge which stands on its own feet, as is the case in other fields, or is their value a matter rather primarily of helping readers to respond more fully?).

Given this diversity, any critic who seizes on a particular normative recommendation and asserts that this is essentially what criticism is or does, implying that it is more important and central than any other possible norm, misconceives the situation unless he makes the primary focus of his recommendation a pragmatic matter; it then becomes a matter of arguing that in the present state of criticism it is more necessary to insist on this particular recommendation than any other. Now if this point is understood, it should be possible to make a single normative assertion as to what criticism should try to do—now, in these circumstances. To this task I now turn.

What seems to me most in need of attention in the present state of criticism is that literary texts are pieces of language whose actual verbal formulations are of unusual importance: we should all resist any attempt to exchange them for other formulations. Their emphases are precisely set, their ideas expressed in a particular manner which has unique force, and in general their expression is memorable. As such, they are unusually demanding pieces of language, demanding of much attention to precisely what it is that they say and demanding of respect for their unique emphasis and individuality. In this respect they are quite unlike most other pieces of language, which rarely have the power to command repeated attention to their unique formulations after they have achieved their purposes in the situations in which they arose. Literary texts may embody ideas which, in a superficial sense, can be said to be found elsewhere; but the precise character and individual emphasis that a literary work gives those ideas make it necessary to see their occurrence in such a context not simply as the reappearance of familiar notions, but also as unique statements of them which demand unique responses. Criticism must surely focus on the unique character and system of ideas of literary works, with the kind of attention to emphasis and detail which will come to terms with the way in which familiar material is modifed and recast so that the result is a uniquely remarkable text. The power to make appropriate abstractions from this demanding material is the most important part of a critic's skills—the ability to grasp how textual details function together to make up the meaning of the whole work.

Why is it necessary to stress this aspect of criticism more than any other? The justification for making a recommendation which might otherwise not seem a remarkable one must lie in the present state of criticism. At the present time, it is necessary to make it for two reasons: first, because never before have critics so determinedly placed themselves (their own emphases, obsessions, personalities and systems of thought) at the center of attention in their criticism; and second, because (probably to justify this displacement of literary texts from the center of critical attention) no attitude toward criticism is more commonly disparaged and caricatured than that which I have just set out.

Modern critics seem less and less inclined to let the text speak for itself, through close attention to *its* emphases; they seem far more concerned to impress than to allow the text to do so, readily substituting their own ideologies and conceptual systems for those of the literary work. They seem often to be trying to rival the uniqueness of literary language by their own dazzling conceptual pyrotechnics, and to display their own erudition and intellectual feats instead of the literary text's subtle individuality. Never have we been faced with criticism which so obviously strains for originality at all costs. Critical essays by well-known and well-regarded critics seem often to ramble from one ill-defined but grandiose concept to another, attempting to enrich a vacuous argument with fashionable jargon and names, as well as bons mots and aphorisms of questionable relevance. The result is a veritable caricature of discussion, a reduction of criticism to an entertainment for scholars, a narrowly clubby kind of discourse. Some protests against this all too familiar kind of criticism have begun to appear; for example, Richard Locke, speaking of structuralists, complains of the "high adventures of solipsistic exegesis and polymorphous jargon," while Gerald Graff, in his caustic article "Fear and Trembling at Yale," objects to the self-dramatization and pretentiousness of an influential group of critics, and David Hirsch has recently complained of a general withdrawal by many critics from the direct experience of the language of literary texts.[9] But for the most part such criticism seems all too readily accepted. While some critics seem more concerned with histrionics and the projection of their own personalities rather than with focusing on literary emphasis, others are more concerned in their criticism with ideologies and systems of thinking of their own choosing, regardless of text. Whether the particular ideology is Marxism, Fruedianism, feminism, structuralism, or whatever, the process seems similar, no matter how dissimilar the emphases of the texts discussed: critics declare themselves adherents of a school of criticism and then expound its ideas rather than looking at each text for the particular work's system of ideas. Uniqueness and complexity are thus quickly reduced to a lowest common denominator. The point is not whether, on occasion, some of these concerns are relevant to a particular text—sometimes they obviously must be. What is really injurious here is the indiscriminate approach with a single set of concerns to texts which all have their own distinct emphases.

From a logical standpoint, it is the nature of abstraction (what abstractions are, how they are justified, and how they relate to other possible abstractions allowed by a text) that is utterly misconceived by such critics. Structuralists commonly abstract very general structures and pronounce them to be a deepest level of meaning, but in so doing they display very little ability to appraise the status or value of such abstractions. The same is generally true of other schools of criticism which deal in "deep" or otherwise very general abstractions, for example, Freudianism or Marxism. But to pursue the issue of the logic of abstractions would require a separate essay; suffice it to say that many different schools mismanage that logic in much the same way.

Strain, oversubtlety, reductionism and self-dramatization are all, then, much evident in modern criticism. Critics, rather than literature, are seen as most central in the process of criticism.[10] And actual criticism—putting first and foremost the attempt to discern the unique emphases of a given text—is commonly scorned and caricatured. It is often thought of as a "narrow" pursuit, especially by the more fashionable histrionic critics, though surely nothing is ultimately more narrow and shallow than a kind of writing which seems designed only to dazzle other members of the critical fraternity. Or it is termed "New Criticism" and, in a nice paradox, written off as old-fashioned, and yet nothing will be as enduring as the plain confrontation of reader and text, the fundamental literary experience which will still be going on long after our current critical fads are forgotten.[11] Or it is labeled "Formalism," with the implication that it is concerned only with formal or aesthetic matters and not with the content of a text, though that is plainly false; reading a document closely and carefully most obviously represents an attempt to absorb its content and its ideas *as completely and accurately as possible,* and it would be hard to see here any restriction to a formal and aesthetic as opposed to a substantive concern. Or it is caricatured as "interpreting in a vacuum," a curious reversal of the more obvious fact that interpreters who place the careful reading of texts first in their critical procedure are placing these texts in a wider context (that of human life in general) than their colleagues who place them in the more restrictive context of a particular historical moment or a particular ideology. One might argue whether the former is too *wide* a context—but surely not whether it is too narrow. Or it is caricatured as subjectivism (i.e., presenting only the subjective view of the reader), an odd charge indeed to make against a mode of criticism that respects the emphases of the text rather than indulges in the idiosyncrasies and pet ideologies of the modern critic.

Why are there currently so many caricatures of this simple, direct view of the task of criticism? Because, surely, to let the text take center stage pushes the critic himself out of that position, and criticism today has become more and more narcissistic.[12] No wonder that our colleagues in other departments of the academy, and even we ourselves, wonder what criticism is.

NOTES

1. Edward Hallett Carr, *What is History?* (New York: St. Martin's Press, 1961).

2. *The Critical Moment: Literary Criticism in the 1960s. Essays from the London Times Literary Supplement* (New York: McGraw-Hill, 1964). The New Zealand Journal *Landfall* 31 (1977): 99–137, recently invited a number of New Zealanders to contribute short articles on criticism and creative writing, thus providing another example of the genre.

3. René Wellek, "The New Criticism: Pro and Contra," *Critical Inquiry* 4 (1977–78): 621.

4. For a more skeptical view, see Gerald Graff, "Fear and Trembling at Yale," *American Scholar* 46 (1977): 467–78.

5. *The Theory of Literary Criticism: A Logical Analysis* (Berkeley: University of California Press, 1974), p. 3.

6. For example, in my *The Theory of Literary Criticism* I argued (chapter 5) that a correct definition of *literature* (though not *criticism*) would lead to a certain view of a work's relevant context excluding others.

7. This does not imply that all approaches are equally valid; many of these approaches seem to me, on the contrary, seriously misconceived. It simply means that argumentation pro or contra the critical position in each case would come not from an examination of the concept of criticism but rather from an examination of the inherent quality of the arguments commonly used to support the position. For example, in the case of structuralism, I assert below that the notion of abstraction, and the status of abstractions, are seriously misconceived. Here it is not inconsistency with the concept of criticism, but logical errors of a broader nature which render the position in question suspect.

8. *The Theory of Literary Criticism,* chapter 3.

9. Richard Locke, "The Literary View: Can These Bones Live?" *New York Times Book Review,* January 29, 1978, p. 3. For Graff, see note 4 above. David Hirsch, "Deep Metaphors and Shallow Structures," *Sewanee Review* 85 (1977): 153–66.

10. See, for example, the reduction of literature to a status similar to that of criticism in Eugenio Donato's "The Two Languages of Criticism," in *The Languages of Criticism and the Sciences of Man: The Structuralist Controversy*, ed. Richard Macksey and Eugenio Donato (Baltimore: The Johns Hopkins Press, 1970), pp. 89–97: "Literature can only be a denunciation of literature and is not therefore different in essence from criticism. Criticism, inasmuch as it is a denunciation of literature, is, itself, nothing but literature. Henceforth the distinction between the two types of discourse is blurred" (p. 95). An intellectual climate which allows serious consideration of such a view surely lacks the ingredient of common sense; and yet this kind of argument is not uncommon today.

11. See especially Wellek's "The New Criticism: Pro and Contra" for effective demolition of some of the myths and prejudices about the New Criticism that are currently in vogue. For further argument against the view that close reading ignores context, see my *The Theory of Literary Criticism*, chapter 5.

12. W. K. Wimsatt's judgment as to the ultimate origin of some modern critical fads seems to me unhappily all too justified: "The explosion of the academic population in the postwar period and the consequently appalling escalation of publishing efforts have worked towards the same revolutionary result. New persons, new professional generations, need new platforms." "Battering the Object: The Ontological Approach," in *Contemporary Criticism* (New York: St. Martin's Press, 1971), ed. Malcolm Bradbury and David Palmer, p. 65.

Demonstration vs. Persuasion: Two Models of Critical Activity

Stanley Fish

In 1954 Kathleen Raine published an influential essay entitled "Who Made the Tyger?" in which she argued that because the tiger is for Blake "the beast that sustains its own life at the expense of its fellow-creatures" it is a "symbol of . . . predacious selfhood," and that therefore the answer to the poem's climactic question—"Did he who made the Lamb make thee?"—"is, beyond all possible doubt, No."[1] In short the tiger is unambiguously and obviously evil. Miss Raine supports her reading by pointing to two bodies of evidence, certain cabbalistic writings which, she avers, "beyond doubt . . . inspired *The Tyger*," and evidence from the poem itself. She pays particular attention to the word "forests" as it appears in line 2, "In the forests of the night":

> Never . . . is the word "forest" used by Blake in any context in which it does not refer to the natural, "fallen" world. (48)

The direction of argument here is from the word "forests" to the support it is said to provide for a particular interpretation. Just ten years later, however, that same word is being cited in support of a quite different interpretation. While Miss Raine assumes that the Lamb is for Blake a symbol of Christ-like self-sacrifice, E. D. Hirsch believes that "Blake's intention . . . was . . . to satirize the singlemindedness of the Lamb": "There can be no doubt," he declares, "that *The Tyger* is a poem that celebrates the holiness of tigerness."[2] In his reading, the "ferocity and destructiveness" of the tiger are transfigured and one of the things they are transfigured by is the word "forests":

> "Forests" . . . suggests tall straight forms, a world that for all its terror has the orderliness of the tiger's stripes or Blake's perfectly balanced verses. (247)

What we have here then are two critics with opposing interpretations, each of whom claims the same word as internal and confirming evidence. Clearly they cannot both be right, but just as clearly there is no basis for deciding between them. One cannot appeal to the text, because the text has become an extension of the interpretive disagreement that divides them; and, in fact, the text as it is variously characterized is a *consequence* of the interpretation for which it is supposedly evidence. It is not that the meaning of the word "forests" points in the direction of one interpretation or the other; rather in the light of an already assumed interpretation, the word will be seen *obviously* to have one meaning or another. Nor can the question be settled by turning to the context—say the cabbalistic writings cited by Miss Raine—for that too will only be a context for an already assumed interpretation. If Miss Raine had not already decided that the answer to the poem's climactic question is "beyond all possible doubt, No," the cabbalistic texts, with their distinction between supreme and inferior deities, would never have suggested themselves to her as Blake's source. The rhetoric of critical argument, as it is usually conducted in our journals, depends upon a distinction between interpretations on the one hand, and the textual and contextual facts that will either support or disconfirm them, on the other; but as the example of Blake's "Tyger" shows, text, context, and interpretation all emerge together, as a consequence of a gesture (the declaration of belief) that is irreducibly interpretive. It follows then that when one interpretation wins out over another, it is not because the first has been shown to be in accordance with the facts, but because it is from the perspective of its assumptions that the facts are now being specified. It is these assumptions, and not the facts they make possible, that are at stake in any critical dispute.

In other words, critical disputes are not, properly speaking, about facts but about the varying perspectives from which the facts will look now one way, now another; and therefore the business of criticism is not so much to demonstrate in *accordance* with the facts as it is to persuade to a point of view within which the facts one cites will seem indisputable. Indeed this is the whole of critical activity: an attempt on the part of one party to alter the beliefs of another so that the evidence cited by the first will be seen *as* evidence by the second. In the more familiar model of critical activity (codified in the dogma and practices of New Criticism) the procedure is exactly the reverse: evidence supposedly available apart from any particular belief is brought in to judge between competing beliefs, or, as we call them in literary studies, interpretations. This is a model derived from an analogy to the procedures of logic and scientific inquiry, and basically it is a model of *demonstration* in which interpretations are either confirmed or disconfirmed by facts that are independently specified. The model I have been arguing for, on the other hand, is a model of *persuasion* in which the facts that one cites are available only because an interpretation (at least in its general and broad outlines) has already been assumed. In one model critical activity is controlled by freestanding objects in relation to which its accounts are either adequate or inadequate; in the other critical activity is constitutive of its object. In one model the self must be purged of its prejudices and presuppositions so as to see clearly a text that is independent of them; in the other prejudicial or prespectival perception is all there is, and the question is from which of a number of equally interested perspectives will the text be constituted. In one model change is (at least ideally) progressive, a movement toward a more accurate account of a fixed and stable entity; in the other change occurs when one perspective dislodges another and brings with it entities that had not before been available.

In short the stakes are much higher in a persuasion than in a demonstration model, since they include nothing less than the very conditions under which the game, in all of its moves (description, evaluation, validation, etc.) will be played. That is why Jonathan Culler is only half right in *Structuralist Poetics* when he says that "the possibility of bringing someone to see that a particular interpretation is a good one assumes shared points of departure and common notions of how to read" (28).[3] Culler is right to insist that notions of correctness and acceptability are institution specific and that knowledge of these "shared points of departure" is a prerequisite of what he calls "literary competence." But he is wrong to imply (as he does here and elsewhere) that literary competence is an unchanging set of rules or operations to which critics must submit in order to be recognized as players in the game. Culler's model of critical activity is one that will hold for the majority of critical performances; for it is certainly true that most of the articles we read and write do little more than confirm or extend assumptions that are already in place. But the activity that is most highly valued by the institution (even if it is often resisted) is more radically innovative. That is, the rewards of our profession are reserved for those who challenge the assumptions within which ordinary practices go on, not so much in order to eliminate the category of the ordinary, but in order to redefine it and reshape its configurations. This act of challenging and redefining can occur at any number of levels: one can seek to overturn the interpretation of a single work; or recharacterize the entire canon of an important author; or argue for an entirely new realignment of genres; or question the notion of genre itself; or even propose a new definition of literature and a new account of its function in the world. At any of these levels one will necessarily begin, as Culler says, "with shared points of departure and common notions of how to read," but the goal of the performance will be the refashioning of those very notions, and the establishment of new points of departure. That is why, as I said, the stakes in a persuasion model are so high. In a demonstration model our task is to be adequate to the description of objects that exist independently of our activities; we may fail or we may succeed, but whatever we do the objects of our attention will retain their ontological separateness and still be what they were before we approached them. In a model of persuasion, however, our activities are directly constitutive of those objects, and of the terms in which they can be described, and of the standards by which they can be evaluated. The responsibilities of the critic under this model are very great indeed, for rather than being merely a player in the game, he is a maker and unmaker of its rules.

That does not, however, mean that he (or you or I) is ever without rules or texts or standards or "shared points of departure and common notions of how to read." We have everything that we always had—texts, standards, norms, criteria of judgment, critical histories, etc. We can convince others that they are wrong, argue that one interpretation is better than another, cite evidence in support of the interpretations we prefer, etc.; it is just that we do all those things within a set of institutional assumptions that can themselves become the objects of dispute. This in turn means that while we still have all the things we had before (texts, standards, norms, criteria of judgment) we do not always have them in the same form. Rather than a loss, however, this is a gain, because it provides us with a principled account of change, and allows us to explain to ourselves and to others why, if a Shakespeare sonnet is only fourteen lines long, we haven't been able to get it right after four hundred years.

Such an explanation, however, is not without its problems, for by making criticism into a game where everything is continually changing, it seems to deprive the critic of any confidence in the position he now occupies. How can someone who believes that the force and persuasiveness of an interpretation depend on institutional circumstances (rather than any normative standard of correctness), and that those circumstances are continually changing, argue with conviction for the interpretation he presently favors? The answer is that the general or metacritical belief does not in any way affect the belief or set of beliefs (about the nature of literature, the proper mode of critical inquiry, the forms of literary evidence, etc.) which yields the interpretation that now seems to you (or me) to be inescapable and obvious. I may, in some sense, *know* that my present reading of *Paradise Lost* follows from assumptions that I did not always hold and may not hold in a year or so, but that "knowledge" does not prevent me from knowing that my present reading of *Paradise Lost* is the correct one. This is because the reservation with which I might offer my reading amounts to no more than saying "of course I may someday change my mind," and the fact that my mind may some day be other than it now is does not alter the fact that it *is* what it now is; no more than the qualifying "as far as I know" with which someone might preface an assertion means that he doesn't know what he knows; he may someday know something different, and when he does, that something will *then* be as far as he knows, and he will know it no less firmly than what he knows today. An awareness that one's perspective is limited does not make the facts yielded by that perspective seem any less real; and when that perspective has given way to another, a new set of facts will occupy the position of the real ones.

Now one might think that someone whose mind had been changed many times would at some point begin to doubt the evidence of his senses, for, after all, "this too may pass," and "what I see today I may not see tomorrow." But doubting is not something one does outside the assumptions that enable one's consciousness; rather doubting, like any other mental activity, is something that one does *within* a set of assumptions that cannot at the same time be the object of doubt. That is to say, one does not doubt in a vacuum, but from a perspective, and that perspective is itself immune to doubt until it has been replaced by another which will then be similarly immune. The project of *radical* doubt can never outrun the necessity of being situated; in order to doubt *everything*, including the ground one stands on, one must stand somewhere else, and that somewhere else will then be the ground on which one stands. This infinite regress could be halted only if one could stand free of any ground whatsoever, if the mind could divest itself of all prejudices and presuppositions and start, in the Cartesian manner, from scratch; but then of course you would have nothing to start *with* and anything with which you *did* start (even "I think, therefore I am") would be a prejudice or a presupposition. To put the matter in a slightly different way: radical skepticism is a possibility only if the mind exists independently of its furnishings, of the categories of understanding that inform it; but if, as I have been arguing, the mind is constituted by those categories, there is no possibility of achieving the distance from them that would make them available to a skeptical inquiry. In short, one can not, properly speaking, *be* a skeptic, and one can not be a skeptic for the same reason that one can not be a relativist, because one can not achieve the distance from his own beliefs and assumptions that would result in their being no more authoritative *for him* than the beliefs and assumptions held by others or the beliefs and assumptions he himself used to hold. The conclusion is tautological but inescapable: one believes what one believes, and one does so without reservation. The reservation inherent in the general position I have been arguing—that one's beliefs and therefore one's assumptions are always subject to change—has no real force, since until a change occurs the interpretation that seems self-evident to me will continue to seem so, no matter how many previous changes I can recall.

This does not mean that one is always a prisoner of his present perspective. It is always possible to entertain beliefs and opinions other than one's own; but that is precisely how they will be seen, as beliefs and opinions *other than one's own,* and therefore as beliefs and opinions that are false, or mistaken, or partial, or immature, or absurd. That is why a revolution in one's beliefs will always feel like a progress, even though, from the outside, it will have the appearance merely of a change. If one believes what one believes, then one believes that what one believes is *true*, and, conversely, one believes that what one doesn't believe is not true, even if that is something one believed a moment ago. We can't help thinking that our present views are sounder than those we used to have or those professed by others. Not only does one's current position stand in a privileged relation to positions previously held, but previously held positions will always have the status of false or imperfect steps, of wrongly taken directions, of clouded or deflected perceptions. In other words, the idea of progress is inevitable, not however because there *is* a progress in the sense of a clearer and clearer sight of an independent object, but because the *feeling* of having progressed is an inevitable consequence of the firmness with which we hold our beliefs, or, to be more precise, of the firmness with which our beliefs hold us.

NOTES

1. Kathleen Raine, "Who Made the Tyger," *Encounter* 2, no. 6 (June 1954): 43–50.
2. E. D. Hirsch, *Songs of Innocence and Experience* (New Haven: Yale University Press, 1964).
3. Jonathan Culler, *Structuralist Poetics* (Ithaca, New York: Cornell University Press, 1975).

Three Notions about Criticism

Morse Peckham

My three notions are possible answers to three questions which to me exhaust the possibilities of questions about criticism, although others, no doubt, will not find them equally exhaustive. These questions are (1) What are the kinds of critical statements? (2) What makes criticism possible? and (3) What is the present state of criticism?

1

Resisting the notion that my thinking must be invalid because I am about to introduce another triad, I discern three kinds of critical statements, of which the first is the *interpretational statement.* I begin with this because it is one of the factors frequently involved in the second kind. It is with some relief that I conclude that there are but two kinds of interpretational statements. In the first, the critic endeavors to determine, either from internal factors or from factors external to the composition of the work, what were the interests (or, somewhat more grandiosely, the ideology or ideologies) which governed the decisions responsible for the salient semantic attributes of the work, or at least what the critic judges to be the salient attributes. In the second kind of interpretational statement, the critic uses the work to exemplify his own interests (or ideologies or ideology). Obviously, in the first kind the critic's interests (henceforth, "ideologies" are to be understood) are also involved, for they govern his decisions about the interests of the writer of the work. The difference between the two kinds of interpretational statement is that exposure, in the first kind, to other interests can have an effect upon the critic's own interests, even to the extent of loosening (if not freeing) him from his bondage to them, while the second kind is unlikely to have any such corrective effect. I use the word "corrective" because I regard all ideologies as necessary but also more or less unsatisfactory, and the blind adherence to any ideology or interest highly damaging both to the individual and his socio-cultural situation.

But this distinction between kinds of interpretational statement cannot be left without some consideration of what makes it possible, and what the effects have been. No utterance controls or determines a response to that utterance. The response is always a determination; the response (a decision, if only metaphorically) involves interpretation, even when the determination is under the severest cultural control, such as torture or the threat of execution. *Hence there is no immanent or necessary connection between any work of literature and any interpretation of the work.* On the contrary, the possibilities of interpreting any work of literature are, if not infinite, at least indefinably great. In the past two hundred years there have been the two interpretational tendencies mentioned above. The first, which is to control possibilities by an effort to determine the interest of the author, has produced increasingly rich and complex interpretations, so that, even if certainty is unattainable, there has been an increasing convergence of interpretation, at least for a number of works to which high value has been traditionally ascribed. The second kind, using the work of literature to exemplify the critic-interpreter's interests, has spread into a delta of interpretational possibilities. The explanation for this spread is that the last two hundred years has seen the emergence of a great many rival ideologies, each of which has developed its particular mode of literary criticism. (If any of these ideologies have not done so, we can safely assume that they probably will.)

The second kind of critical statement consists of *judgments of competence*. These, as I have suggested, can be based upon interpretation. Thus from the interpretation can be derived some general proposition or "truth," philosophical, ethical, historical, sociological, psychological, and so on. Thus we may praise Balzac, say, because of the competence of his "profound sociological insights." On the other hand, we might deny his authorial competence on the grounds of "stylistic" incompetence. As ideologies change, and as styles change, the grounds of judgments of competence change. John Sparrow once judged what was then "modern poetry" to be simply incompetent; the poets hadn't learned how to write poetry. Free verse was initially judged to be the consequence of incompetence; then judgments of competence in writing free verse were gradually developed. Like interpretational statements, judgments of competence can always be countered by drawing upon some rival justification or determination of competence. "My Last Duchess" can be judged prosodically incompetent because one does not notice the presence of the rhymes. (A surprisingly large number of professional students and teachers of literature think that the poem is in blank verse.) But it can also be judged extraordinarily competent for precisely the same attribute: that is, for the "subtlety" of its rhymes. A poem may be judged competent because it is charming, delicate, touching, and straightforward; or it may be judged incompetent in spite of all these attributes because it does not offer an ironical conclusion. Or a poet may be judged less competent because he invariably offers a "mechanical" ironical conclusion (as the common judgments of O. Henry stories illustrate). It seems obvious that judgments of competence, like interpretational statements of the second kind, are traceable to the critic's interests (which we call "biases" when we do not accept them). As with ideologies, the immense delta-spread of styles emerging in the last two hundred years, the result of the ideology that a competent writer must develop a unique style rather than developing competence in an existent style and then modifying it, has brought about an equivalent delta-spread of rationalizations for judgments of competence. As a counter to this, there is a critical tendency to judge that what from one determination of competence is a flaw may indeed have served the writer's interests and therefore be justifiable. Thus what is said to be the crudeness or banality of Balzac's style may be determined to serve the interest of directing the reader's attention to characters, situations, and events; while the marvelous complexity of Proust's style may be determined to be a flaw in that it directs the reader's attention from what Proust is saying—or away from the semantic aspect or content of the novels. The stylistic surface of Swinburne has persuaded a great many readers that he had nothing of interest to say. These (or other readers), if persuaded that Swinburne had indeed something of interest to say, might then determine him to be an incompetent poet. The gnarled and knotted syntax and the "ugly" phonic character of Browning's later poetry has been responsible for the fact that it has been pretty much neglected. On the other hand, both of these stylistic attributes can be judged to be challenges which are richly rewarding when overcome and when one penetrates to the interpretation of Swinburne and Browning. Thus their respective styles could be judged not as incompetent but as supremely competent.

What it appears to come down to is that if one values a work of literature, it is not difficult, at least for someone trained and experienced in the rhetoric of literary criticism, either to determine that the ascription of value is justified by the writer's high competence, or that, correspondingly, an ascription of negative value can be justified by a determination of the writer's incompetence.

We come then to the third kind of critical statement, *ascriptions of value*. The fact that to the same work can be, and constantly is, ascribed negative and positive value, justified by a determination that the identical literary attribute can be judged as an indication of either competence or incompetence, suggests that though the same language is used for judgment of competence and judgments of value, the two judgments are quite different in kind, even though judgments of competence can be used to justify and rationalize judgments of value. Let me use an example from my own recent experience. In the first six months of 1979 I had occasion to reread six of the major novels of Dickens, from *Pickwick Papers* to *Little Dorrit*. All six were novels I had once admired and delighted in. But now, in my sixty-fifth year, I found all of them, except *Pickwick Papers*, simply execrable. I can read no more of what I now regard as drivel. With little trouble I can construct a justification for my position. For example, I could say that the novels are marked by Romantic formal strategies but that these strategies are in the service of an Enlightenment ideology. And I could even, perhaps, argue this rationalization at such length and with such a command of the devices of literary critical rhetoric that some readers might take it seriously. But I cannot honestly justify by rationalization a judgment I regard as too easily justifiable. If those were Dickens's interests, it is impossible to deny that he was superbly competent in exploiting that ideological incoherence. Thus there is no necessary connection between judgments of competence and judgments, or ascriptions, of value. No matter what justification for my present judgment I construct, it seems clear that my former ascription of value to Dickens's fiction and my present withdrawal of that ascription to the point of detestation are matters of personal history and temperament. That is, I once could use Dickens to serve an interest, but now I cannot. But what is that interest?

I would suggest that ascriptions of value to a literary work, to any work of art, to any being or to any human activity, or to a tree, or to a landscape are all the same kind of behavior. We may call it the value experience to distinguish it from the verbal (or verbally justified) ascription of value. Probably the most common term used to verbalize that experience is "beauty," though currently "meaningful" seems to be at least as popular. Central to the value experience is the ascription of value to oneself, evidently learned during the socialization of the child. Parents engage in two quite distinct ascription activities in bringing up children (or at least that is the norm—

exceptions may account for sociopaths); on the one hand the child is constantly judged competent or incompetent in the performance of various specific activities; but on the other hand, he is given generalized praise for being such a good child, or the nicest little boy in the world. That is, *value is ascribed to him without reference to competence,* and in the course of his further development and in adulthood, that value continues to be ascribed, maintained, and stabilized by various institutions, membership in which constitutes value ascription: clubs, religions, honorary societies, nations, and so on. Religious rituals, mass, communion, animal or human sacrifice, patriotic celebrations—all those behavioral strategies which anthropologists call the "sacred"—are the most obvious modes of experiencing the self-ascription of value. In secularized cultures, such as ours, psychotherapy has assumed the function of restoring and stabilizing the self-ascription of value, at least for a respectably large portion of the population. All psychotherapies work for somebody, and, except for cases involving a physiological abnormality or trauma or lesion, they all appear to work the same way, i.e., by teaching the patient to ascribe value to himself. For others, those to whom psychotherapy is unacceptable or too expensive, new religions emerge, or are revived, such as white witchcraft or Druidism, or are imported from alien cultures, a phenomenon of increasing frequency in our culture during the past one hundred and fifty years. Now, just as certain perceptual configurations that are displayed by value institutions are signs to the individual of his own value (in childhood, Christmas and birthday presents; in adult life, communion or even the mere listening to a sermon or an invitation from a socially exclusive hostess), so there can be extra-institutional signs to which the individual responds in the same way—that is, as *signs of his own value.* Having learned from institutions to respond to value-signs, he can now select them for himself.

In artistic matters for quite some time the capacity to use a work of art to maintain or restore or improve the self-ascription of value has been known as "taste." And that is why it is idle to argue about taste, although, as I have indicated, it is always possible to *justify* a taste; but that is simply because language makes it possible to justify anything. If we say, then, that someone has excellent taste in poetry, for example, we are saying no more than that the individual's poetry value-signs have been validated as value-signs by the small subgroup of those interested in literature of a high cultural level. It is not, then, a question of whether I was right or wrong in ascribing value to Dickens up to fiften years ago, when I last read one of his novels, or right or wrong in my current inability to do so. Rather, at one time I could use Dickens as a value-sign (a sign that maintains my own value), but now I cannot.

The explanation in my particular case is probably at the present time inaccessible, but a general explanation can be offered. The self-ascription of value subsumes judgments of both competence and incompetence, but there is no inherent or necessary connection between value and competence. Consequently, the self-ascription of value is necessarily unstable. Thus the individual, as his experiences modify his personality, finds it necessary to abandon some value-signs and to establish others. His taste in literature changes. Psychotherapy, then, is primarily the socialization and institutionalization of a behavioral process which is a constant norm in the individual's own behavior. That process is essential because, as emotional depression shows—an experience in which there is a striking loss of the self-ascription of value and most commonly a decrease in competence in performing behavior in which the depressed individual had previously been competent—the self-ascription of value is necessary to maintain and improve competence, the coin and barter of interaction.

To return to literary criticism: there appears to be, in any culture, a writer or two whose works have been canonized (a term significantly derived from religious practices). In our culture it is obviously Shakespeare, and very little Shakespeare criticism is devoted to denigration. Almost all of it is aimed at providing further justification, either of competence or interpretation, for the verbal ascription to his works of supreme greatness. To deny that greatness is to bring upon oneself, at least from others, denigration, a withdrawal of value-ascription. Thus, an individual who agrees with you on the ascription of value to a particular work or writer becomes, for you, a value-sign. Such agreements are an important, even a central, factor in the totality of behavior in response to works of art, and suggest very strongly that ascribing value to others and receiving such ascriptions is central to the socializing process. A good term for the interactional (or social) arrangements for ascribing value to others and receiving ascriptions of value is *agape system*, i.e., the system of interactional and intra-actional "love." Ascriptions of value to works of literature, then, can be understood as a factor in a culture's agapic system, or better, as one of the many agapic systems in a culture.

Some words can perhaps profitably be added here concerning the kind of critical statement this paper represents, and presumably the other papers in this volume. If criticism is response to works of literature, then this kind is responses to responses. It can be variously called critical theory, or metacriticism. The history of such metacriticism suggests that it is an activity best subsumed by philosophy, or, to more modern tastes, such as my own, by the behavioral sciences. I must add, however, and hastily, that I do not consider the behavioral sciences as they are presently practiced to be in much of a position to subsume anything. Thus the possibility that metacriticism properly belongs to the behavioral sciences must, at the moment and for the foreseeable future, remain in the realm of the ideal.*

2

I come then to the second of my questions: What makes criticism possible? One answer to this is simple and obvious; we criticize literature because we criticize everything else. That is, we determine its meaning, we judge its competence, and we ascribe value to it. And we do all three in response to both natural and man-made configurations. It would seem odd, for

*The above highly condensed discussion of value is given extensive and detailed presentation in my recent *Explanation and Power: The Control of Human Behavior* (New York: The Seabury Press, 1979).

example, to say that a tree is incompetent, but there is no significant difference between saying that loblolly pines are useless and even dangerous as fireplace wood and saying that a swimmer is performing the breaststroke very poorly. In both cases one is saying that the configuration is useful or not useful for some particular human interest. In the same way a lumberman can say that a tree is "beautiful," meaning that it will make fine wood for expensive furniture, and a painter can use the same word to mean that it will make a splendid subject for a watercolor. Both are acts of interpretation as well as judgments of competence. Thus one can convert a tree into a value-sign by leaving milk and flowers for a dryad living in it.

But all this leaves us where we started: What makes any of these judgments possible? We may begin with a phenomenon that has long puzzled me. If the role is sung by a great artist, such as a Callas, we can be completely involved in the sufferings of Lucia di Lammermoor, and nevertheless burst into applause for the singer when she finishes the mad scene. The traditional terms for that involvement, "dramatic illusion" and "the willing suspension of disbelief," are, to me, quite useless, merely pointing at the problem but making no contribution to understanding it and solving it. Evidently in the twinkling of an eye we can shift our modes of apprehension. For the sake of some stability in terminology, I shall call our involvement in Lucia the apprehension of the behavior as an *act,* and our applauding Callas as the apprehension of the same behavior as a *performance.* The almost interchangeable use of "act" and "perform" both in the theater and out of it is an indication that any behavior can be apprehended as either an action or a performance. Indeed, in daily life we are constantly making that discrimination, in, for example, disagreements about whether a particular sequence of behavior was or was not ironical, or sincere, or hypocritical, or whether the individual was or was not lying, or conning us.

The explanation for this duality of apprehension and interpretation is that the protocols of all behaviors, behavioral patterns, and behavioral assemblages are learned as appropriate to particular situations. However, once a behavior is learned, it can be presented in kinds of situations other than those for which the connection between behavior and situation was taught as appropriate. In child culture, though often transmitted by parents, this eternal possibility of human behavior is learned in games of "let's pretend." I shall use "action" for behavior in accordance with the protocols appropriate to a given situation, and "performance" for behavior not in accordance with those protocols. If our behavior is inadequately learned, we do not present the appropriate verbal and nonverbal signs; our behavior is error-ridden. But when we lie, our behavior violates the protocols of a situation in which the situational demand is that we tell the truth, and at the same time we present the verbal and nonverbal signs appropriate to a truth-telling situation. However, when we lie, we are judging that it is *not* appropriate for us in that situation to tell the truth. Hence, our behavior as *performance* is insincere and dishonest, but as *action* is sincere and honest. The complement to our judgment is the judgment of the individual with whom we are interacting; that is, he can judge either that we are telling the truth or lying, either that we are acting or performing. If the latter, he can, instead of merely condemning us, propose an explanation (one that may or may not be a justification) for our performance, that is, judge it as sincere. Thus one of the oddities of human behavior, the factor that gives behavior its irresolvable and inconsolable strangeness, is that insincerity, hypocrisy, lying, and conning are always and necessarily sincere and honest.

The theater is a two-level situation. We apprehend Lucia in relation to her situation and judge her behavior as action, and as appropriate or inappropriate, and whether or not inappropriate behavior is action or performance. But we applaud Callas for her behavior as performance of Lucia, as appropriate for the theater situation. As Callas she is sincere; as Lucia she is either sincere or insincere as the case may be. Likewise, we can judge Callas as having a bad night, and her performance as error-ridden; or we can judge that she is having a bad night, even though her performance is without flaws, because her performance is "unconvincing," or that she "is just going through the motions." We make the same judgment when we decide that an individual is lying because there is a certain quaver or hesitation in his vocal production or some other failure or error in the presentation of certain nonverbal signs (or even because his behavior is *too* flawless a performance). In both cases we are responding to what we apprehend as an incoherence in the semiotic assemblage we are being offered. In the actual apprehension of a theatrical performance our interpretation is constantly flickering between apprehending the behavior in relation to the dramatic situation and apprehending it in relation to the theater situation. (In nontheatrical situations this flickering takes the form of doubt; in theatrical situations it tends to appear as doubt about the competence of the performance.) We find a theatrical experience most rewarding when that flickering is eliminated by an apprehension of the behavior solely in relation to the dramatic situation, that is, as action. As an example, on my fourth viewing of Visconti's film, *Death in Venice,* my apprehension occasionally, though rarely, flickered because of my judgment that Bogarde's performance was at times a bit exaggerated. But only on my fourth viewing. On the other hand even on first viewing I was aware that the frames were shot to eliminate certain modern aspects of Venice. For a moment or two I shifted from apprehension of action to apprehension of performance, but only because I know Venice well. In the same way, while listening to an electronically reproduced performance of music, I apprehend the sound as action; but if there is flaw in the recording technique or a bit of dust on the record or a scratch, I shift to apprehending the sound as performance.

This distinction between action and performance, common to the theater and ordinary nontheatrical experience, this dual possibility of apprehension, is what makes criticism possible. We say of the first appearance of a new department chairman before his faculty that he performed his role very well. The metaphor of the theater is one of the oldest metaphors for talking about behavior, not only in everyday language but also in the basic terminology of the behavioral sciences. Nevertheless, when we speak of the "role" of the department chairman we are quite aware that we *are* speaking metaphorically, that what we mean is that his behavior was in accordance with the protocols learned for that kind of behavior in that kind of situation. By using the word "role" we announce that we are engaging in criticism. Because of this distinction between action and performance we may condemn a man for lying, but admire him for lying so well—or we may regret that Tennyson was insincere in concluding *In Memoriam* with an optimism he himself, he said, had never arrived at, and yet admire him for fulfilling the protocols for an elegiac lament. We can apprehend a literary work as either action or performance. If we interpret it as offering some large generalization about the human situation, we may judge it as appropriate or inappropriate to our understanding of the human situation, or to the understanding of the human situation culturally available at the time it was written. If we judge it as competent or incompetent, we are judging it either as error-ridden or as insincere or as both, or as sincere but error-ridden. Or we may judge it as corresponding to our taste, that is, as to whether or not we can use it as a value-sign. But if it does serve us as a value-sign, we are apprehending it as pure action. However, it is of great importance to realize that if we apprehend it from the point of view of taste, and find it incapable of serving us as a value-sign, we are also apprehending it as an action, even though we may subsequently rationalize that response by judging it inappropriate in its meaning or incompetent in some way or other. Finally, it would seem to follow from this that to apprehend a work as action is to facilitate our own actions as interpreters and perceivers of competence.

3

We come finally to my third question: What is the present state of criticism? My answer to that is: Not very satisfactory, even, Very unsatisfactory. One factor responsible is an economic factor. I refer to the infamous requirement of publication for tenure and promotion of university and, increasingly, college faculty members. Publish-or-perish should be recognized as a policy of *publish-and-perish*, intellectually and morally. It is a policy responsible for a moral and intellectual corruption unparalleled even in the higher education establishment of this country. The enormous expansion of that establishment, dependent as it has been on the massive exploitation of graduate students for freshman and sophomore instruction, has meant a corresponding decline in the overall or average quality of graduate instruction and a similar decline in the quality of graduate students, many of whom are now themselves giving graduate courses. Two examples are enough to show what has happened.

Throughout the country there has been a proliferation of regional scholarly-critical associations, meeting at least annually, the unavowed purpose of which is to provide opportunities to give papers which are then entered in one's *vita* for promotion and tenure. There has been a similar enormous expansion of journals devoted to the publication of papers written solely for the same purpose. Two results are worth noting. One is that the probability of an important paper or even book being read by someone who can profit from it is increasingly remote; the other is the increasing rate of expansion of the number of ideologies exemplified in the second kind of interpretational criticism discussed above. And these ideologies are increasingly bizarre. It almost seems that the more bizarre the mode of interpretation one chances upon, the better the chances for publication.

The major explanation, however, lies in the peculiar place of literature (and art in general) as an institution in our culture. In the course of the nineteenth century, as a consequence of the Enlightenment secularization of culture, two novel value institutions emerged, the Nation and Art. Nationalism, emerging from Enlightenment ideology and quantitatively the dominant of the two, turned individual nations into value institutions, so that even religious institutions became subsumed by nations. From Romanticism emerged what came to be known as the Religion of Art. That is, art became for many individuals, perhaps the majority at the higher cultural level, the dominating value institution. In spite of some superficial indications to the contrary, in academic circles and their non-academic adjuncts (that is, for most writers and critics) literature continues to be a value institution, a source of stabilizing the self-ascription of value. Hence arguments about taste, about which it is pointless to argue; such arguments are not merely analogous to arguments about whether a candidate for sainthood should be canonized or not; both kinds of arguments belong to the same category of behavior. Hence, also, the pietistic tone of most criticism and metacriticism. The bulk of literary critics are to literature as theologians are to religion. Thus there is a vital distinction between accepting a literary work as a value-sign because it has been institutionally canonized, and independently determining it as a value-sign. To argue about whether or not a work should be or has been properly canonized is not to take taste seriously. To take taste seriously is to recognize it as a function of the inherent variability and instability of one's unique personal history and one's interpretation of that history. The value of the institutionalization of literary value-signs lies not in their presentation as articles and objects of faith, but solely in their presentation as possible and at best traditionally recommended value-signs. Literature, after all, is merely something that some human beings do, the deposit of a particular kind of behavior. But so long as literature is predominantly a value institution, a comprehension of literature's place in human life will continue to be eluded, as will any rational comprehension of literature itself, including a firmly grounded theory of criticism, and especially, and above all, a firmly grounded theory of interpretation.

Criticism, Pleasure, and Truth: A Typology of Critical Statements

Marie-Laure Ryan

When speaking of criticism, we usually mean a discourse fulfilling a particular function and concerning a particular type of communicative event. To characterize this type of event, let us consider the following exchange. A professor, lecturing on physics, declares: "The composition of atoms is conveniently described by a specific number of protons and neutrons that are present in the nucleus." Interrupting his lecture, he turns toward a student and asks: "By the way, Jack, what is a proton?" Before the student answers, another whispers in a nasalized voice: "If you answer this question correctly, you'll win a 13-inch color TV."[1]

In speech act theory,[2] the first and the third utterances belong to the same class—representative statements—as opposed to the second, which belongs to the directive class. While the second sentence is supposed to get the hearer to perform an action (in this case demonstrate his knowledge of physics), the first and third utterances constitute attempts to describe a state of affairs. Since the third utterance is obviously false as a description of the actual situation, speech act theory would regard it as an unfelicitous assertion. But if the utterance fails as an assertion, it remains successful, at least potentially, as an act of communication. The class may demonstrate its recognition of the speaker's intent, and its approval of the communicative act, by bursting into laughter. To grasp the function of such a statement, we must probe more deeply into the speaker's intent than just to the level forming the explicit concern of speech act theory. We must not only ask, with speech act theory, "what can a speaker do with a proposition P"—a question whose possible answers are types of illocutionary forces, such as *ask*, *assert*, *order*, and *promise*—but we must also ask, with a more general theory of communication, "what can a speaker do with a complete speech act?" We must investigate the speaker's possible motivation for producing an utterance with the illocutionary force F and the propositional content P.

Each of the utterances of the above exchange illustrates a different type of motivation. The first is oriented toward *information*, the second toward *action*, and the third toward *pleasure*.[3] Everyday conversation is a patchwork of mostly spontaneous utterances belonging to one or the other of these categories. On the textual level, the three basic orientations are constitutive of genre. Laws and recipes are action-oriented, biographies and news reports information-oriented, and novels, poems and jokes are illustrations of the pleasure category.[4] The difference between action, information, and pleasure utterances can be captured by examining the criteria by which the hearer evaluates the message, and the conditions which have to be fulfilled if the utterance is to be successful as an act of communication. An utterance oriented toward action is characterized by a lack of relevant criteria for evaluation. The speaker does not invite the hearer to form any particular opinion of the message, but simply to accomplish a specific action. When the hearer responds in the appropriate manner, whatever his private thoughts may be, the transaction is successful. The hearer's evaluation of the message may determine his choice of action—hence the importance of rhetoric in action-oriented genres such as political speeches and advertisements—but while forming a specific opinion of an action-oriented text can be instrumental, it is never essential to the success of the exchange.

With information and pleasure-oriented texts, on the other

hand, the hearer's evaluation is of prime importance. The sender of an information text invites the hearer to extract a message and to use it as material in forming his image of the world. Since the point of the transaction is to increase the hearer's knowledge of reality, the relevant evaluative criteria are the *truth* and, given the truth, the *novelty* of the contents. Insofar as they claim to convey true facts about the world, informational utterances create a competition with other messages: accepting one of them means rejecting as false a number of actual or possible conflicting utterances.[5] No such competition exists in the world of pleasure utterances. We can accept a pleasure text as satisfactory, without taking an implicit stand as to the validity of other messages. This is so because pleasure-oriented texts do not offer something worth extracting and using, but rather, something worth experiencing. The hearer expects immediate satisfaction from a pleasure text, and this satisfaction must come from the act of *receiving* the text. Which criteria are used in the evaluation process cannot be stated uniformly and definitively for the entire class. Pleasure, unlike information, is a highly diversified phenomenon. Evaluative criteria differ from person to person, from genre to genre, and within the same genre they must be adjusted for each individual text. All we can say is that the reader's/hearer's satisfaction is independent of the truth of the contents.

The irrelevance of the question of truth does not mean that all pleasure-oriented messages must remain unverified in the actual world and fall within the category of fictional statements. Reports of facts may very well be meant by their authors to be read for the sake of pleasure. This is presumably the case with Truman Capote's *In Cold Blood* and with the autobiographies and published correspondences of many literary authors. Conversely, fictionality is not restricted to the pleasure category: many advertisements include the verbal or visual representation of a fictional situation. But if the categories pleasure and fiction do not coincide entirely, the theoretical importance of their relationship should not be overlooked. When a nonfictional text is offered for the sake of pleasure, the author is implicitly telling the reader: this text would still be rewarding if it were a fiction. It should not really matter to the reader whether or not *In Cold Blood* reports a true story, or whether Elizabeth Barrett Browning's *Sonnets from the Portuguese* express the author's real feeling. If a pleasure-oriented text is to be successful, it should be worth reading as a piece of fiction.

Of the three categories action-, information-, and pleasure-oriented messages, the concern of criticism is clearly the last one. We have seen above that the evaluative criteria relevant to the pleasure orientation can only be defined negatively for the entire class, as *not* being the truth and novelty of the contents. The function of criticism is to fill in the blank in this definition by elaborating tailor-made criteria for the specific text under consideration. Insofar as its concern is a text's ability to provide a pleasurable reading/hearing experience, criticism is not restricted to those messages whose primary *raison d'être* is to create pleasure. Action and information texts may also be subjected to criticial inquiry if they are worth reading for the sake of pleasure. On the other hand, not all statements about pleasure-oriented texts fulfill a critical function. While Roman Jakobson's attempts to uncover pleasant phonic patterns in the political slogan "I like Ike" is an act of criticism, the statement "*Madame Bovary* was published in 1857" is not, because it is not relevant to the text's ability to yield pleasure to the reader.

In contrast to the texts with which it is mainly concerned, criticism is not aimed toward pleasure, but toward information. Rejecting a critical act means endorsing a competing statement. That criticism is evaluated as informational discourse is demonstrated by this imaginary refutal, which could appear in the "Forum" section of a critical journal: "The argument of Professor Nebelmacher's article 'The Concept of the Self in John Smith's Late Fiction' is fallacious and mistaken. When he claims that Smith's hero retreats inward in order to kill his old self, Professor Nebelmacher ignores internal evidence, and misses the real point of the novel." This statement exposes the paradox of critical discourse: while truth is irrelevant in pleasure-oriented texts, it remains relevant in the metadiscourse relating to these texts. To see under which conditions criticism can satisfy the criterion of truth and constitute a successful act of communication, let us review the various types of statements which enter into the composition of critical essays.

First of the distinctions to be made is among *judgments, descriptions,* and *interpretations*. Judgments represent the critic's subjective opinion of the text, and their truth or falsity is a question of sincerity. A judgment P is true of a text if the critic thinks that P is true, and it is successful as an act of communication if the reader is led to form the same personal opinion.

The truth condition pertaining to judgments is clearly not sufficient in the case of descriptive and interpretive statements. I take it that "Madame Bovary is the wife of a country doctor" is a descriptive statement with respect to Flaubert's novel, and that "Madame Bovary is led to suicide by her inability to distinguish fiction from reality" is an interpretive statement. A recent attempt by R. J. Matthews to define the distinction between the two categories is formulated in terms of the epistemic relation of the speaker to the subject matter.[6] A description, Matthews argues, is a statement uttered by a speaker who is in a position to know whether or not what he says is true, while an interpretation is a proposition advanced as simply plausible on the basis of some data. Another way to characterize the distinction would be to say that descriptive statements are immune to the introduction of additional evidence, while interpretive statements are liable to be overturned if additional relevant data become available. By probing more deeply into Flaubert's novel, a critic may be led to attack the above statement about Emma Bovary's reasons for committing suicide, but no matter how many other facts this critic discovers about *Madame Bovary*, he will not challenge the statement that Emma is the wife of a country doctor.

The descriptive statements found in critical discourse fall into two subcategories. The first comprises metalinguistic statements of the form "the text has x," where x stands for a linguistic or discourse entity with a qualifier, such as "three strophes," "rhymes in /aj/," or "sentences with multiple embedding." In the second subcategory are paraphrases of the text's component sentences and accounts of the propositions which are semantically entailed by the propositions asserted in the text. The stating of these propositions is what gives rise to summaries. A summary is a set of propositions which are necessarily true of the same states of affairs for which the text is true.

Interpretive statements are also divided into several categories. The first is exemplified by this passage, quoted from Jonas Spatz's article, "The Mystery of Eros: Sexual Initiation in Coleridge's 'Christabel'":

> Christabel sees in her stepmother the daughter who can compete for her father's love the only way the conscious Christabel cannot: sexually. Geraldine embodies the Oedipal feeling that Christabel's conscious mind has repressed.[7]

Since Coleridge's poem is a fiction, and since Christabel and Geraldine do not exist in reality, these statements are as indeterminate in truth value as the famous logical example, "The king of France is bald." The critic advances them as true in an alternate possible world[8]—the world of "Christabel"—and the reader assesses their truth value with respect to that world. To determine their validity, the reader applies a criterion to which I shall refer as "the principle of minimal departure." This principle, which I derive from the work of David Lewis on fiction and counterfactuals,[9] is that whenever we interpret a message about an alternate possible world, we reconstrue this world as being the closest possible to the reality we know. This means that we will project upon the fictional universe as many as possible of the propositions which we take to be true for the actual world, and that we will make only those adjustments which we cannot avoid. For instance, if a fairy tale tells us about a blue flying horse, we will reconstrue an animal possessing all the properties of real-world horses, except for the color and the ability to fly. Through the principle of minimal departure, literary theory can achieve a satisfactory compromise between the Aristotelian view of literature as mimesis, and the modern doctrine of the radical autonomy of the literary text and of the world it calls into being. If the doctrine of mimetism were adopted literally, authors would be at fault for departing from reality, and the creation of fictional universes would constitute an illicit activity. On the other hand, if the world of the text were radically autonomous, the reader would have no firm basis for filling in the space left open by the text, and interpretation would become impossible.

By allowing a fictional universe to differ from the real world, while at the same time maintaining some ties between fiction and reality, the principle of minimal departure overcomes both of these difficulties. If the principle holds, the conditions for evaluating interpretive statements about fictional worlds will be spelled as follows: Imagine a world A where a given interpretive statement is true, together with the facts established by a text.[10] Imagine a world B where these facts are also true, but in which the same interpretive statement is false. The interpretation will be considered valid with respect to the text if world A differs less than world B from the reality we know. (This is a rephrasing of Lewis's principle.) Accepting the statement, "Christabel's conscious mind has repressed the Oedipal feeling," thus means entertaining the opinion that the reconstruction of an alternate possible universe in which Christabel represses her desire for her father involves a more economical adjustment of our representation of reality than the reconstruction of a world where Christabel's thoughts or behavior, as described by the text, are compatible with the statement that she has surrendered to the Oedipal feeling. Or to put it in a simpler way: it means that the reader who agrees with the interpretation would make a similar statement of a real-world person about whom he had similar information.

The principle of minimal departure means not only that the reader can use his direct experience of reality to fill in the fictional universe, it also means that the statements which interpret the real world have potential explanatory power for the world of the text, as long as their objects are members of both worlds. Since the world of "Christabel" possesses human beings living in nuclear families and experiencing desire for members of the opposite sex, a critic is justified to seek explanation in the writings of Freud. This does not mean that Freud's writings are a member of the world of "Christabel." Since the text never refers to them, the proposition "Freud's writings exist" is indeterminate or false for Coleridge's poem. (Existential propositions constitute an exception to the principle of minimal departure in that they cannot be directly carried over from the real to the fictional world.) What makes the propositions advanced by Freud applicable to other worlds than the one in which they were uttered is that, as R. J. Mathews puts it, "propositions are rules for picking out a set of worlds—namely the worlds for which this proposition takes the value true."[11] This definition permits Freud's theories to take the value false for the real world, but the value true for a given fiction. The consequence of this possibility is that a critic who proposes a Freudian reading of a literary work does not necessarily take a stand as to the validity of Freud's doctrine for the actual world, nor does the reader who accepts his reading.

The second type of interpretive statement concerns the message of the work for the *actual world*.[12] An example of this type would be: "George Orwell's *1984* warns us against the dangers of totalitarian systems." The acceptability of the critical act of deriving a real world message from a fictional text does not depend on the truth of the message, but on whether or not it was correctly derived. The derivational mechanism consists of approaching the text as an instance of *exemplary discourse*. The interpreter views the state of affairs obtaining in the fictional universe as the illustration of a general principle. If P explains the fictional facts, and if P has explanatory power for the facts of reality, then P can be reconstrued as a possible message. It will be noted that this procedure inverts the principle of minimal departure. Since the reader completes and interprets the facts of the fictional world on the basis of his experience of reality, the message he extracts will reflect his experience, and the process will never be completely free of circularity.

The third type of interpretive statement concerns the text as a verbal entity. Since a text is a real object, the truth value of such statements will be assessed for the actual world. The critic does not simply advance them as potentially satisfiable in reality—as he does with the propositions aimed at capturing the message of the work—he takes personal responsibility for their validity. A sample of this type of statement includes: (1) "The novel's unity lies in its symbolic structure," (2) "The poem's mythical foundation comprises elements of what Joseph Campbell calls the monomyth of the hero," and (3) "The serpent symbolizes Christabel's sense of guilt." Each of these interpretations entails a proposition of the type "x is a sign or verbal entity, and x has property y." For instance, the first of the above statements contains the proposition "x is a symbol, x enters into a structure, and this structure gives unity to the novel." And the second statement really means "x is the plot of the poem, and x shows a resemblance to the plot of the 'monomyth of the hero'." The difference between statements concerning signs as signs, and statements concerning the worlds created by these signs, can be illustrated by the contrast between "The serpent symbolizes Christabel's sense of guilt" (third type of interpretation) and "In *Paradise Lost,* the serpent is commissioned by Lucifer to cause the fall of mankind" (first type). While the first example can be paraphrased as "the image of the serpent," the second cannot: its subject matter is not a sign, but a blood and flesh member of a possible world.

The statement about the symbolism of the serpent in "Christabel" finds its truth value in the actual world, but it embeds a proposition which, when considered by itself, provides an interpretation of the textual world: "Christabel feels guilty." This example demonstrates the dependency relationships linking the various kinds of critical statements. The three basic types and their subtypes rarely occur in pure form in a critical essay: most sentences are multilevel groupings of propositions concerning different worlds, and therefore following different truth conditions. Consider for instance the following sentence, from the abstract of Spatz's "Christabel" article:

> In a series of poems written from 1797 to 1801, Coleridge dramatized the problem of sexual maturation by focusing on the betrothal of a girl threatened by her own sexuality.

In this sentence are hierarchically combined: a statement of literary history ("Coleridge wrote a series of poems from 1797 to 1801"), introducing a description of the poems' content (the betrothal of a girl), which the critic completes with an interpretive statement concerning the textual world ("the girl is being threatened by her own sexuality"), so as to derive an interpretive statement capturing the message of the works for the actual world: "Sexual maturation, in Coleridge's opinion, is a threatening process." Getting at this latter statement is clearly the point of the whole utterance.

As this example suggests, the different types and subtypes of critical statements present various degrees of self-sufficiency. (I call self-sufficient a statement which may form the *point* of a critical text.) The least autonomous are descriptive statements. The reader who is already familiar with the text under consideration has automatic access to the information conveyed by descriptions. If criticism is to satisfy the criteria of truth and novelty, descriptive statements should not be used as an end in themselves, but as a basis for judgments and interpretations.[13]

The first type of interpretive statement is often used to support interpretations of the second category. But explaining how things are, and why they are the way they are in the world of a text may also constitute the *raison d'être* of a critical essay. Since this brand of criticism tells us nothing about the real world, its only conceivable communicative function is to increase the pleasure which we take in the text. The postulate underlying its production is that if we enjoy the world of a text, the more we learn about this world, the greater our gratification. Accepting an interpretive statement as both true and new in the world of a pleasure text means discovering additional reasons to appreciate the text. It is in this rather indirect sense that our first type of interpretation can be said to produce criteria for evaluating the text, and to be concerned with its ability to yield pleasure to the reader.

The second type of interpretive statement is usually self-sufficient. If the rules of the pleasure game are to be respected in an essay whose point is to extract the message of a text, critic and reader should share the assumption that reconstruing such a message is a source of pleasure, regardless of its truth value in the actual world. Disagreeing with the message of a work should not prevent the reader from enjoying the text. In most cases, however, the second type of interpretation leads to considerations which do not fit the above definition of critical discourse. Interpreters may engage in a discussion of the originality and validity of the message, thereby treating the work as an information text. (A message will, of course, be doubly rewarding if it satisfies the evaluative criteria of two distinct categories!) Or interpreters may use the message of the work as a basis for statements pertaining to literary history, history of ideas, or even biography. For instance, Spatz invokes his own reading of "Christabel" to refute other scholars' suggestions that Coleridge was either impotent, repressed, or homosexual. This sort of conclusion could have been reached through other types of evidence, such as letters, diaries, or the testimony of contemporaries. In making such a statement, the interpreter is therefore using the work as a mere *document.*

The third type of interpretation has two different uses. In its analytical form, "x is a sign and x means y," it leads to interpretive acts pertaining to the textual world. In the form "x is a sign and x has effect y on the reader," it explores directly the sources of the text's ability to provide pleasure, and it supports personal judgments.

Of all types of critical statements, judgments are the most autonomous. They can be fed by all other types—and they lead back to none of them. In conjunction with the statements upon which they are built, however, they provide basic data for poetics, a discourse whose concern is not the individual text as a pleasure object, but the general principles underlying the activity of using language for the sake of pleasure.

Since the coming of age of semiotic studies, great emphasis has been placed on the institutionalized, culture-bound aspects of discourse phenomena. Being widely practiced as an academic discipline, criticism is now indeed a cultural institution, as are poetics and literary history. But unlike history and poetics, criticism does not owe its existence to the academic institution. The three types of statements which constitute critical discourse occur as spontaneously in conversation as do utterances embodying a pleasure orientation. Returning to our opening example, we can imagine that the student's remark prompted reactions such as the following: "You know what Bill said in class today when the prof asked Jack a question? Something about winning a 13-inch color TV if he could answer correctly" (description). "He spoke through the nose, and the whole thing was so funny" (judgment). "He pretended the prof was conducting a TV game show" (interpretation/filling in of fictional universe on the basis of real-world knowledge). "He seemed to be just kidding, but I think he was trying to tell the prof that P" (interpretation/reconstruction of a real-world message). Just as the speaker who joked about the classroom situation was engaging in an activity which underlies all institutionalized pleasure-oriented genres (literary or not), so the speaker who later describes, judges, and interprets the joke lays down the foundations of critical discourse.

NOTES

1. The last utterance of this exchange is adopted from Mark Hansell and Cheryl Seabrook, "Some Conversational Conventions of Black English," in *Proceedings of the Fourth Annual Meeting of the Berkeley Linguistic Society* (Berkeley: Berkeley Linguistic Society, 1978), p. 577.

2. As outlined by John Searle in *Speech Acts: An Essay in the Philosophy of Language* (Cambridge: Cambridge University Press, 1969) and other publications.

3. For a more detailed discussion of these categories, see my "Toward a Competence Theory of Genre," *Poetics* 8 (1979):307–69.

4. The three categories are valid not only for verbal exchanges, but also for visual and nonlinguistic auditive communication. Paintings and music are pleasure-oriented, traffic signs and the whistles of a dog-trainer are action-oriented, and the illustrations of a textbook convey information, as does the ringing of a bell to mark time or a special event.

5. On the problem of competition between different messages, see Michael McCanles, "All Discourse Aspires to the Analytic Proposi-

tion," in *What Is Literature,* ed. Paul Hernadi (Bloomington: Indiana University Press, 1978), pp. 190–205.

6. "Describing and Interpreting a Work of Art," *Journal of Aesthetics and Art Criticism* 36 (Fall 1977):5–14.

7. *PMLA* 90, no. 1 (1975):113.

8. By possible I mean in fact imaginable. A fictional universe may transgress the laws of nature and be consequently materially impossible.

9. See *Counterfactuals* (Cambridge: Harvard University Press, 1973), and "Truth in Fiction," *American Philosophical Quarterly* 15, no. 1 (1978):37–46.

10. A problem which deserves further consideration is how we decide what counts as a fact in the world of a text. Should we assume that the text, as world-creating utterance, has absolute authority, and that whatever its speaker asserts should be entered as true for the fictional universe? This position leads to serious difficulties. If the set of propositions over which this universe is defined were immediately given in the text, the reader would have no choice but to take ironic statements at face value, and to accept all the declarations of unreliable narrators. To avoid this pitfall, we must assume that the propositions which hold in the world of the text are themselves abstracted, rather than mechanically derived, from the sentences which constitute the text. The act of establishing the facts which hold in the textual world thus straddles the borderline between description and interpretation.

11. See "Literary Works Express Propositions," in *What Is Literature,* p. 108.

12. In the case of nonfictional pleasure texts, this category falls together with the preceding one.

13. The only context in which descriptions retain their informational value are reviews intended to introduce a literary work to a circle of prospective readers. But this critical genre would be incomplete without the critic's personal judgment, so even there descriptions must be subordinated to another type of statement.

2

Criticism as Re-presentation

What Can Structuralism Do for Us?

Susan Rubin Suleiman

Despite the touch of parody the astute reader may detect in my title, my impulse in this essay is nothing if not serious. I wish to explore what structuralism can (still) do for us, we being the self-conscious members of the American academic establishment, teachers and students of literature and the humanities.

Why structuralism? Because, of all the intellectual "isms" of the late twentieth century, even discounting the element of modishness that accompanies such "isms," structuralism looked for a while as if it promised the most: not only a rigorous method of analysis grounded in the science of linguistics and applicable to every kind of human activity (to the extent that every kind of human activity could be thought of as a language, a system of signs), but also a philosophy, a vision capable of renewing our whole sense of what human life was about. Structuralism, wrote Roland Barthes in 1963, "brings to light the properly human process by which men give meaning to things. . . . *Homo significans:* such might be the new man of structural research."[1]

This kind of optimism is now gone. Although structuralism as a method and semiotics as the general science of signs continue to flourish in Europe and even in the United States, and although they have produced over the past two decades an impressive body of works, few structuralists or semioticians writing today would make the sweeping claims for their activity that Roland Barthes made twenty years age. Barthes himself repudiated his structuralist positivism as early as 1971 (in the opening pages of *S/Z*) and used the authority of his chair at the Collège de France to proclaim the futility of all systematization, all pretentions to scientific discourse about culture. The only semiology he was still prepared to offer was a "negative" one.[2]

Barthes was of course not the only radical French critic of structuralism. In the very year that Barthes published his programmatic essay on "The Structuralist Activity," Jacques Derrida was already attacking the abstraction and reductionism, the static formalism and the "metaphysics and simultaneity" that characterized "every structuralism and every structuralist gesture."[3] Not long afterward, Julia Kristeva and the *Tel Quel* group were proclaiming the need for a new semiotics that would be none other than a subversion of the "old" one.[4] Thus in the very years when French structuralism, having absorbed the works of its predecessors the Russian Formalists and the Prague Structuralists (works that became available in France in the early 1960s), was elaborating its own methodology and producing its own great monuments (Lévi-Strauss's *Mythologiques*, Foucault's *Les Mots et les choses*, Althusser's *Pour Marx*, Barthes's *Eléments de sémiologie* and "Introduction à l'analyse structurale des récits," Greimas's *Sémantique structurale*, Genette's three-volume *Figures*, Todorov's *Poétique de la prose* and *Introduction à la littérature fantastique*, Bremond's *Logique du récit* were all published in the decade between 1963 and 1973), it was already being doubled by a discourse whose main thrust was to undermine or radically redefine the most basic notions of structuralism, beginning with the Saussurean notion of the sign and extending to every major binary opposition: synchrony/diachrony, presence/ absence, subject/object, rule/manifestation, code/message.

What must be stressed, however, is that in France this simultaneity of opposing discourses was not felt as such. As the term *post-structuralism,* which has come to designate the enterprise of Derrida and his followers, indicates, the relationship between structuralism and its radical critique was felt to be one of temporal succession.[5] One consequence of this sense of historical succession was that structuralism, both in literary theory and in other fields, had a chance to sink in and attain a certain dominance before the challenges to it became manifest. The term post-structuralism is thus fully appropriate in the French case, for it indicates a *traversing* of structuralism rather than a going around it. The intellectual trajectory of Roland Barthes is a particularly clear example.

In the United States things have been different, and it is precisely the difference that occasions this essay. Structuralism and post-structuralism reached the American universities almost at the same time, with the result that the first did not have time to be absorbed before being already displaced by the second. This was especially true in the field of literary theory. Whereas Lévi-Strauss and Foucault were translated early (at least as such things go—with a three-to-five-year gap), most of Todorov's and Genette's work remains untranslated; Bremond's work is little known except by a few specialists, and of Greimas there exists almost nothing in English. The relatively quick translation of Barthes's works is an exception, but it is significant that his most "structuralist" article of all, the "Introduction to the Structural Analysis of Narrative," had to wait nine years before appearing in English.[6] By then it was past history for Barthes himself; for the large majority of American students of literature, whose reading knowledge of French is at best shaky, the article was new. But it appeared well after Paul de Man's *Blindness and Insight* (1971), which was already a celebration of Derrida and of post-structuralism. Compared to the impact that Barthes's article had in France, its impact here was minimal. It had come too late.

At this point, I can foresee two possible objections to my argument. First, am I not exaggerating in claiming that structuralism "hit" the universities much later here than in France? Students and professors of French literature are, after all, members of the university, and they don't need translations.

The influential *Yale French Studies* issue on *Structuralism*, which was in English, appeared in 1966, and *The Structuralist Controversy*, with a line-up ranging from Todorov to Derrida, was published in 1970. Granted, but all this does not alter the fact that in university departments of English and Comparative Literature, whose students, faculty, and degree of influence on the intellectual life of the country far outweigh those of French departments (many of which, let us not forget, were, and still are, fiercely split over "la nouvelle critique"), structuralism has never been fully understood or assimilated. This is partly due to the absence of translations of structuralist literary theory and criticism and partly to more complex historical reasons, the chief of which, I suspect, is that structuralism's surface similarities with the New Criticism impeded its acceptance at a time when the dominant mood in the United States was anti-New Critical. The most adventurous of the anti-New Critics (I am thinking especially of the so-called "Yale School") were, however, perfectly receptive to Derridean post-structuralism, which allowed them to inject into American theory a whole strain of Continental philosophical thought going from Nietzsche to Husserl to Heidegger. One foreseeable consequence has been that some of Derrida's American opponents have tended, in the heat of battle, to confuse post-structuralism with structuralism—a step that benefits no one and that can only cause further misunderstanding.[7]

A second possible objection follows closely on the first: why should I deplore the fact that an early work like Barthes's 1966 article on the analysis of narrative has had little impact in the United States? The article is largely outdated, even in terms of structural analysis; it belongs at best in a course on the history of structuralist criticism. Although the objection has some validity, I would challenge it on both specific and general grounds. Specifically, one cannot fully understand *S/Z*, which is perhaps the one work of structuralist orientation—but already veering away from classical structuralism—that graduate students these days are exposed to, without knowing the 1966 article, of which *S/Z* was both a continuation and a major modification.[8] More generally, and more importantly for our present discussion, the lack of firsthand knowledge (and for students I mean by that classroom study under the guidance of a well-informed instructor) of seminal structuralist works has led to some blinding misconceptions about structuralism, misconceptions that tend to be passed on in the classroom and even in print. Despite the popularity and usefulness of works of synthesis like Jonathan Culler's *Structuralist Poetics* (1975) or Robert Scholes's *Structuralism in Literature* (1974), structuralism is bound to be misunderstood as long as knowledge about it is limited to secondary sources.

It is by discussing some of the more commonly held misconceptions about structuralism (most often formulated as a reason for dismissing it) that I will try, in what follows, to suggest the positive uses to which structuralism may be put. My reason for proceeding in this way is not merely polemical. Critical misconceptions can be instructive, since they usually reflect in a distorted way what are, or have been, genuine criticisms. The misconceptions I shall deal with are interesting because they each touch on what might be called a sensitive nerve ending of the structural approach to literature.

1. *Structuralism is a pseudo-science; it tells us in jargonized language and by means of complicated graphs, diagrams and tables, what we already know anyway. As such it is not only useless but pernicious, for it deprives literature and criticism of their humane qualities.*

This is recognizably the "traditional rearguard" objection to structuralism. It reflects the very deep suspicion that humanists have of science, systematization and metalanguage in general. It is as though a language about literature which lays claim to scientific precision somehow threatens the humane values that literature embodies. Beneath this noble suspicion there may of course also lie the simple fear of, and resistance to, learning a difficult new vocabulary: why bother, if structural analysis only tells us, in technical language, what we already know—know perhaps not so clearly, but sufficiently for our purposes?

Despite its apparent obtuseness and self-serving quality, the argument is not without power. I can think of two responses to it. First, it is not at all certain that an explicit account of, and accounting for, what we "already know" implicitly or intuitively is useless. Barthes anticipated a similar objection when he defined the structuralist activity as the decomposition and the recomposition of an object, the fabrication of its simulacrum:

> At first glance it is not much (which is what makes some people say that structuralist work is "insignificant, uninteresting, useless, etc."). And yet, from another point of view, that not much is decisive; for between the two objects [the original and its simulacrum], the two moments of the structuralist activity, something *new* is produced, and this new thing is nothing less than general intelligibility: the simulacrum is intellect added to the object. . . .

To make explicit what we "already know" about a work of literature is to bring our own intellect to bear on it. Far from being antihumanistic, it is the very sign of our humanity: "this addition . . . is man himself, his history, his situation, his freedom, and the very resistance that nature opposes to his mind."[9] Professors of literature know perfectly well that there is a difference between "knowing what we know" and "saying what we know that we know." The whole enterprise of teaching literature in a classroom would become derisory if that were not true.

But that still does not answer the objection to the use of "jargon." Granted that all commentary on a text is metalanguage, why choose a metalanguage as technical and as bristling with neologisms as the vocabulary of structural analysis? There would be no reason for doing so, *unless* the introduction of new technical terms allowed us to see things we had not seen before—indeed, to know things we had not known before. Structural analysis at its best (and here we can only be concerned with it at its best) allows precisely that. The examples one could adduce range from Saussure's enabling distinction between *langue* and *parole* (Did we really "know" the difference before? All of contemporary linguistics is founded on it.) to Gérard Genette's distinction between *voice* and *mode* in narrative. Genette is a good case in point, for his comprehensive study of narrative discourse, *Discours du récit,* has enabled us not only to speak more precisely about what we already knew, but also to perceive differences where we saw none before.[10] By disentangling, among other things, the question of "who tells" from the question of "who sees" the events of a story, Genette has completely renewed our conception of narration and point of view. He could not have done this without the use of a highly refined, minutely differentiated classification and nomenclature. As Saussure's work already made clear, to name a thing is in a sense to bring it into existence.

Where, in this case, is the critical insight behind the misconception? It lies in the humanist critic's intuitive sense that the only real value in an analytic method, especially where literature is concerned, is in the results it produces. The danger of structural analysis, like that of any highly sophisticated methodology, is that it may become an end in itself, or worse still, a substitute for thought. But the abuse of a method is no indictment against the method itself. Critics who write in "ordinary language" can also produce nonsense.

2. *Structuralism ignores history. It is all right as far as static description goes, but it cannot deal with temporal phenomena.*

This might be called the vulgar Marxist misconception of structuralism, not to be confused with the subtle and informed Marxist critique formulated by, say, Fredric Jameson. The misconception is based on the fact that structuralism privileges synchrony over diachrony and tends to "transform stories into permanent states." This observation, made by the eminent structural semantician A. J. Greimas, shows that structuralism is not unaware of its own problem with temporality; as Greimas again notes, "the fact of placing oneself in the attitude of the receiver of messages has as its consequence that historical algorithms present themselves as states, in other words as static structures."[11] For Greimas, the transformation of story into structure is the inescapable consequence of understanding, since in order to understand the "meaning" of a story (or of history) one has to grasp it all at once. A structural understanding is more like a map one can take in at a glance than like a journey along a road.

This does not mean, however, that structuralism is incapable of dealing with diachrony. As Jameson, whose critique of structuralism concentrates precisely on the question of history, acknowledges, "It would be wrong to conclude that no diachronic development whatsoever is possible in the Saussurean model."[12] Structuralism treats history as a succession of systems or states, each of which can be described with great detail and precision—whence Jameson's perfectly just assessment that for structuralism, history is the "history of models" or the description of successive states, each of which can be thought of as a transformation of a preceding one. Foucault's *Les Mots et les choses (The Order of Things)* stands as a monumental example of this kind of history. Jameson insists, however, that a methodological problem still remains: "the methodological problem . . . is not so much related to the content of the moments described, but rather to the passage from one moment to another. . . ."[13] Structuralism, in other words, cannot explain how and why one state is transformed into another.

This charge seems accurate enough as far as *Les Mots et les choses* is concerned.[14] It is no reason, however, to dismiss wholesale what structuralism offers the historian: a methodological tool for uncovering, beneath the linearity of events and the multiplicity of surface phenomena, the structures of thought, of social and economic organization, that determine the "shape" of a historical period.

As far as literature is concerned, it seems not insignificant that the most interesting contributions of structuralism so far have been in the domain of the analysis of narrative—definitely a temporal phenomenon. Although it is true that structuralists have been for the most part concerned with the logic of narrative rather than with its chronology, the notion of transformation allows for algorithms that account for the development of a narrative from an initial to a final state; and the notion of syntagmatic (as opposed to paradigmatic) organization allows for quite detailed analyses of the sequential unfolding of individual narratives.

Yes, but can structuralism deal with literary history? We know that the Russian Formalists already attempted to account for literary evolution by their theory of "defamiliarization"—the history of literary forms being the continuous process whereby formal devices are renewed, become banalized through repetition and imitation, and are renewed again. This view, as F. W. Galan has pointed out, is "already a far cry from the traditional view of literary 'progress' as a succession of masters and their influences—an approach that produced what Viktor Sklovkij sarcastically termed the literary history of the generals."[15] As Galan further points out, the Formalist notion of literary evolution was expanded and modified by the Czech Structuralists to include not only the internal evolution of forms but the interaction of literature with the larger cultural system as well.

Some of the work being done today by semioticians as far-flung as the Moscow-Tartu semiotics group or the Porter Institute for Poetics and Semiotics at Tel-Aviv University suggests that the meeting ground between structuralism and literary and cultural history is becoming a well-populated place. The notion of the literary polysystem (i.e., the complex and many-layered organization of the literary domain in a given culture during a specific period), as it has recently been developed by I. Even-Zohar in the tradition of the Czech structuralists, seems to me especially fruitful.[16] A history of literature that would consist of the description of successive states of the literary polysystem in one country (or of neighboring polysystems at a given time), taking into account both the intrinsic dynamism of the system and the extrinsic intervention of other factors, would be an extremely important structuralist contribution to literary and cultural history.

3. *Structuralism is like New Criticism: it treats the text as an autonomous object, cut off both from its context and from the reading subject.*

4. *Structuralism neglects meaning; it is irredeemably opposed to hermeneutics.*

These two accusations, which are interrelated and which one sees repeated in various forms by critics advocating a new philosophically or hermeneutically or subjectively oriented criticism, are at first glance the most damaging to structuralism. If they were correct, there would indeed be little that structuralism could do for us today. They are not correct, however; those who accept them without further examination show a lack of awareness both of the historical development of structuralism and of its most fundamental notions, beginning with Saussure's notion that no isolated element, whether in language or anything else, has meaning except insofar as it is integrated into a signifying system.

The idea that structuralism is like New Criticism and suffers from all the latter's limitations is based on a misunderstanding which equates structuralism with a narrow formalism. This is not the place to show that even the Russian Formalists were not nearly as narrow in their conception of criticism and of the literary work as they are sometimes made out to be. Their insistence on the *specificity* of literature and on the status of literary works as objects of study independent of social, historical, and biographical events—in other words, their claim that the study of literature must accede to a discipline and a methodology of its own—in no way implied that they considered individual works to exist in a vacuum. Their analyses of single works were always theoretical in orientation, the work being seen as a means of studying a general problem in poetics. Furthermore, as Boris Eichenbaum noted in his 1927 essay on "The Theory of the 'Formal' Method," the Formalists very soon realized that even general poetics could not do without a consideration of literary history: "Our moving into the area of the history of literature was no simple expansion of our study; it resulted from the evolution of our concept of form. We found that we could not see the literary work in isolation, that we had to see its form against a background of other works rather than by itself."[17] This is quite different from the New Critics' insistence on the autonomy of "the work itself," just as the

Formalists' claim to a rigorous scientific method is different from the New Critics' "practical," empirical, essentially antitheoretical approach to the text.

In a recent polemical essay, Geoffrey Hartman has laid much of the blame for the present isolation of the humanities from social and political life in the United States on the excesses of practical criticism: "The tradition of practical criticism," he writes, "so narrow at present, has limited our awareness of the relation of literature to the practical life, which includes law, religion, economics, and the process of institutionalization itself."[18] Although Hartman does not make the mistake of confusing structuralism with New Criticism, he nevertheless dismisses structuralism on the grounds that it is against interpretation (p. 497). Before turning to that question, I would remark that structuralism at present offers precisely the bridge between literature and the "practical life" that Hartman calls for in his essay. It is true that the first wave of structuralism was concerned almost exclusively with the development of generic and logical models for narrative and poetic structures, independently of the larger cultural system in which literature existed. The emphasis was on the internal organization of literature and literary works, on typologies and taxonomies. As early as Roland Barthes's pioneering work on modern mythologies, however, and certainly as early as Lévi-Strauss's study of primitive myths, structuralism showed itself capable of relating the structure of individual narratives to the society in which they functioned. As Paul Ricoeur has pointed out, Lévi-Strauss's analysis of the Oedipus myth showed that "the myth is not a logical operator between just any proposition, but between propositions that point toward extreme situations: origins and ends, death, suffering, sexuality."[19]

Increasingly today, structuralist critics and theorists of literature tend to view the individual work not only as part of a larger, specifically literary system—the genre, the literary production of a period or of a culture—but to view the literary system itself as only a subsystem in a more general system of cultural productions which includes law, religion, economics, and the process of institutionalization itself (among other things). The way to open up the study of literature to the study of the practical life is not to dismiss the scientific aims of structuralism but to extend them, not to confine structuralism to an outdated and simplified view of it but to build on its most fruitful insights. One of these, already perceived by the Russian Formalists, was succinctly stated by Tzvetan Todorov in 1964: "The exhaustive description of a phenomenon without recourse to the general system into which it is integrated is impossible."[20]

This brings me to the question of the relation between structuralism and hermeneutics, which is perhaps the major question confronting literary theory today. The immense popularity and influence, both in the United States and Europe, of what has come to be called reader-oriented or audience-oriented criticism, testifies to the growing concern with problems of interpretation. Whatever the approach one adopts—sociological, historical, phenomenological, psychoanalytic, rhetorical—and whatever view of interpretation underlies it—the hermeneutic absolutism of E. D. Hirsch, the radical questioning of Derrida, the relativism of Stanley Fish, the pluralism of Wayne Booth, the militant subjectivism of David Bleich, or some intermediate position along the way—the importance accorded to the question of reading and interpretation remains central.[21]

Does structuralism have any place here, or is structuralism indeed against interpretation, indifferent to meaning? The source of this misconception lies no doubt in Saussure's often-quoted dictum that "in language there are only differences." To conclude from this statement, which says that no element in language has meaning in isolation, that structuralism is indifferent to meaning, is a gross oversimplification. Structuralism has not been primarily concerned with *stating* the meaning of, say, a work of literature. It has always been concerned, however, with "how meaning becomes possible, at what price and along what paths."[22] As I noted earlier, Barthes's name for "structuralist man" was *Homo significans*.

In recent years, the possibilities of convergence between

structuralism and hermeneutics have begun to be explored in a serious way. Jonathan Culler has defined structuralist poetics as "the theory of the practice of reading."[23] To my mind it is Paul Ricoeur, however, who has demonstrated most convincingly the way in which structural analysis and hermeneutics complement rather than oppose each other. In his magisterial essay, "Qu'est-ce qu'un texte? Expliquer et comprendre," Ricoeur argues that the Diltheyan dichotomy between explanation and understanding (the first being the province of the natural sciences, the second the province of textual interpretation) is a false dichotomy where the reading of texts is concerned. Rather than opposing the scientific explanations of structural analysis to the hermeneutic understanding of the interpreter, Ricoeur sees the two activities as continuous movements along a single "hermeneutic arc." Structural analysis, according to him, "far from evacuating [the] radical questioning [of the interpreter], restitutes it to a level of greater radicalness." The function of structural analysis, as shown by Lévi-Strauss's work on the Oedipus myth, is "to reject a surface semantics, that of the myth as it is told, in order to uncover a deep semantics."[24] Structural analysis becomes thus a "necessary stage between a naive interpretation and a critical one"; the movement along the hermeneutic arc becomes a series of mediations between the work of interpretation as it is practiced by the text on itself and the final appropriation of the text by a reader (pp. 198–200).

Ricoeur's essay was published in 1970; the authors of a more recent volume on the interpretation of narrative arrive at strikingly similar conclusions.[25] The volume itself, based on a colloquium held at the University of Toronto in 1976, is indicative of the convergence I have been discussing, for its chief concern is with the relationship between a formalist-structuralist and a phenomenological-hermeneutic approach to texts. Despite the differences in orientation and vocabulary, there is a surprising degree of agreement among the contributors regarding the interdependence and complementarity of the two approaches. Rather than being seen as deadly enemies, structuralism and hermeneutics are coming to be perceived as potential collaborators, each one providing the other with a dimension it lacks.

What can structuralism do for us? Certainly not everything. Nor, of course, have I been suggesting that a structuralist approach to literature is the only valid one. But it would be a pity if, blinded by easy slogans and seductive misconceptions, we rushed to consign structuralism to the dustbin of history. It was not a structuralist but one of structuralism's harshest critics who wrote, over fifteen years ago, what still seems pertinent today: "Since we are living on the fecundity of structuralism, it is too early to flog our dream. We must think instead about what it *could* mean."[26]

NOTES

1. "L'activité structuraliste," in *Essais critiques* (Paris: Éditions du Seuil, 1964), p. 218. All translations from the French are my own.

2. See the text of his inaugural lecture at the Collège de France: *Leçon* (Paris: Éditions du Seuil, 1978), pp. 35–36. In one of his last interviews before his untimely death in March 1980, Barthes reiterated his preference for "what is not systematic," and remarked that he himself no longer did any criticism. (Nadine Dormoy Savage, "Rencontre avec Roland Barthes," *The French Review*, February 1979, pp. 435, 437.)

3. "Force et signification," in *L'Écriture et la différence* (Paris: Éditions du Seuil, 1967), pp. 41–42. The essay was first published in *Critique* in June-July 1963.

4. Julia Kristeva, *Semeiotikè. Recherches pour une sémanalyse* (Paris: Éditions du Seuil, 1969), p. 31 and *passim*. The essay referred to here was first published in the Marxist journal *La Nouvelle Critique*, new series no. 16 (September 1968):15–20, and was also reprinted in the volume *Théorie d'ensemble* (Paris: La Collection *Tel Quel*, 1968).

5. This may have been due to the "events" of May 1968, which were unquestionably a major dividing line in the social and cultural life of the country. Structuralism was considered to have been "killed," or at least dealt a serious blow, by the "événements de mai,"

when one of the slogans posted on the walls of the Sorbonne proclaimed: "Une structure ne descend pas dans la rue."

6. Originally published in 1966 in *Communications* 8; the English version appeared in *New Literary History* 6, no. 2 (Winter 1975): 237–72.

7. See, for example, M. H. Abrams's widely read and otherwise well-informed attack on Derrida and his American followers, which begins with the statement: "What is distinctive about Derrida is . . . that, *like other French structuralists*, he shifts his inquiry from language to *écriture* . . . ." ("The Deconstructive Angel," *Critical Inquiry* [Spring 1977]:429; my emphasis).

8. For a more detailed discussion of *S/Z* as a "two-faced" work, see my "Introduction: Varieties of Audience-Oriented Criticism," in Susan Suleiman and Inge Crosman, eds., *The Reader in the Text: Essays on Audience and Interpretation* (Princeton: Princeton University Press, 1980), pp. 18–21.

9. "L'activité structuraliste," p. 215.

10. *Discours du récit* forms the bulk of *Figures III* (Paris: Éditions du Seuil, 1972). An English translation has at last been published: *Narrative Discourse: An Essay in Method*, trans. Jane E. Lewin (Ithaca, New York: Cornell University Press, 1979).

11. Algirdas Julien Greimas, "Structure et histoire," in *Du Sens. Essais sémiotiques* (Paris: Éditions du Seuil, 1970), p. 104.

12. Fredric Jameson, *The Prison-House of Language. A Critical Account of Structuralism and Russian Formalism* (Princeton: Princeton University Press, 1972), p. 18.

13. Ibid., p. 194.

14. Jameson's critique applies less to Foucault's most recent work, *La Volonté de savoir* (Paris: Gallimard, 1976), announced as the first in a multivolume history of sexuality. Here Foucault's controlling metaphor shifts from "archeology" to "genealogy" (*Volonté*, p. 159), with all that that shift implies. One thing it does *not* imply is that Foucault has "renounced" the structuralism of his youth, as I have occasionally heard argued. If he was ever a structuralist (he himself is ironically evasive on that point), he remains one now. Structuralism also has a history; it can evolve without ceasing to be.

15. F. W. Galan, "Literary System and Systemic Change: The Prague School Theory of Literary History, 1928–48," *PMLA* 94, no. 2 (March 1979):279.

16. See Itamar Even-Zohar, *Papers in Historical Poetics*, no. 8 in the series *Papers on Poetics and Semiotics*, ed. Benjamin Hrushovski and Itamar Even-Zohar (Tel-Aviv: The Porter Institute for Poetics and Semiotics, 1978); also "Polysystem Theory," *Poetics Today* 1, nos. 1–2 (Autumn 1979):287–310. For a recent overview of the work of Moscow-Tartu group, see the special issue of *New Literary History* de-

voted to *Soviet Semiotics and Criticism*: Vol. 9, no. 2 (Winter 1978), as well as the continuing series of English translations edited by Ann Shukman and L. M. O'Toole, *Russian Poetics in Translation* (University of Essex).

17. "The Theory of the 'Formal' Method," in *Russian Formalist Criticism: Four Essays*, translated with an introduction by Lee T. Lemon and Marion J. Reis (Lincoln: University of Nebraska Press, 1965), p. 119.

18. "A Short History of Practical Criticism," *New Literary History* 10, no. 3 (Spring 1979):507–508. Other page references will be given in parentheses in the text.

19. "Qu'est-ce qu'un texte? Expliquer et comprendre," in *Hermeneutik und Dialektik* II, ed. Rüdiger Bübner, Konrad Cramer, Reiner Wiehl (Tübingen: J. C. B. Mohr [Paul Siebeck], 1970), 197. My translation. An English version of the essay appeared in David M. Rasmussen, ed., *Mythic=Symbolic Language and Philosophical Anthropology* (The Hague: Martinus Nijhoff, 1971).

20. "L'héritage méthodologique du Formalisme," in *Poétique de la prose* (Paris: Éditions du Seuil, 1971), p. 20.

21. I have discussed the theoretical implications of the major contemporary approaches to reading and interpretation in my introduction to *The Reader in the Text*.

22. Barthes, "L'activité structuraliste," p. 218.

23. *Structuralist Poetics* (London: Routledge & Kegan Paul, paperback ed., 1975), p. 259.

24. Paul Ricoeur, "Qu'est-ce qu'un texte?," p. 197; further page references will be given in parentheses in the text.

25. See Mario J. Valdés and Owen J. Miller, eds., *Interpretation of Narrative* (Toronto: University of Toronto Press, 1978).

26. Jacques Derrida, "Force et signification," p. 11.

Critical Truth as Necessary Error

Wallace Martin

The function of criticism is to mediate between literature and culture—in Robert Langbaum's words, "to turn the work of art into a cultural acquisition."[1] Those who disallow the mediating function of criticism point out that works of art are by definition products of culture. But unlike social customs, political institutions, architecture, and handicrafts, the status of imaginative literature in Western societies remains problematic. Neither creative writers nor critics have accepted the conclusion that literature is simply a cultural product. In the classical tradition, literature was said to incorporate both art (the cultural component) and nature. The antithetical terms commonly employed in criticism (knowledge and pleasure, universal and particular, representation and expression, conscious and unconscious) indicate that literature is seen as containing a "non-cultural" component that supplements or subverts its purely cultural functions.

Quite apart from disagreements about the "intrinsic" nature of literature, its place in culture is in fact determined by criticism. As Jean Starobinski says, "the very status of creative works in the universe of culture depends upon an act of consciousness and a discourse which at once recognize and validate their existence." Geoffrey Hartman describes the cultural function of literary interpretation as follows: "it fuses with the art-work or helps it to integrate . . . with other structures. . . . While literary criticism is not commerce, it does make works of art negotiable from generation to generation, or affects their value."[2] It is the critic's responsibility to find or create an ordered set of elements in the culture of his time that will make literature intelligible. More often than not, he must create the requisite structure in order to account for the "natural" amorphousness of literature, but unlike the imaginative writer, the critic functions within a system of constraints defined by his culture and the purpose of his activity. He is comparable to a *bricoleur*—a handyman who ingeniously adapts a heterogenous collection of objects to the solution of a practical problem. The critic (to paraphrase Lévi-Strauss) proceeds from a set of elements—a literary work and a cultural situation—to the *discovery* of its structure. The meaningful order posited in a critical essay cannot by its nature be isomorphic with the work it treats or with any of the cultural terminologies it employs. In order to combine the two, the critic is forced to alter both. Because the integration achieved in an authentic work of criticism emerges from the materials being integrated, its structure "*can never be postulated in advance*. It can only be discovered *a posteriori* . . . by experience."[3]

The observation that criticism distorts literature is not a new one, but rational discussion of its implications was long precluded by the apologies and invectives that it prompted. Recently a number of critics have recognized that literary works must be subjected to torsions if they are to be aligned with the larger literary and cultural frameworks that constitute the tradition. M. H. Abrams says that this conception of criticism as structural integration is confirmed by an examination of critical practice:

> Random leafing through the pages of any critic whose writings we find illuminating will reveal how large a part of what he says involves, by various linguistic means, classifying features of the

> work in hand with those of a shifting variety of other works—works written by the same author, or written by other authors of the same period, or else types of works produced over many periods. . . . The physical features of the work do not change; but it is only when we compare the critical analysis with an analysis of the same work by another critic, equally rewarding in his discriminations, that we recognize how much of the evocation of particular aesthetic aspects is the result of the critic's deployment of linguistic devices for classifying and cross-classifying things in any number of distinctive, unpredictable, and illuminating ways.[4]

What changes when we shift from one method of classification to another? Abrams implies that our perception changes, while assuring us that the "physical features" of the work remain the same. But it is becoming increasingly difficult to think of the literary work as an object which, like an animal or a piece of furniture, can serve as an invariant referent despite differences in the ways it is discussed. Literature is neither a physical nor an ideal object; it is made of language and cannot escape the ambiguous attributes of its medium.

Just as a word belongs to no grammatical category and has no determinate lexical content apart from its use in a sentence, so the meaning of a literary work cannot be said to exist apart from its functional place in a cultural syntax. There is no end to the relations between literature and culture as a (posited, created) whole. The literary text, says J. Hillis Miller, is not a

> thing in itself, "organically unified," but a relation to other texts which are relations in their turn. . . . The boundaries, finally, between literary texts and other kinds of texts are also perforated or dismantled. If insights or methods developed in psychology, anthropology, philosophy, and linguistics are appropriated by literary criticism, linguistics, on the other hand, broadens out imperialistically to redefine all those other disciplines.[5]

Hayden White has commmented ironically on the "imperialistic" ambitions of this "form of intellectual practice": "Modern literary critics recognize no disciplinary barriers, either as to subject matter or to methods. In literary criticism, anything goes. This science of rules has no rules."[6] Setting aside the question of "rules" for the moment, and emphasizing only the critic's intellectual responsibilities, we might ask: how many other disciplines can criticism do without? If we begin by eliminating linguistics, we might go on to discard psychology, philosophy, history. . . . It is apparent that criticism, even at its narrowest, has always made use of other disciplines. One might reply that criticism need not refer to other disciplines as such; it can be based on common sense, without reference to thought as philosophy or to feeling as psychology. But much that passes for common sense is in fact the formal doctrine of a discipline as it existed at some time in the past. The fiat that would separate criticism from current thought would isolate literature from contemporary culture. Such isolation is impracticable, if not impossible; it has never been prevalent. Perhaps, then, it would be enough to ask that criticism, in drawing on other disciplines, represent them accurately. Unfortunately, that request can never be honored.

Let us grant, to begin with, that we can never know enough, and that critics should not refer to extraliterary subjects with which they do not have detailed acquaintance. Is it possible to allude to a philosophic doctrine, in the course of a literary discussion, in such a way that its tradition and implications will be accurately represented? The significance of concepts can seldom be conveyed apart from the systems of which they are a part. Can an adequate sense of the system ever be embodied in a passing reference? More important: even if accurately embodied, could the reference be properly understood? The reader of criticism is seldom trained in more than one discipline; he has no special talent for correctly apprehending fragments of knowledge that are meaningful only in relation to entire fields of study foreign to him. These limitations are, unquestionably, disabling, but they have never hindered men from making use of imperfectly understood insights, as Nietzsche recognized:

> *Philosopher's error.*—The philosopher supposes that the value of his philosophy lies in the whole, in the structure; but posterity finds its value in the stone which he used for building, and

> which is used many more times after that for building—better. Thus it finds the value in the fact that the structure can be destroyed and *nevertheless* retains value as building material.[7]

Given that there is no such entity as "culture as a whole," there is nevertheless a nexus of overlapping discourses that embodies reference to a wide range of cultural concerns, into which no philosophic system, no psychological construct, and little precise knowledge of history and society has ever entered in its integral form. This state of affairs is neither unusual nor deplorable; it is inevitable. Culture, as an assimilable and communicable common heritage, cannot absorb entire systems of thought. It must break down the materials it employs so that they can enter into new forms of coherence. Here the vast edifices of philosophy have been reduced to rubble and used to create new structures—public monuments and the shrines of new cults, dwellings and gazebos. Such reconstructions as are preserved at archeological sites or in museums serve functions entirely different from those that they originally served. The humanistic departments of universities are in part conceptual museums. The disciplinary autonomy and accurate representation of the past that they encourage serve important cultural functions. While not acting as an apologist for the more ambitious kinds of literary criticism that take all knowledge as their province, I cannot see any logical way to disallow them; they are clearly sanctioned by the critical tradition.

Emphasis on the distortions of literature and culture that are unavoidable when criticism attempts to join the two in new structures is not meant to imply that "anything goes" in criticism. Lacking recourse to rules or an *a priori* delimitation of the discipline, we must assay each critical act individually, appealing to fact, reason, judgment, and taste in the measure appropriate, given the regional diversity of the critical field. To say that such constraints are culturally determined is not to say there are no reasons for them. What we ask of the critic is that regardless of his methods and the materials to which they are applied, some internally consistent structural integration be revealed.

Once they enter criticism, ideas from other areas of knowledge are only partially sanctioned by their origins. We cannot know in advance that a theory which has proved useful elsewhere will yield reliable results when applied to literature, even if the application is rigorous. Since it has probably been altered in the process of its transfer to criticism, a theory begins a new life there: its fundamental terms will be reshaped by the exigencies of the literary field, and the analogy that served important psychological functions in prompting its transfer will be less important than empirical applications in determing its success.

The principles of order employed in discussing literature vary immensely. Chaucer used the planets, the value-scale of the metals, and ten subsidiary principles of classification in ranking authors in the *Hous of Fame*; Northrop Frye associates "generic plots" with the four seasons in *Anatomy of Criticism*; grammar is a source of distinctions between rhetorical figures and fictional points of view; psychology, philosophy, and biology have contributed important metaphors to criticism; and almost any critical essay treating one or more literary works will propose its own set of categories, since we still expect of criticism (despite the other liberties we allow it) some revelation of significant order. Theory does not determine the strategies employed in criticism, the purposes for which it is written, or the materials it will use to achieve its ends. Broadly defined as including any principle of coherence, theory is one among many components of critical discourse.

Despite their disagreements about other matters, critics now seem to think that "theory" in this general sense is an inescapable part of criticism. But they remain divided on the question of how it functions. Although in the sciences theory sanctions and serves as a means of extending knowledge, many critics see it as an unavoidable liability in the humanities. The most interesting recent discussions of the problem attempt to account for the seemingly paradoxical fact that critical theory leads away from "truth" (in that no theory is ever acceptable) but that the individual truths occasionally appearing in criticism are usually embedded in theoretical discussion. Theory is the source of error, but it is only through the creation and recognition of theoretical error that the truth can be discovered.

As represented by Murray Krieger, the problem results from the fact that theoretical statements, which are of necessity generalizations, can never account for the unique qualities of literary works:

> With the best of our critics—those who will not permit their theoretical commitments to blind them to the unpredictable demands of the single literary work—critical discourse at certain points becomes a reasoned disorder, or a disordering of reason. . . . Often the critic's inner person asserts itself at the expense of his systematic allegiance, so that what confronts us is a theoretical inconsistency that we welcome in preference to the insensitivity and neglect produced by theoretical dogma uncontested.[8]

After analyzing examples of the phenomenon in the works of major critics, he says that they testify to "the continuing need for theoretical inconsistency" in criticism (*Theory of Criticism*, p. 54). "Insight" and "theory" are clearly opposed to one another: the latter results from the critic's persona and man's inescapable tendency to generalize, whereas the former issues from the critic's person.

Paul de Man has a more paradoxical explanation of the connection between truth and critical theory. Not only does theory fail to reveal the truth about literature, he says, but it also blinds us to the truth; and yet this theoretical blindness is necessary if we are ever to achieve literary insight. The presence of such blindness is in fact evidence of the profundity of a critic's work. De Man appears to have been driven to this conclusion by the critics he has studied:

> In all of them a paradoxical discrepancy appears between the general statements they make about the nature of literature (statements on which they base their critical methods) and the actual results of their interpretations. Their findings about the structure of texts contradict the general conception that they use as their model.[9]

This conclusion is more forcefully expressed in passages that evoke the situation of Oedipus: "Critics' moments of greatest blindness with regard to their own critical assumptions are also the moments at which they achieve their greatest insight" (*Blindness and Insight,* p. 109); critics can "grope toward a certain degree of insight only because their method remained oblivious to the perception of this insight" (p. 106). If the critic himself does not present the insight that is at odds with his theory, he at least leads his readers so close to it that they are able to discover it by themselves.

Despite the differences in their assumptions and arguments, Krieger and de Man both see critical theory as a necessary evil: it is present so that truth can be discovered elsewhere. The useful feature of the position they take is that they are able to preserve an intersubjective conception of critical insight without resorting to perspectivism or relativism, while at the same time granting some importance to theory and explaining the pervasiveness of critical error. However, the advantages of their position must be weighed against their strenuous subtlety. They cannot explain *why* theory, as error, is necessary for the discovery of critical truth. While it is possible that the perennial problems of criticism result from forces at work in the critic's psyche, or from some aspect of literary language that "causes blindness in those who come in close contact with it" (de Man, p. 106), the possibility that they can be explained more simply deserves exploration. In identifying insights that have escaped the conceptual nets of the critics they discuss, Krieger and de Man cite evidence and make use of convincing explanations—indicating that regardless of the unconscious genesis of truth and error, we are for better or worse compelled to understand them consciously and to appeal to reason in doing so.

In what ways does commitment to a theory preclude discovery of a truth? Or, to rephrase the question, why does the search for truth preclude certain kinds of literary insight? From one point of view, the exclusion of certain insights is a necessary rather than an unconscious or paradoxical feature of human understanding. Any theory, if it is to have explanatory power, must presuppose some limit to the number of concepts relevant to a situation or event. As J. Hillis Miller has observed, critical disagreements often concern the delimitation of the context to be employed in literary study: a text can be analyzed intrinsically, or in relation to its author, genre, historical period, mythological or psychological content, etc.[10] Selection of a context is necessary not only because explanation (and essays) must end somewhere, but also on the basis of the assumption (accepted by all but cosmic mechanists and mystics) that everything does not necessarily influence everything else.

What W. Ross Ashby says of scientific explanation is equally true of criticism:

> [Every phenomenon] *embodies no less than an infinite number of variables,* all but a few of which must of necessity be ignored. Thus if we were studying the swing of a pendulum in relation to its length we would be interested in its angular deviation at various times, but would often ignore the chemical composition of the bob, the reflecting power of its surface, the electric conductivity of the suspending string, the specific gravity of the bob, its shape, the age of the alloy, its degree of bacterial contamination, and so on. The list of what might be ignored could be extended indefinitely. Faced with this infinite number of variables, the experimenter must, and of course does, select a definite number for examination—in other words, he defines an abstracted system.[11]

Delimitation of the factors relevant to a theory involves specification of its context, or "boundary conditions." In literature, as in nature, the factors that may be relevant to an explanation are innumerable, "bounded only by the imagination of the writer" (*Design for a Brain,* p. 71). Scientists assume that most of these can be disregarded or controlled in particular cases, and their laws concern only the variables that they have selected to study. But the critic, unlike the scientist, cannot "repeat" the object/event that is the literary work and manipulate its features in such a way as to determine which are important. Indeed, it is doubtful that he can repeat his own experience of the work with the assurance that no relevant factor in himself or the context has changed.

In light of these considerations, the relationship between theory and "error" or "blindness" in criticism appears less problematic. A critic, armed with a theory, sets out to explain an aspect of literature that he considers worthy of attention. He will of necessity treat a limited set of the indefinite number of factors that can affect literary response. Some readers may find his explanation convincing; others may simply reject it because of the explanatory framework it entails. As a rule, there is a vast middle ground within which large numbers of readers will find the critic's work helpful and at the same time frustratingly unsatisfactory. Usually, they conclude that he has failed to consider one or more crucial factors which, when seen in relation to those he has discussed, reveal an entirely different configuration both of the problem he was attempting to solve and the theory he used in doing so. How could he have failed to see the answer which is (to me) so obvious? Stated differently—why did he exclude one of the innumerable factors that can, and in my view must, be included in the explanation? My objection to his work is not capricious, and it does not result from a rejection of his theory. As the passage from Ashby indicates, the revision of the theory that I see as necessary may involve factors that are of explanatory significance but that happen to have been excluded by the boundary conditions that the critic established.

Thus considered, the "reasoned disorder" that Krieger finds at certain points in the writings of great critics can be seen not as a disintegration of theory, but as the integration into their theories of explanatory elements that had hitherto been excluded. The critic's conceptual network determines what insights his theory will be able to catch, but it does more than that: by serving as a grid on which he can focus his attention, it makes him particularly aware of what has slipped through his categories. As a result he (or his readers) may catch the glint of a new perception and ravel and reweave his theory so that it will not slip through. Even when it is unsatisfactory, theory serves a positive function, because without the articulation it creates, contrary insights cannot be perceived. After a theory has filtered out certain kinds of perceptions, those it has missed become apparent—but not before. As Bacon said, "Truth emerges more readily from error than from confusion" (*Novum Organum*, II, 20). Both error and truth involve theory; confusion does not.

This account of critical theory explains a phenomenon that is common among readers of criticism: even if an essay appears to be completely wrongheaded, it is often the occasion of new perceptions about the literary work it treats. A hitherto unarticulated theory forces itself to the surface of the reader's mind, bringing with it perceptions that had been unavailable to him. In most of our quarrels with critics, however, we want to revise and supplement their theories in order to explain some important aspect of literature that has escaped their notice. There is no end to the possibility of such revisions because critical explanation does in fact involve all problems at once—the literally endless list of features that can be important in literature—and it is impossible to know *a priori* that any one of them is of no explanatory consequence.

Because of the control he is able to exercise over the parameters of explanation, the scientist can make his theories precise and credible: his experiments can be replicated. The only way that a critic can amass evidence for his theory is by applying it to different situations (other literary works) or by showing that it sheds light on areas of literary study to which it had not hitherto been applied (literary history, genre study, reader response, etc.). Controlling variation, science repeats the same; criticism can only repeat with difference, or elsewhere. Because a structural theory (one based on a concrete logic) gains in credibility through extension of its scope, it tends to expand the sphere of its explanations across disciplinary boundaries. In this realm, as Barthes says, "the force of meaning depends on its degree of systematization: the strongest meaning is the one whose systematization includes a large number of elements, to the point where it appears to include everything noteworthy in the world."[12]

No systematic account of literature has proved generally acceptable, and some critics argue that the very attempt to create such accounts is what leads criticism astray. However, a convincing demonstration that all critical theories are erroneous would not lead to this conclusion. As Popper and Bachelard have shown, what we require of an explanation is not that it be demonstrably true, but that it admit the possibility of being falsified. Thus any argument that succeeds in showing what is wrong with a critical theory shows that the theory satisfies the only requirement we can make of an explanation—that it be decidable. Disproofs of theories validate theory.

There is not one set of criteria for identifying critical error and another set for discovering truth. Confusion about this point may result from the temporal dimension of understanding. No theory or system, scientific or critical, provides a means of *discovering* truth; they can be used only to verify or validate it. A failure to distinguish heuristic procedures from verification procedures leads to otiose objections to a theory on the grounds that it has not led to the production of interesting criticism, or defense of a theory because it is suggestive. As we know from the philosophy of science, it is to a model—an analogy or metaphor that in itself asserts nothing—that we must look for discovery. Theories, properly speaking, justify assertions, but do not produce them.[13]

Through quotation and citation, criticism segments and redistributes texts in order to posit relationships between literature and culture.[14] The fact that criticism is a rhetorical form does not lessen its dependence on theory because, as Aristotle said, "we entertain the strongest persuasion of a thing when we conceive that it has been demonstrated." For better or worse, then, reason remains an inescapable tool of critical construction and deconstruction. The alternative to erroneous systems and structures is not none at all, but only better ones.

NOTES

1. "The Function of Criticism Once More," *Yale Review* 54 (1965):218.

2. Starobinski, "On the Fundamental Gestures of Criticism," *New Literary History* 5 (1974):493; Hartman, *The Fate of Reading* (Chicago: University of Chicago Press, 1975), p. 14.

3. *The Savage Mind* (Chicago: University of Chicago Press, 1966), p. 58.

4. "A Note on Wittgenstein and Literary Criticism," *ELH* 41 (1974):549.

5. "Stevens' Rock and Criticism as Cure, II," *The Georgia Review* 30 (1976):332.

6. "The Absurdist Moment in Contemporary Literary Theory," *Contemporary Literature* 17 (1976):378.

7. *Mixed Opinions and Maxims*, no. 201, trans. Walter Kaufmann and R. J. Hollingdale in *On the Genealogy of Morals* (New York: Vintage, 1967), p. 176.

8. *Theory of Criticism* (Baltimore: Johns Hopkins University Press, 1976), pp. ix–x.

9. *Blindness and Insight* (New York: Oxford University Press, 1971), p. 9.

10. "The Antitheses of Criticism," *Modern Language Notes* 81 (1966):560.

11. *Design for a Brain* (London: Chapman & Hall, 1960), p. 15.

12. *S/Z*, trans. Richard Miller (New York: Hill and Wang, 1974), p. 154.

13. French philosophers of science have traditionally viewed scientific models as a contamination of theoretical purity: see Pierre Duhem, *The Aim and Structure of Physical Theory*, trans. Philip Wiener (Princeton: Princeton University Press, 1954), p. 70, and Mary Hesse's reply on behalf of the Anglo-American tradition in *Models and Analogies in Science* (Notre Dame: University of Notre Dame Press, 1966). As Derrida shows in "White Mythology," *New Literary History* 6 (1974):60–68 (originally published in 1971), the French suspicion of structural models has been kept alive by Bachelard and Canguilhem. When Derrida says that a challenge to the traditional French view might lead to "a rewriting of the meaning of science, of knowledge, of truth" (pp. 65–66), he appears to be endorsing views long held in the Anglo-American tradition, though he may not be aware of them.

14. See Michel Charles, "La lecture critique," *Poétique*, no. 34 (1978):129–51.

Viva Voce: Criticism and the Teaching of Literature

Roger Shattuck

Literature has two advantages over wine. A good book ages forever, and you can read it as often as you wish without diminishing its substance. The literary critic is like a wine lover whose dream has come true. His stock can never spoil or be consumed. He can choose, enjoy, share, and discuss his cellar; it will grow as he grows. He need never go thirsty.

But my subject reaches far beyond the pleasure a person of cultivated taste may find in the art of literature. It is worth insisting on how large and varied the domain of criticism has become today. Several loose and overlapping categories come easily to mind. The journalistic reviewer addresses himself to the general public, usually on the subject of recent works. A recognized writer like Edmund Wilson is permitted to try the wide-ranging form of the literary essay. Teachers at all levels choose works to present to their classes for discussion, interpretation, and evaluation. Scholars, whether they lean toward biography, history, or interpretation, contribute to the stock of tools and materials with which all critics must work.

A slightly different version of this essay was previously published as "How to Rescue Literature?". Reprinted with permission from *The New York Review of Books*.

Literary theorists and philosophers try to give it all a shape and a name and often attach literature to adjacent fields, as if to provide a safe dock in the perilous seas of critical dispute. Many individuals, of course, practice all forms. Yet individual versatility and the constant interchange among categories do not remove their distinctness. Because it is by far the most widely practiced, the most influential, and the least acknowledged as a branch of criticism, I shall talk principally about teaching, and refer to other branches as they support or disrupt it.

LITERATURE IN THE PROFESSORS' DEN

In a university I recently visited, my path took me regularly by two classes which I found myself observing with fascination through the open doors as I passed. In the first, five or six students sat around a table listening to the elderly professor read to them in Spanish from a beautifully bound book propped in front of him. What I heard of his voice was expressive and very clear. His histrionic gestures and shifts in emphasis played constantly between the comic and the passionate. At frequent intervals a student would read from his own text—haltingly, yet catching some of the professor's feeling and even a few of his gestures. My host informed me that some faculty members considered Professor M's teaching the scandal of the Spanish department; in his Cervantes seminar he simply read the *Quijote* aloud, with running commentary on the language, historical background, and cross references in the novel, and with little systematic interpretation. Yet a few graduate students always stated that they had learned a great deal from Professor M and expressed great loyalty to him. The question was moot; he would retire next year.

Further down the corridor an intense young man in a corduroy jacket and no tie had always, by the time I passed, covered the blackboard with carefully lettered diagrams, assorted symbols, and equations. He stood gesticulating with the chalk at the large class, all of whom were taking notes with a concentrated expression. According to my host, Assistant

Professor N had a strong following among the graduate students in English and had attracted some good undergraduates. He had published two stunning articles combining communications theory and speech act theory in an analysis of comic strips. He was a candidate for early promotion and had received offers from two universities to participate in special interdisciplinary programs.

Both these classroom critics faced the same problem: how does one fill the forty hours of class or lecture time we call a "course"? In the past the accepted activities in the teaching of literature seemed limited in number and free of serious challenge. The life and times of the author, a close reading "on many levels," and an accompanying history of ideas combined personal response with the Great Tradition and usually led to some form of appreciation and evaluation. "Appreciation" grew out of an attempt to relate a work as interpreted to other literary works and to the dynamics and tensions of our lived experience. I. A. Richards fluttered the pedagogical chicken coops a bit back in the twenties. It took the wider ideological challenges of the sixties to leave a lasting mark on classroom behavior. Professor M has reverted almost to the Middle Ages, when students often spent their time copying a precious manuscript read aloud by the teacher. Professor N would probably feel a certain malaise about a Great Tradition and about attempting any form of appreciation, a word now consigned to music departments. His methods of interpretation and analysis give him an apparent command or mastery of literary works that has turned the activities of English and foreign literature departments on their heads.

An early pastiche version of what is happening today can be found in Oscar Wilde's entertaining dialogue, "The Critic as Artist." Gilbert, by far the more eloquent speaker, acclaims the critic's role.

> For it is the critical faculty that invents fresh forms. The tendency of creation is to repeat itself.
>
> Criticism, being the purest form of personal impression, is in a way more creative than creation, as it has least reference to any standard external to itself. . . . [1]

Gilbert's aggressive posing has gradually been systematized and institutionalized to the point where literature may be looked upon in the most respected circles as a pretext for criticism, as a convenient armature for theory. I sense that in some graduate literature programs around the country today more extensive and more careful reading is expected of students in literary theory and methodology than in works of literature—let alone in literary history. It is not just that literature has been submerged in doctrinal thinking. A literal usurpation has begun which would depose literature and grant sovereign authority to one or more of several competing disciplines. It is impossible to describe these pretenders in any detail, but a partial roll call may help.

Various forms of structuralism appropriate literature to a set of myths that rule us through a strong binary logic. "We do not claim," writes Lévi-Strauss, "to show how men think in myths, but how myths think themselves in men, and without their knowledge . . . myths think themselves *among themselves*."[2] The slippery doctrine of *écriture* (writing? scripture?) has delivered literature into the hands of linguistics and set out to eliminate the author in favor of language itself. Barthes stated it categorically in the sixties: "Language is not the predicate of a subject . . . it is the subject."[3] (By "subject" he means not topic but the seat or agent of thought and consciousness.) It is the phenomenon, the possibility, of having significance, of being a sign, that lies at the heart of semiology (or semiotics), a discipline founded on the supremacy of a universal theory of signs. Communication and information theory has staked a major claim to the territory of literature since Roman Jakobson's "Linguistics and Poetics" speech in 1958.[4] So far as I can discern in the writings of J. L. Austin and J. R. Searle (both philosophers) and their followers, speech act theory originally took no interest in literature except marginally as "etiolated" or stagnant speech. This mode of analysis recently grafted onto criticism has the effect of converting literary studies into a form of sociolinguistic philosophy. Reader-response theory tends to look around and beyond the text to the reactions it elicits. Promising as a basically experimental approach, it often becomes enmeshed in interview statistics, transactional psychology, and curious notions about communities of readers. These recent theories have defined and refined their methods while Marxist and Freudian criticism remain very active.

All these approaches can widen our horizons and challenge us to reexamine the relations between criticism and its host, literature. What we should beware of is the temptation to subordinate literature to the claims of any extraliterary discipline to superior authority or knowledge. Literature is not autonomous and unrelated to our daily lives; on the contrary, we all to some degree live by and through it. But it does not belong to any domain outside the domain of art, and we are shirking our responsibilities if we look the other way while self-styled "literary" critics deliver literature into the hands of one or another branch of the social sciences. We would do well to remember something of the past. It has taken two hundred years approximately to free literature from the authority of established religion, royal patronage, and bourgeois values. The heroes of that struggle—Swift and Diderot and Goethe, Flaubert and Dostoevsky, Joyce and Proust—were before all independent writers who submitted their work to no authority beyond the conflicting traditions of literature itself and the demands of their own sensibilities. Do we now, out of loss of confidence in literature or out of doubts about how to spend class time in a difficult season, want to surrender literature—or criticism—to a new set of masters?

A disturbing aspect of these raids on literature and criticism by outlying disciplines is their common aspiration to the objectivity and certainty of science at the very moment when the tendentious and teleological nature of much scientific activity is coming to light.[5] Not the existence of this ambition (already pronounced in Taine's theory, not in his practice) but its spread should trouble us. In the introduction to *Cours de linguistique générale* Saussure, a consistently exciting and clearheaded thinker on language, called for the creation of "a science which will study the life of signs in the midst of social life" and named it semiology. In a beautifully self-fulfilling prophecy, comparable to the gaps in Mendeleev's periodic table anticipating the discovery of new elements, Saussure wrote that "its place is determined in advance."[6] Some powerful literary critics—I quote Frye and Barthes—have followed his lead.

> It may also be a scientific element in criticism which distinguishes it from literary parasitism on the one hand, and the superimposed critical attitude on the other. . . . Everyone who has seriously studied literature knows that the mental process involved is as coherent and progressive as the study of science. . . . If criticism is a science it is clearly a social science.[7]

> Linguistics can give to literature that generative model which is the principle of all science, since it is always a question of making use of certain rules to explain certain results.[8]

Do we wish to adopt this stringent approach to enter a field that, for many readers, still encompasses individual consciousness, free will, accountability, and human values? Should we as critics postulate the perfect uniformity and coherence of literature and deal with it systematically in terms of laws and equations, models and statistics and nonlinguistic symbolic systems? Such projects should indeed be tried out and the results evaluated; we have reason to take alarm when they begin to undermine the study and teaching of literature as one of the humanities.

I would trace yet another important aspect of this scientism to Saussure. For it is he who, by fiat, in his introduction, banishes individual or personal speech from the house of linguistic study.

> The study of language contains two parts: one, the essential part, takes *langue* for its object, which is essentially social and independent of the individual; . . . the other, the secondary part, takes individual speech (*parole*) for its object. . . .
>
> Such is the first bifurcation one comes upon as soon as one sets out to form a theory of language. One must choose between the roads, both of which one cannot follow at the same time.[9]

Since Saussure omits any consideration of individual speech (except to call it "diachronic"[10]) this bifurcation amounts to a beheading. When combined with the thought of Marx or

Freud, of Lévi-Strauss or Lacan (as is often the case), this proclamation incinerates the whole humanistic tradition of persons and scatters the ashes across a landscape composed of language, myth, the unconscious, and other collective entities. To dismiss *parole* means to dismiss individual acts of communication, including literary works. True, the willful and perverse crotchets of such acts do not submit readily to scientific study, linguistic or otherwise; stylistics has succeeded in dealing far more adequately with individual cases. Nevertheless, linguistics as a science seems to have invaded literary criticism brandishing its claim to be the central human social science that holds the key to all the others. The claim will not stand up; the price of dismissing persons is too high.

We all behold the obvious results of this growing scientism among literary critics: aggressive and often turgid new terminologies, the displacement of discussions of literary works by discussions of theory and method—even in the classroom; and the growing demand of critics (without Wilde's wit) to stand as the full peers of "creative" writers. We have not reckoned fully yet with feedback effects whereby writers may be composing linguistically generated, nonpersonal, systematically ambiguous works in order to provide critics with the fodder they seek. For, increasingly, particularly in the United States and France, writers are critics and are also professors of literature. This plurality of offices can lead to an intellectual conflict of interest unforeseen by Baudelaire when he insisted that "all great poets naturally and fatally become critics."[11]

WHAT THEN CAN WE DO?

In the face of these efforts to use literary works as the subject matter for a science that anatomizes literature, what can we do to keep literature whole, especially as it is taught, and to encourage an integral process of reading? For it is as if each province of criticism today wanted to limit itself to only one element in the communication-theory model I referred to earlier. Structuralism works away on the message or text sealed off from author and reader and recircuits it into myth and language. Semiotics "breaks" or "cracks" the literary work like a code to produce not so much a set of interrelated meanings attributable to author or audience as a protracted commentary on the infinite possibilities of meaning. Speech act theory concentrates on a segment of intentional performance linking speaker to message ("illocutionary act" is a particularly infelicitous term for it) and shuns literature as parasitical. Reader-response theory finds its pertinent evidence in the addressee. Much criticism today is characterized above all by its myopia.

The rest of us would do well to keep our heads, eschew intellectual fashions, avoid cleaving to one method as suitable to all circumstances, and attempt to approach a work of literature without rigid preconceptions, without a grid of theory. No, there is no"innocent reading" any more than there is an "innocent eye." But it is possible to temper experience and mastery with a kind of induced innocence—negative capability of *lâcher prise*—which discourages the kind of usurpation I have been deploring. And, in the domain of teaching literature which concerns us here, I would also favor certain kinds of exercises—busy work even—that have fallen totally out of favor: word for word copying, dictation, reading aloud, summarizing (précis writing), memorization, and translation. All of these activities enforce close attention to what a piece of writing is actually doing, without requiring an elaborate theory of literature to begin with. One of these methods in particular impresses me as both a fruitful form of reading and a sturdy antidote to some of the abuses I have been attacking. Another anecdote will make the point.

A visiting professor from France widely respected for his command of semiological approaches gave a lecture recently on Apollinaire's poem, "Le Pont Mirabeau." At the start he handed out copies of the two successive versions of the poem Apollinaire published, which differ markedly in format and punctuation. After giving the audience time to read the two texts, the lecturer began a highly perceptive analysis, with diagrams and symbols, of the poem's verse structure, rhyme, sound pattern, and syntax. A number of neglected relations emerged. In his conclusion he detected in filigree behind the consonants the name of the woman (Marie Laurencin) whose love the poem celebrates. Then he stopped. That was all.

In what it said the talk was brilliant. Its omissions outraged me and led me to protest. First the lecturer failed to mention a third version: Apollinaire's own recording of the poem in a strikingly mannered and haunting voice—a version that without being definitive, would throw into question some of the lecturer's insistence on the nonlinear qualities of the text. (He was indeed acquainted with this recording.) Second, even though the bulk of his talk addressed itself to auditory aspects of the poem, he never tested any of his hypotheses by reading the poem aloud—not a stanza, not a single line. The audience had to create all these effects for itself in its inner ear—and in a foreign language. Once taken apart by the lecturer's detailed analysis, the poem was never reassembled and set in motion by means of an oral performance articulating the sounds and projecting its complex emotional effects. "Le Pont Mirabeau" was left in pieces on the blackboard.

I do not propose here to enter the ancient debate over the priority of the visual or the auditory in our perception of the world and in the formation of our sensorium. John Hollander, Walter J. Ong, Marshall McLuhan, Rudolph Arnheim, and Jean Piaget have published important works on the subject, which I recommend to all persons concerned with the connections between the arts.[12] Rather I wish to suggest that at our present cultural juncture, the critical activity of teaching literature should include as one of its essential and valorizing goals the *oral* interpretation of literary texts. The analytical dismantling of a work or passage would then lead up to a performance serving as verification and demonstration, a means of actually experiencing the forms and features previously discussed at the remove of critical interpretation. No approach to literature can separate itself from this elementary responsibility to contribute some element to a live reading of the text under consideration. If the author's biography or the work's narrative structure do not help us hear the voice and tone of the whole, the articulation of its parts, and the pacing of its language, then they are irrelevant to the study of that work—though they may interest us for other reasons. At least for literary criticism as it is practiced in the classroom and lecture hall, where a living audience sits with eyes and ears ready to respond to almost any stimulus, the acid test is not the intellectual brilliance of the teacher's argument but the demonstrability of his interpretation in an actual reading aloud of a sizeable passage.

The fact that modern linguistics as shaped by Saussure restricts itself to competence (*langue*) and neglects performance (*parole*) need not influence our reading of the special class of texts called literature. No matter how much we would like it to happen, no text "speaks for itself." Some person must read, construe, and finally speak the words.

FIVE CONSIDERATIONS

Five major considerations lead me to speak out in favor of voicing literary texts as a way of interpreting and appreciating them.

1. Oral interpretation brings texts alive, restores the freshness and urgency of older works, and situates them in a collective setting which improves on the intimist convention of the author murmuring directly into the reader's ear. Performance requires the creation of another projected voice, that of "the text itself," not for all time but for this time. And, in the delicate process of locating that voice, criticism can reinsert itself into the physical act of reading, rather than having to trot along always after or before the fact, as commentary.

2. The kind of practical attention to the physical words enforced by reading aloud serves as a bulwark against the usurpation that characterizes much contemporary criticism. I would not maintain that every literary effect is transposable into an elocutionary act by the reader. But the continuous challenge of oral interpretation keeps us alert to gesture and tone of voice, and to the burden of argument and figurative language which they weave together. And in these circumstances

the speaker implied or projected by speech act and communication theories can no longer remain a phantom, a putative off-stage role never available for examination. He enters and speaks his text for us to hear and respond to.

Oral interpretation also obliges us to register literary works first in linear human time, with its subtle aspects of evanescence and renewability, before the text can be converted into a synchronic structure out of time and subsumable under a diagram. The presence in live performance, however informal, of all three elements of the communication transaction (addresser, message, addressee) discourages premature concentration on one of these as the object of criticism. Oral interpretation can at least delay the abduction of the text by method, theory, or system.

A performed reading affirms the existence of the literary work in the true domain of art, which is *leisure*—not playtime exactly, but a form of recognized openness to new experience and sensibility, the goal of all our busy activity according to Aristotle, "the thing most dear to human beings" according to Euripides. Oral literature has always been closely associated with the basic institutions of leisure: social gatherings, festivities, and ceremonies. Those of us who are teachers might remember that the Greek work for leisure was *scholē*. School itself should be one of those privileged institutions.

3. An emphasis on oral interpretation in literary criticism will restore our sense of the power and centrality of the speaking voice in human transactions. Unlike the ideographic languages of the East, which aspire to picture thought directly, Western phonetic languages have articulated sound as their first "meaning." Since the production of sound, unlike a text once it is written or printed, requires the expenditure of energy, speech must arise from the active physical presence of the speaking agent. And because of the way it is produced and received, vocal speech conveys states of interiority not available to vision. Sound rather than vision appears to be the most effective and sensitive transmitter of human thought and feeling and therefore capable of uniting us in the experience of the

total present. Writing records this experience without reproducing it.

The most deep-seated reason for this privileged status of sound in our lives probably springs from its close relation to the rhythms lodged in our fundamental biological processes. In *The Biological Foundations of Language* Eric Lenneberg places the development of vocal speech in a specific nexus. "It has long been known that the universal rhythmicity of the vertebrate brain . . . is the motor for a vast variety of rhythmic movements."[13] He refers to breathing, heartbeat, walking, and speech. The physicality of speech and its reliance on the presence of two parties at least marginally in communication with one another keeps it in touch with the whole of our being, mind and body, reason and feeling.

Even though our culture powerfully propels literary authors toward the written word, many "writers" insist on the role of oral delivery to provide the true test of quality. The gradual dissociation after Socrates of thought from speech and the ultimate displacement of oratory and dialectic by the privacy of print[14] have not prevented literature from remaining deeply oral—even the novel. Flaubert shouted his sentences to himself in his *gueuloir* in Croisset. Tolstoy read his chapters aloud to his family as he wrote them. The innovations of modernism, such as free verse from Whitman to Cummings, stream-of-consciousness in Joyce, verbal inventions from Gertrude Stein to Barthelme, and even Proust's long-distance periods, are all essentially oral. How can we read, let alone *teach*, any of them without assaying their auditory nature?

A human being manifests his presence, both as an individual and as a member of a society, by many means—among them dress, carriage, facial expression, gesture, locomotion, and voice. Literature has refined voice into an expressive art with roots planted deep in articulate sounds and in the body that produces them. Insofar as we leave those physical sounds behind, we are also drifting away from literature's capacity to convey individual consciousness in a manner distinct from painting and mimetic gesture, which are reliant on the eye.

4. The oral approach to literature can help establish in schools the opportunity to improve voices for expressive and pleasing speech. A large part of religious training and military discipline is based on the ancient belief that by learning and performing the outward physical signs of emotions and moral attitudes we will come to experience those emotions and attitudes inwardly. In kneeling and close order drill, the body sways the mind. We teach children manners on the same principle. Training the voice in control and expressiveness very probably enlarges the scope of mental states available to us—particularly in a culture where the tonalities of speech have fallen badly into neglect and abuse. "The quality of life," to which we now pay close attention, depends deeply upon the tonality and dynamics of the voices with which we communicate with one another. Those vital sounds influence our moods more subtly than the weather and music. Why not consider the voice as a feature of our lives to be trained in the educational process—not separately as elocution or public speaking, but integrated into the study of literature interpreted orally?

5. The arguments that oppose the ideas I have been voicing belong to a tradition as old as the invention of printing. "The pen is the tongue of the soul," wrote Cervantes. Emily Dickinson, protective of all the nuances she compressed into her tiny verses, made her conviction clearer: "a Pen has so many inflections and a Voice has but one."[15] Such direct or implied declarations of faith in silent reading are rarely assembled and systematically examined.[16] The clearest presentation of the arguments I have discovered is contained in the few pages Susanne Langer devotes in *Feeling and Form* to a criticism of the oral performance of literature. In chapter 9 she argues that poetry differs from music in that music arises from our perception of "the passage of time made available by purely sonorous elements." Poetry "is not a fabric of *tönend bewegte Formen*," and therefore lends itself to silent reading. In chapter 15 she pits the "strict view" that literature begins with letters against the "popular theory" that all literature should be read

aloud. After granting that some poetry "profits by, or even demands, actual speech," she states her position.

> But much poetry and nearly all prose should be read somewhat faster than the normal rate of speech. Fast speaking does not meet this demand, because it becomes precipitous. Silent reading actually is faster, but does not appear so, because it is not hurried at the quicker tempo, whereas physical enunciation is. The images want to pass more swiftly than the spoken word. And furthermore, in prose fiction as well as in a good many poems, the voice of a speaker tends to intrude on the created world, turning formal lyric address such as: *I tell you, hopeless grief is passionless* . . . into genuine speech, addressed by the poet's proxy—the speaker—to another real person, the listener. A novel that centers chiefly in the creation of virtual personalities almost always suffers, when read aloud, by the peripheral presence of the reader. . . . [17]

Susanne Langer's observations on the relative qualities of silent and oral reading do not, as I see it, establish the primacy or superiority of the former. Rather they underline their complementary nature. The burden of my argument here is not to suppress silent reading but to advocate the need for both. I am trying to repair the present imbalance and give oral reading its deserved place. These two modes of approach to the text feed each other; the classroom offers a particularly good opportunity to combine silent and live reading. An oral interpretation may well extend our understanding of a work beyond the range of our own experience and imagination more convincingly than a commentary could do. This enlargement of our experience can take place precisely because reading aloud is a public act, open to examination, shared by many observers who can then discuss the "reading" as they cannot so readily discuss their several private and silent readings. The manifestness of the public reading thus facilitates criticism of a shared version whose existence is too easily taken for granted when a group of people are discussing a printed text they have previously read to themselves. They assume they are talking about the same object, whereas they probably have widely differing impressions of its voice and pace, its tone and color.

It is not a definitive or authoritative version of the work that I am suggesting will come out of this cultivation of oral interpretation. The purpose of reading aloud is basically heuristic. By trying out different oral versions a group explores the meanings released by a passage more effectively than by discussing an incompletely shared set of private readings. A similar assumption lay behind the once universal exercise of translating classic texts—not to produce a perfect version but to show students the subtleties of language and literary discourse through translation.

Now it is true, as Emily Dickinson's one-liner states with beautiful economy, that an oral reading may require us to choose between an ironic or a naive tone of voice, whereas a silent reading would allow these two moods to flicker in the mind. The performer has to decide on a reasonably coherent interpretation that can suggest many undertones and nuances without being all inclusive. Yet if literature is to be valued as a shared enterprise we must find a common ground of meaning and a limit on the splash and overflow of divergent interpretations. Even information theory sets a ceiling to the number of "bits" the human mind can process; every channel has a capacity.[18] Oral interpretation serves as a kind of test or verification to discover just how much of a work can be transmitted by speech to a community of listeners. In a reading by a competent performer, the meanings thus gained will more than compensate for those set aside.

If not all critics, at least most teachers are performers, and all of us can develop our skills in that direction according to our gifts and opportunities. Even more important, we can encourage our students to read works aloud, to interpret them orally, and to memorize them in order to savor the sonorous qualities too often buried in the printed text. The pervasive force of television confronts us with what is only a phantom oral culture: it offers no presence (the visual side is often redundant and dispensable), no participation, no exchange, no sense of collectivity—a depressingly one-directional enterprise. Those of us who deal with language and literature, who profess the word, can do far more than we are now doing to keep the spoken word alive and responsive to its expressive resources. We need constantly to reconsider our theories of literature and our methods of approaching it. But the vast exercise of criticism that goes on in the form of teaching literature in school and college will serve its purpose handsomely if it turns a substantial part of its attention to the trials and rewards of oral interpretation. The best literary works will grow with each reading.

Perhaps old Professor M should be kept on a year or two to teach the *Quijote*.

NOTES

1. Oscar Wilde, "The Critic as Artist," 1890; rpt. in *The Soul of Man Under Socialism and Other Essays*, ed. Philip Rieff (New York: Harper and Row, 1970), pp. 121, 132.
2. Claude Lévi-Strauss, *Le Cru et le cuit* (Paris: Plon, 1964), p. 20.
3. Roland Barthes, *Critique et vérité* (Paris: Éditions du Seuil, 1966), p. 70.
4. Roman Jakobson, "Concluding Statement: Linguistics and Poetics," in *Style in Language*, ed. Thomas A. Sebeok (Cambridge: MIT Press, 1960), pp. 350–77.
5. The basic references on the subject are Karl Popper, *The Logic of Scientific Discovery* (New York: Basic Books, 1959) and *Conjectures and Refutations: The Growth of Scientific Knowledge* (New York: Basic Books, 1962); F.A. Hayek, *The Counter-Revolution of Science* (Glencoe: Free Press, 1952); and most recently Lewis S. Feuer, "Teleological Principles in Science," *Inquiry* 21 (1978):377–407.
6. Ferdinand de Saussure, *Cours de linguistique générale*, ed. Tullio de Mauro (Paris: Payot, 1976), p. 33.
7. Northrop Frye, *Anatomy of Criticism* (1957; rpt. New York: Atheneum, 1966), pp. 7, 10–11, 16.
8. Barthes, p. 58.
9. Saussure, pp. 37–38.
10. Saussure, p. 138.
11. Charles Baudelaire, "Richard Wagner et Tannhauser à Paris," (1861); rpt. in *L'Art romantique*, vol. 4 of *Oevres completes de Charles Baudelaire*, ed. F. F. Gautier (Paris: Éditions de la Nouvelle Revue Française, 1923), p. 288.

12. John Hollander, *Vision and Resonance* (New York: Oxford University Press, 1975); Walter J. Ong, *The Presence of the Word* (New Haven: Yale University Press, 1967); Marshall McLuhan, *The Gutenberg Galaxy* (Toronto: University of Toronto Press, 1962); Rudolph Arnheim, *Visual Thinking* (Berkeley: University of California Press, 1969); Jean Piaget, *The Language and Thought of the Child* (New York: Meridian Books, 1955).

13. Eric Lenneberg, *The Biological Foundations of Language* (New York: Wiley and Sons, 1967), p. 119.

14. See William K. Wimsatt and Cleanth Brooks, *Literary Criticism: a Short History* (New York: Knopf, 1964), chapter 4; Walter J. Ong, "Transformations of the Word" in *The Presence of the Word*.

15. Quoted in Stanley Burnshaw, *The Seamless Web* (New York: George Braziller, 1970), p. 247.

16. For a lightly sketched historical exploration, see Elias Rivers, "Literature As the Disembodiment of Speech," in *What Is Literature?* ed. Paul Hernadi (Bloomington: Indiana University Press, 1978).

17. Susanne K. Langer, *Feeling and Form* (New York: Charles Scribner's Sons, 1953), p. 278.

18. See the remarkable exploratory article by George Miller, "The Magical Number Seven, Plus or Minus Two: Some Limits on Our Capacity for Processing Information," *The Psychological Review* 63 (1956), 2:81–97.

Criticism, Indeterminacy, Irony

Geoffrey Hartman

1. "Indeterminacy" is a word with bad vibes. It evokes a picture of the critic as Hamlet, "sicklied o'er by the pale cast of thought." It is often said to involve an attack on the communicative or edifying function of literature. A pseudoscientific or antihumanist bias is ascribed to critics when they do not replace words by meanings quickly enough. We like to consume our literature. We like to think of critics as service stations that keep readers fueled for their more important business, refreshing them and speeding them on.

Yet indeterminacy, though not an end to be pursued but something disclosed by liberal and thoughtful reading, is more like a traffic sign warning of an impasse. It suggests (1) that where there is a conflict of interpretations or codes, that conflict can be rehearsed or reordered but not always resolved, and (2) that even where there is no such conflict we have no certainty of controlling implications that may not be apparent or articulable at any one point in time. This "tacit component" will be mentioned again. But two things should already be

Reprinted by permission of the publishers from *Criticism in the Wilderness: The Study of Literature Today* by Geoffrey Hartman, New Haven: Yale University Press, Copyright © 1980.

clear. The referential function of words in ordinary situations, where the context is easily determined, is not in question. At the same time, all statements are potentially overdetermined and have a circumference larger than their apparent reference.

A statement made in a novel is subject to a different kind of interpretation than a statement made in a restaurant, but it is not a different statement. This look-alike (sound-alike) quality is disconcerting because the frame or setting (restaurant/restaurant-in-a-novel) is interchangeable—and often played with, in works of art. Quotation marks are a generalized frame of this kind: any phrase can be put in question, or echoed that way.

Phrases do echo crazily in some minds, and in one's own mind at times. Othello is a victim of this echoing. There is the joke of one spouse saying "Good Morning" and the other snarling "You want to pick a fight?" Shakespeare, to return to him, has his fun with a word that echoes itself: "Cuckoo! Cuckoo! O word of fear, / Unpleasing to a married ear." Or as Valéry says elegantly and generally: "La résonance emporte sur la causalité." The creation or drawing in of strange reverberations of unexpected contexts—frames of reference—is a mark of literature; and this "interanimation" will always have a tacit component. (See I. A. Richards, *The Philosophy of Rhetoric,* chap. 3; Kenneth Burke, "Semantic and Poetic Meaning" in *The Philosophy of Literary Form;* and Michael Polanyi, *Personal Knowledge,* part 2.) What is inexplicit is as functional as what is patently there, though it is hard to describe in a rigorous manner the relation between marked and unmarked features, between what is provided and what elided, what is verbal and what situational, what is foregrounded and what understood.

In "The Voice of the Shuttle" (*Beyond Formalism,* pp. 337–53) I described the structure of verbal interanimation as it governs figures of speech. They have overspecified ends and indeterminate middles, so that the elision or subsuming of the middle terms (a received story, a traditional theme, a current idiom) creates a sense of mediated immediacy that provokes interpretation. But I have done no more than provide a graded progression of examples; and these may require not only modification or completion but also an understanding that cannot be totally anticipated or constrained. This understanding is like a frame or context always beyond the horizon.

Even in the absence of a competent theory, however, we should recognize the fact that with the Symbolist poets, from Mallarmé and Rimbaud to Hofmannsthal, Yeats, and Valéry, a reflection on language accompanies explicitly the writing of poetry—a poetry we are still, at present, trying to *theorize*. Iris Murdoch puts the matter well. "Precision of reference had been sometimes more, sometimes less, important to the poet; but now suddenly it seemed that the whole referential character of language had become for him a sort of irritant or stumbling block." Characteristic of Symbolist or post-Symbolist poets, she continues, "is the way in which language appears to them like a metaphysical task, an angel to be wrestled with. Their attention is fixed upon language itself to the point of obsession, and their poems are thing-like, non-communicative, non-transparent to an unprecedented degree; they are independent structures, either outside the world or containing the world."[1] This, then, is part of the context in which literary criticism moves at the present time. The poets were there before Saussure.

2. To some extent every developed theory attempts to separate criticism from sheer scepticism or "nihilism." But how it does this can be very diverse. The diversity is itself of interest and perhaps not totally reducible. Can we understand anything without an inner movement of assent? Is that question best approached through a "grammar" of assent or through a Husserlian analysis of the "positional" and "intentional" structures of thought? Through existential dialectics or through speech act theory? Should we perhaps eschew all technical philosophy and be content with hints derived from fusion or identification theories, by Vico, Dilthey, and psychologically oriented authors? For the literary scholar, is it sufficient to follow the debates concerning the relation of understanding to belief in Richards, Eliot, and the New Criticism?

In terms of systematic thought I have nothing to add. But I

would like to recall that fiction itself, our very capacity for it, is what is threatened by both oversceptical and overaffirmative (dogmatic) philosophies. The destinies of fiction and criticism are joined; and the fact that criticism takes the form, so often, of commentary, is a sign of this. Even a negative commentary tends to save the text by continuing it in our consciousness. The relation of criticism to fiction, in any case, is more intrinsic than of thought to a found object. If, as in the Anglo-American tradition, we approach this issue through an insistence on meaning, I would continue to preface it as follows:

> The problem of meaning cannot even be faced without considering the necessity or fatality of some primary affirmation. Religious belief is such a primary act, but a special form of it. The founding of a fictional world is such a primary act. Fiction reveals something without which the mind could not be, or could not think. The mind needs a world, a substantialized Yes. Yet every great artist rebels against this, and today his rebellion is conventional. By beginning to question the necessity of fiction, i.e. the inherently affirmative structure of imagination, he joins the philosopher who sees a truth greater than that arbitrary Yes. (*Beyond Formalism*, p. 74)

3. Indeterminacy as a "speculative instrument" should influence the way literature is read, but by modifying the reader's awareness rather than by imposing a method. To methodize indeterminacy would be to forget the reason for the concept. It does not doubt meanings, nor does it respond to an economy of scarcity and try to make reading more "productive" of meaning. Quite the contrary: it encourages a form of writing—of articulate interpretation—that is not subordinated naively to the search for ideas. From this perspective the apparently opposite demands for *objective interpretation* on the part of E. D. Hirsch and for *subjective criticism* on the part of Norman Holland ignore equally the resistance of art to the meanings it provokes. Reduction of multiple meaning, according to Hirsch, is achieved through the postulate of a determinate and determinable authorial intention. Holland places the reduction of meaning in the "defensive mastery" of the artist

and the defensive misery of the reader. Hirsch would regulate the understanding, so that it does not waste itself; Holland would deregulate it, since the problem is not subjectivity but our overreaction to it, an excess of social rules and psychic defenses.

Though the issue of multiple meaning and its reduction is raised by both critics, they eventually leave art behind. Holland evangelizes the very difficulty of gaining an interpretation of art, suggesting that the interpretive work builds up, by way of the classroom, a community of readers who share this interpersonal, reflective experience; Hirsch seeks to rationalize literary studies by arguing that interpretation of art must abide by the rules of interpretation generally, that meanings are hypotheses subject to canons of verifiability. The concept of indeterminacy, however, explores the "blind lawfulness" (Kant) of imagination, or how art allows the understanding to produce its own form of meaningfulness. "As it must not, so genius cannot be lawless," Coleridge wrote in his *Lectures on Shakespeare*, "for it is even this that constitutes its genius—the power of acting creatively under laws of its own origination."

I realize that reduction of meaning and the role of the principle of indeterminacy would need more exposition than I can offer here. May I emphasize the following. As a guiding concept, indeterminacy does not merely *delay* the determination of meaning, that is, suspend premature judgments and allow greater thoughtfulness. The delay is not heuristic alone, a device to slow the act of reading till we appreciate (I could think here of Stanley Fish) its complexity. The delay is intrinsic: from a certain point of view, it is thoughtfulness itself, Keat's "negative capability," a labor that aims not to overcome the negative or indeterminate but to stay within it as long as is necessary.

How long, though? That cannot be abstractly answered. Forms of closure will occur, precipitated by acts of writing or reading. But it is the *commentary process* that matters: the taking away, modification, elaboration, of previous meanings. As long as criticism is also commentary, the work of art that is its "referent" is established as a constant variable, and its successive actualization (its "history") must itself be studied, as in the reception theory of the School of Konstanz associated with Hans Robert Jauss and Wolfgang Iser.

To compile an inventory of meanings in their structural relations ("structuralism") or of the focusing and orientative acts of consciousness in *their* relations ("phenomenology"), seems rather distant from what we do as critics, even when unusually introspective. This is where the gap between humanistic criticism and "scientific" approach to literary studies is most apparent; and I have not been able to bridge it. The gap is like that between *langue* and *parole* in Saussure, or between grammar and the living language, or between a principle and its application. (In hermeneutics, as Hirsch reminds us, a difference was often discerned between subtlety of understanding and subtlety of explication—of articulating and applying one's understanding. Gadamer, however, thinks these are or can be fused.) On the whole, I favor moving "indeterminacy" from the area of semiotic, grammatical, or phenomenological reduction to that of humanistic criticism itself: that is, we take back from science what is ours, we do not allow ourselves to depend on the physical or human sciences for the model of a *mechanism* that fascinates by its anonymous, steely, impersonal character. (So, for example, on the strange foundation of unconscious process the most elaborate structures, including art, are built up.) Through interpretive criticism we ascertain the kind of relation we have to that mechanism, as writing and reading disclose it. Wordsworth's "dim and undetermined sense / Of unknown modes of being" is also what moved him to autobiography, and to define that which has no single, exclusively personal, locus. Yet what is being disclosed may be, precisely, the absence of one and only one context from which to view the flux of time or the empirical world, of one and only one method that would destabilize all but itself, of one and only one language to rule understanding and prevent misunderstanding.

To put it another way: we read to understand, but to understand *what?* Is it the book, is it the object (in the world) revealed by the book, is it ourselves? Or some transcendental X?

It is not difficult to insist that all these aspects must participate; and philosophical reflection from the side of phenomenology, as well as the critique of phenomenology by semiotics, hermeneutics, and linguistic analysis have distinguished among these aspects.[2] But the literary critic remains the "delegate" of the common as well as of the uncommon reader, and so cannot at each point rehearse distinctions that would displace reading as the enjoyable and liberal activity it is. Reading should always remain, on one level, an exemplary grappling of mind with text for the sake of immediate intellectual and moral benefits, such as "seeing" an idea, a sharper view of the relation between style and moral action, or between the comprehension *(Verstehen)* of literary sentences and intersubjective consensus *(Verständnis)*. I will therefore risk bracketing various philosophical considerations in asserting the following.

We read, as we write, to "be understood," yet what we gain is the undoing of a previous understanding. Indeterminacy, as a concept, resists formally the complicity with closure implied by the wish to "be understood" or the communication-compulsion associated with it. Criteria of correctness or correspondence (of *truth*) may be caught up in this complicity. Indeterminacy functions as a bar separating understanding and truth. Understanding is not disabled but is forced back on the conditions of its truth: for example, the legitimacy of its dependence on texts. If this seems too radical a perspective, there remains the puzzle that the reception of literary works is usually accompanied by an uneasiness about their reduction to meaning. Reduction *of* meaning, that is, may work against reduction *to* meaning. Reading itself becomes the project: we read to understand what is involved in reading as a form of life, rather than to resolve what is read into glossy meanings. As in collage or conceptual art, meanings (Rilke's "gedeutete Welt") are part of the medium of art, part of its *matériel*.

To keep a poem in mind is to keep it there, not to resolve it into available meanings. This suspensive discourse is criticism, and it can be distinguished from the propaedeutics of scholarly interpretation as well as from the positivity of applied teacherly interpretation. The reader's "willing suspension of disbelief" is really a suspension of accommodating and allegorical meanings, the sort that would comfort a seduced yet disbelieving mind. What many consider "figurative" reading is but a way of avoiding the pressure of fiction on the mind, while a nonallegorical reading can insist on the plain presumption of the text. Thus, though I recognize the genre of "Leda and the Swan" as a *transposition d'art* or a vignette from Yeat's *légende des siècles,* I must refuse to let that divert me from questions about the authority of its author, the literalness of his claim, the mimetic texture of his vision. The seduction of understanding through a fiction should provoke something more active than bemusement or suspended disbelief: it should provoke me to break, however provisionally, the very frame of meaning I bring to the text. Perhaps "bracket" in Husserl's sense of the *epoche* would be better than "break" to describe this suspension of anticipatory ideas or theories (*Ideas,* pars. 30–33), for nothing is really broken but rather freed for contemplation, analysis, and play.

4. "Indeterminacy" is not a word to insist on. "Irony," if its history were kept in mind, would be preferable; when it was used by the New Critics it raised smaller fears. That may have been because they separated irony from a philosophical context that can be made to include, as in Kierkegaard's *The Concept of Irony,* the doubting of appearances, of phenomena, from Socrates on. This context includes the history of scepticism as well as of the overcoming of scepticism. Cleanth Brooks, among the New Critics, saw that irony had a similarity to paradox, that is, to statements or a type of statement that went against (*para*) established belief or received opinion (*doxa*); and he rescued it from being a simple and determinate figure of speech. It was presented as an open or tacit but always constant feature of works of art that a critic could formalize as a source of their value. Irony itself became, paradoxically, a value ascribed to art, and the analyses that showed this, particularly in *The Well-Wrought Urn,* were so tactful that one could not suspect them of being ironical. The urn lost its

death-related character, and criticism gained a new and businesslike stability.

So irony's "practicality" was assured, and it became domesticated in literary studies. But its strange, featureless, even daimonic flexibility (able to assume any shape) was reduced to the status of serviceable Elf or Kobalt, the kind that helps poor shoemakers cobble shoes as long as no one tries to catch spirit in the act. The literary critic, indeed, was advised to be precisely that: a practical person who should not look beyond his last. Everything that was subversive or exalting, indeterminacy of meaning, or infinite negativity, or disruptive subjectivity, was embargoed. The embargo leaked, of course; also because literary-historical studies kept reintroducing the importance of irony as a larger theme, a more heroic and even pathetic—or counterpathetic—virtue, with religious and philosophical ramifications.

Hegel considered Friedrich Schlegel a playboy philosopher because of his emphasis on irony in every realm of life; Kierkegaard considered Hegel's dialetic as not existential enough, and so comparably negative or prematurely universalizing in its effect on ethics. Kierkegaard valued the depth of Romantic irony and the seduction of "the aesthetic"—but he categorized the latter as an inadequate and ultimately unserious mode of dealing with either mortal anguish or immortal thoughts. The importance of Kierkegaard to philosophical thinkers in the twentieth century is related to his critique of Hegel's dialectic as an "aesthetic" maneuver, one that universalizes falsely, deprives existence of its "particularity" (a term that becomes important when aesthetics, as in Lukács, tries to overcome aestheticism), and so removes philosophy from the sphere of religious and social action. The relation of thought to *praxis* becomes, in one way or another, the crucial problem. The difference in traditions—empiricism in Richards and the British critics; Hegelianism or Marxism in Lukács, Adorno, Sartre, and Ortega; hermeneutics or Freud or Heidegger (or all of these) in Gadamer, Ricoeur, and certain American critics—does not affect this common aim of purging thought of aestheticism or similar evasions.

One need only open the first major books of Benjamin and Adorno respectively to recognize this common aim. Benjamin's "Epistemo-Critical Prologue" to *The Origin of German Tragic Drama* (1927, though conceived ten years earlier) emphasizes the disparity between philosophy and doctrine, a disparity that can only be overcome through the very *form* of philosophy. "In its finished form philosophy will, it is true, assume the quality of doctrine, but it does not lie within the power of mere thought to confer such a form."[3] Where, then, does that authoritative form come from? The fact that there must be representation, and that this representation is verbal ("the area of truth toward which language is directed"), leads Benjamin into an involved and fascinating series of Platonic, Kantian, Kabbalistic (name-mysticism) reflections. These include the formulation of a concept of *prose form* or *philosophical style*, which is clearly meant to save philosophy from the imputation of being on the side of poetry rather than truth—the charge that caused Plato to banish the poets from his Republic. Benjamin, turning Plato against Plato, defines philosophical style as "the art of interruption in contrast to the chain of deduction; the tenacity of the essay in contrast to the single gesture of the fragment; the repetition of themes in contrast to shallow universalism; the fullness of concentrated positivity in contrast to the negation of polemic" (p. 32). And he goes through Plato beyond Plato when he writes:

> It is the task of the philosopher to restore, by representation, the primacy of the symbolic character of the word, in which the idea is given self-consciousness, and that is the opposite of all outwardly-directed communication. Since philosophy may not presume to speak in the tones of revelation, this can only be achieved by recalling in memory the primordial form of perception. Platonic anamnesis is, perhaps, not far removed from this kind of remembering; except that here it is not a question of the actualization of images in visual terms; but rather, in philosophical contemplation, the idea is released from the heart of reality as the word, reclaiming its name-giving rights. Ultimately, however, this is not the attitude of Plato but the attitude of Adam. . . . [P. 36–37]

As for Adorno, his *Habilitationsschrift*, published in 1933 as *Kierkegaard: The Construction of the Aesthetic*, begins so revealingly that I can dispense with further commentary: "If one insists on understanding the writings of philosophers as poetry [*Dichtungen*] then one has missed out on their truth-content. The law of form in philosophy demands the interpretation of reality in agreement with the way concepts relate. Neither a proclaiming of the subjectivity of the thinker, nor the pure closure of a construct in itself, may decide its character as philosophy but only the following: whether reality has entered the concepts and identifies itself through them and substantiates them perspicuously."[4]

The importance of being earnest takes a somewhat different form today than in the 1920s and 1930s. But it still contains a perplexed meditation on the relation of philosophy and poetry, truth and method, ideas and representations. Nothing might seem nearer to the life we lead than the language we speak; and philosophical thinking has become primarily a thinking about language. But one feels trapped in language that is about language, or has the sense that one cannot emerge from a verbal universe—not even into an Adamic essentialism of the Name. Nor has the spread of semiliteracy helped. Every statement, idiom, or idiolect has now its rights; and this situation of *surnomie*, where there are too many styles, terms, interpretations, leads to a low-grade *anomie* that is expressed in TV sitcom, its endless and insipid comedy of errors, or in the excessive theatricality of novels peopled by caricatures rather than characters, or in the witty and deliberate charlatanism of advertisements in a consumerist culture.

There is no presence; there is only representation, and worse, representations. The crisis focuses on that, not on language as such. It is a crisis of *evidentiality*. How do we save phenomena that cannot save themselves? Our mediating role is bound to be suspect, if truth is thought of as self-evidencing, as "the death of intention" (Benjamin). Yet we must think of it *also* as that. The reflective person has to avoid being a mere reflex of others; a bundle of inherited intentions, a mediated rather than mediating will. The paradox is clear enough.

This is no new crisis; it is the old one; but a shift has indeed occurred. We ask not only what truth may be in distinction from beauty or opinion or positive knowledge. We ask about the truth of evidence in a world where there are only representations; and about the tension between language and representation. What authority do texts enjoy? Why do we continue to rely on them? Are we investing them with the missing "ocular proof," or do they become documents of the resistance in us to the conversion of representation into presence?

The oldest detective story keeps being reenacted. On every side there is a self-incriminating lust for evidence. Hermeneutics is an art that grows out of perplexity, out of finding an enigma where we expected a kerygma. Evidence fails or is disabled, and unusual or ungovernable types of interpretation come into play. Science fiction too creates worlds in which the forces are unknown, and all appearances and testimonies risk being false.

No wonder some are scared witless by a mode of thinking that seems to offer no decidability, no resolution. Yet the perplexity that art arouses in careful readers and viewers is hardly licentious. It is the reality; it is only as strange as truth. It recalls the artificial nature or purely conventional status of formal arguments or proofs; the fact that human agreements remain conveniences with the force of law, metaphors with the force of institutions, opinions with the force of dogma. It recalls the prevalence of propaganda, both in open societies that depend on conversation, jawboning, advertising, bargaining, and in controlled societies that can become sinister and inquisitorial, adding to their torture chamber the subtlest brainwashing and conditioning devices without giving up the brazen and reiterated lie. Can any hermeneutics of indeterminacy, any irony however deeply practiced and nurtured by aesthetic experience, withstand either society while they are still distinguishable?

NOTES

1. *Sartre: Romantic Rationalist* (New Haven: Yale University Press, 1958), pp. 29–30. Distinguished earlier attempts to theorize the Symbolists are, principally, Edmund Wilson's *Axel's Castle* (New York: Charles Scribner's and Sons, 1931) and Charles Feidelson's *Symbolism and American Literature* (Chicago: University of Chicago Press, 1953). Even Northrop Frye's *Fearful Symmetry* (Princeton: Princeton University Press, 1947) is still an attempt, in the light of Yeats, to present Blake as a great precursor, a Romantic Symbolist. A significant shift in the critical spectrum comes when a theory of specifically Romantic poetry is recovered in the 1960s and breaks up the powerful Symbolist-Modernist axis.

2. See, for example, Wolfgang Iser, *The Act of Reading* (Baltimore: The Johns Hopkins University Press, 1979); Jacques Derrida, *Speech and Phenomena*, trans. David B. Allison (Evanston: Northwestern University Press, 1973); and Ernst Tugendhat, "Phänomenologie und Sprachanalyse" in *Hermeneutik und Dialektik*, 2, ed. Rüdiger Bübner, Konrad Cramer, and Reiner Wiehl (Tübingen: J.C.B. Mohr, 1970), 3–23. Tugendhat suggests that Husserl's "intentional act" is modeled on understanding names rather than sentences, with the result that the subject-object schematism is retained as primary instead of being subordinated to a hermeneutic and intersubjective perspective.

3. Walter Benjamin, *The Origin of German Tragic Drama*, trans. John Osborne (London: NLB, 1977), p. 27.

4. *Kierkegaard*: *Konstruktion des Ästhetischen* (Tübingen: J.C.B. Mohr, 1933), p. 1; I can render Adorno's difficult German only approximately. The original runs: "Wann immer man die Schriften von Philosophen als Dichtungen zu begreifen trachtet, hat man ihren Wahrheitsgehalt verfehlt. Das Formgesetz der Philosophie fordert die Interpretation des Wirklichen im stimmigen Zusammenhang der Begriffe. Weder die Kundgabe der Subjektivität des Denkenden noch die pure Geschlossenheit des Gebildes in sich selber entscheiden über dessen Charakter als Philosophie, sondern erst: ob Wirkliches in die Begriffe einging, in ihnen sich ausweist und sie einsichtig begründet."

A Functional View of Criticism

Mario J. Valdés

It is not uncommon to read a statement of critical purpose which maintains that there is a dark side to the literary work and that the function of criticism is to cast light on this dark side, to explain to the reader what is not clear, and in general to act as an interpreter between the text and the reader. To be sure, there are a number of statements of purpose which differ in detail or in substance from this one. Yet critics as a rule do not ask the question which must come before the question of value: why explain, if that is what the critic is to do, literature, and not history, philosophy, or some other body of writings? The value, if there is one, of literature is not a self-evident truth; and that value must be established before the critic can go on to fix his position in relation to literature and readers of literature.

Literature has two fundamental attributes which are the justification for its existence and its study; it is of value as language, as the most elaborate expression of a language community's identity, and it is of value as one of the most direct forms of self-knowledge attainable for those who read and those who write. Certainly self-knowledge has also been the quest of philosophers and religious teachers throughout history, but the basic difference between literature and philosophy is that in literature the full realm of subjectivity is freed to engage itself in its conception of reality, and the difference between religious teaching and literature is that religious thought depends on faith which is sometimes unavailable. We must not lose sight of the fact that the truth of literature is a subjective and intersubjective truth which cannot purport to reflect an extrasubjective reality. The modern novel has been used as a sociological document by a number of contemporary investigators; nevertheless, its worth does not rest on the information it provides about the world depicted within. It is valuable as a social document in the sense that the novel expresses the subjective and intersubjective structures which operate within a given community.

If the value of literature is subjective and intersubjective, it follows that the aims of criticism should also be related to these kinds of value. Consequently, the statement of purpose we considered above, which I believe is the prevalent one today, must be reoriented toward the reader. In this way we can restate the aims of criticism as directed to the reader rather than to a text upon which an objective status has been conferred. There is not a dark side to the work of literature, but there are deficient readers of literature. An important critical activity thus aims at producing a certain necessary competence in the reader. A second and higher aim of criticism is to engage in a critical dialogue with the tradition of literature as we have inherited it. This second aim seeks to attain for us participation in culture. The highest aim of criticism, however, must be the enrichment of our self-awareness as readers.

The competence of readers is an attainable goal if they are willing to share the text directly with others and explain the basis for their observations. Most literary critics engage in this dialogue of readers, but only those who explicitly share their method of analysis can contribute much to the reading of others. The scholar-critic who is largely concerned with cultural participation already assumes that he is addressing competent readers who have mastered the texts in question, but who have not yet fully appreciated the specific works within the cultural tradition. Consequently, the scholar examines the text against its historical background. But the historical dimension of the text is or should be only a part of the reading experience. The reader's own historicity is the only valid historical base; we in the twentieth century can only read a seventeenth or twelfth-century work from our historical position. We cannot separate ourselves from our historical ground. Participation in the cultural tradition consists of an acute awareness both of our historical distance from the text and of the universal bonds which transcend that distance. The critic whose aim is to enrich the reader's experience is concerned not only with enlarging the reader's competence and degree of cultural participation but also with seeking to open the reader's awareness to his own subjectivity. When the reader can recognize the paths which his subjective response to the text has taken in the reading experience he is engaging in hermeneutical interpretation.

Obviously the reader attains competence only with a formal understanding of the work and achieves the more demanding cultural participation through the diachronic knowledge of the changing modes and developments in the history of literature. The third aim of criticism—enrichment of the reading experience—demands an open form of classification which can integrate the formal and historical aspects of the work. This requirement is unmistakably pressing because the realm of enquiry is the intersubjective structure of the reading experience and not the isolated text nor the historical milieu.

I propose a complete redirection of the critical purpose from the text to the reader. Two observations on human activity can be our base for an ethics of criticism. First, taken as a whole, man's personal actions constitute a continuous effort at expression. "Living" for the individual can thus be considered as a continuous but faulty process moving from personal intentions and aspirations to partial realization. A second observation is that the human perception of reality is constituted within a value structure. Consequently an expression of values is present in everything we do. We see our world within our order of discriminations, needs, and urgencies. A table appears very differently to the furniture salesman, the craftsman, the freezing man in the mountains, the drowning man in the sea, because of the personal context of each man's values. Consequently we can say that value to us is the mode of perception, implicit in our actions, through which we encounter the world and appropriate it to ourselves.

In a recent interview (*Psychology Today*, February 1973, pp. 56–69), George Steiner was asked what relation literature has to ethics. His response can serve to further our consideration of values:

> I had been brought up in a world that believed that if people read good books, went to museums, subscribed to the opera, and loved symphonies, certain decencies would follow. There was a deep belief that human savagery and hatred and killing were caused by lack of education. People who read won't believe in stupid murderous slogans. People who love Beethoven are not going to do certain things to other people. People who spend their lives reading Virgil or Goethe or Shakespeare or Racine will understand each other across disagreements. If we can say with a cold laugh today, "How stupid. We should have known it wouldn't work," well, we are the poorer for that knowledge. It was a very reasonable thing to hope for and a very noble hope. I desperately wanted to find out what went wrong. Why did this deep, tremendous house of culture go over like a house of cards the moment it faced political terror and violence? [P. 57]

Steiner's ensuing discussion presents the frustration and failure of humanistic education, but without finding the reasons why those expectations proved to be false. What was mistaken in the ideal concept that man can substitute dialogue for violence? Let us examine the question within the context of literary criticism and the novel.

The traditional answer, which was echoed in Steiner's views, is based on the theory that value is a personal judgment and reality is objective, separate, and value-free. With such an approach it is almost inevitable that a liberal individualism would propagate the notion that the value of literature is the making of the educated man whose cultural sensibility demonstrates that he is at the pinnacle of civilization. Similarly the traditional view has been that the value of literary criticism is in the aid it provides in the education of such an elite man. I propose that the traditional view of these values is mistaken because the premise of the opposition between value and reality is an error.

No man's reality can be conceived as independent or free of values. The universe for each individual is the cohesive unity brought about by his value structure. The moment we appropriate a thought or a thing it enters into our value structure. Thus, instead of a theory of opposition between value and reality, let us begin with a radical unity. We know the feeling of satisfaction precisely when our value system is in accord with our milieu. This is to have what we need and desire when we need it and desire it. What, we may ask, is the value of literature and of criticism if man's experience at all levels is a value experience? My answer is that literature has value only if it promotes and satisfies the needs of the reader, and criticism has value only insofar as it also fosters the satisfaction of the reader. We must, of course, search beyond subjective exigencies for the intersubjective structure of value to all readers. For each reader, value is an anticipation of some measure of fulfillment in the reading experience in which he is about to engage himself; it is in this sense the project of reading itself. Consequently if he does not find that the experience has justified his value anticipation, he will judge the activity to have been deficient.

We can now turn our full attention toward the question of value in the literary critic's activity. If the critic refuses to grant the work an objective reality divorced from the reader, his undertaking can only be directed to the reader. The value of criticism therefore lies in the dedication to the human reality of the reading experience, the critic's own and that of other readers. This is a concept of mutual enrichment which has been with us for a long time as the ideal of the teacher-learner, but unfortunately has been overlaid with countless layers of self-promotion.

The individual reader must remain the beginning and the

end of criticism, for the value of criticism is to be found in the enrichment of the personal reading experience. The experience of this value is an experience of shared subjectivity. Yet the value concept of enrichment of the reading experience must be further explored in order to recover its practical sense within the framework of action.

Consider the reader's experience of a novel. Because there are two referential aspects to any experience of language, there are also two aspects of value involved with reading a novel. First, we can attain knowledge in the third person. Here the language refers to an exterior world, and there is an openness and a receptivity in the reader who will refer the milieu of the novel to the milieu of his life-world. We try to fix the meaning of words in our intercourse with the novel, for we are engaged in trying to understand its world in relation to our own. We thus seek a pattern which we can grasp as a social reality. We hope to triumph over diversity by unity, over unrelated incidents by pattern. This form of knowledge is the domain of our participation in life as social beings. The greater enrichment of the reader's social being is achieved through dialogue with other readers, and the critic in this context is a reader's reader who seeks to engage him in dialogue.

In addition to third-person knowledge we can also attain first-person knowledge. The self-reference, a fundamental aspect of the narrative's language, ultimately comes to bear on the reader's self-knowledge. The reference of most narrative words is away from ourselves and into the third person's world, but we also have the dimension of the narrator's self-reference which elicits self-reference in the reader. When the reader becomes aware of his relationship to the narrator and to the narrative world he has achieved a radical self-awareness as a reader and as a coproducer of the experience which is the novel. The ultimate achievement of this radical self-awareness is self-knowledge.

Thus literature offers two varieties of enrichment. One is the enrichment of the reader as a social being, and the other is the enrichment of the reader as the subject of self-knowledge. These are not opposed to each other; indeed, they are complementary facets of the central concept of reality as the experience of the world through the subjective value structure. Thus these two versions of value are interdependent as the social and personal sides of reality.

The critic as a reader's reader shares the same experience and participates in the same value. The only difference is that the critic seeks openly to engage in the dialogue of interpretation that will bring forth with clarity the position of the reader and will make the reading experience itself the object of attention. Consequently, by achieving an enrichment of the reading experience for himself as a social man and as a person, the critic can fulfill the same function for other readers as well.

Criticism can never rival the literary text without denying it. If criticism overshadows the original text, the critic has become a rival author and has substituted his text for the original. The critical act is devoted to the original text and to an analysis of it in order to facilitate understanding the experience of reading it. Thus, the critic serves other readers by first establishing the internal distance of the text and secondly by exposing his own subjectivity in response to the text in search of an intersubjective dialogue with other readers. The basic subdivisions of the critical activity are analysis and interpretation. Each has its own logic, its own laws of operation, and its own aim, but both are part of the same integral activity which pursues the enrichment of the reading experience as knowledge of social participation and as self-knowledge.

The ethics of criticism is linked to the enrichment of readers through mutual respect. Just as we can never have true dialogue without mutual respect, the critic will not achieve a genuine enrichment of the reading experience without respect for the reader.

The double path of enrichment is open to all critics whatever their specific function among the multiple facets of criticism, for I have discussed an ethical goal and not a method in this essay. An ethical sense of literary criticism comes from the consideration of those radical questions: why study literature, and for whom do we write our commentary? There are other goals than those which I have described, but in my opinion there are insufficient grounds for giving serious dedication to them. The ivory tower concept of the pursuit of truth and beauty is meaningless if we objectify truth and beauty. The only meaning of the two words which I have been able to understand is that of a human value judgment born out of the dialogue among human beings.

Literature and Hermeneutics

Hans Robert Jauss

TRANSLATED BY TIMOTHY BAHTI

The founding of a *literary* hermeneutics, and its methodological development, are tasks that present themselves anew to us today. Certainly there exists a long-standing secular tradition of *philological* hermeneutics. This tradition can take pride in an honorable origin—the intepretation of Homer in antiquity. It can appeal to an extensive theory guiding the exegesis[1] of canonical writings and can claim as its proudest post-Renaissance monument the restored texts of, and commentaries upon, the classical authors of Greece and Rome. The historical interpretation of the past texts of all of world literature is no less rich a product of this tradition which, since the nineteenth century, has adhered to the ideal of objective and thus "scientific" knowledge. Yet as is well known, these

A longer version of this essay was published in German as a contribution to *Text und Applikation: Theologie, Jurisprudenz und Literaturwissenschaft im hermeneutischen Gespräch*, ed. Hans Robert Jauss, Manfred Fuhrmann, and W. Pannenberg (Munich: Fink, 1980), vol. 9 of *Poetik und Hermeneutik*. The original version appeared under the title "Überlegungen zur Abgrenzung und Aufgabenstellung einer literarischen Hermeneutik." It is excerpted and translated by permission.

accomplishments do not uniquely belong to philological hermeneutics. It shares them with theological, juridical, philosophical, and historical hermeneutics, in short, with all disciplines that are occupied with editions, "source criticism," and the historical exegesis of texts of the past. Thus, from the perspective of the history of disciplines, one can speak of a common philological foundation of all "regional" hermeneutics, and the initial question must rather be posed as follows: Where does the unique and independent character of a literary hermeneutics actually begin? How did it, and how does it today proceed when it wants to do justice to the aesthetic character of its texts?

This question is quite likely to embarrass the philologist, even today. Traditionally, it was referred to rhetoric as a question of the effect of literary discourse, or it was considered the business of nonacademic literary criticism as a question of aesthetic value. Where, since the beginning of our century, the question has actually been posed—as the question of the "literariness" of texts—and where it has been turned into an exegetical premise, hermeneutic reflection was dismissed. This was true for the projects of the Russian Formalists as well as for Leo Spitzer's stylistics;[2] but even the later linguistic or semiotic poetics and the most recent theories of *écriture, jeu textuel,* and *intertextualité* either scarcely inquired about the hermeneutic implications of the new descriptive methods or, under the spell of formalistic scientific ideals, presented an antihermeneutic position. Susan Sontag's *Against Interpretation* was well received because her ardent attack upon the objectivism of traditional exegetical practice highlighted the contradiction that exists between modern literature and traditional interpretation when the latter reduces the polyvalence of the "open work" (*opera aperta*) to an ostensibly pre-given meaning, hidden in the text or to be sought behind it.[3] On the other hand, neighboring textual disciplines—especially theology and jurisprudence—have by now succeeded in distinguishing their own hermeneutic praxis of understanding, exegesis, and application from the generally shared presuppositions of all philological-historical interpretation. If one glances at recent developments in hermeneutic theory, one can only agree with Peter Szondi, who in 1970 lamented that literary hermeneutics had so far been content to play the role of the "poor relative" in this discussion.[4]

Szondi called for a revision of the traditional philological methods that had become blind to theory, and he saw the goal of a new literary hermeneutics in the task of developing "a theory of interpretation which is not, to be sure, unphilological, but which reconciles philology with aesthetics."[5] This theory would have to distinguish itself from the traditional hermeneutics of classical philology in that it "will not only consider the aesthetic character of the text to be interpreted in an evaluation which follows after the exegesis, but rather it will make the aesthetic character a premise of the exegesis itself."[6] Contrary to the generally widespread tendency toward a theory of understanding which, since Bultmann, would go beyond all regional hermeneutics, Szondi pleaded for the return to a material hermeneutics which would respect the practice of literary exegesis and be based upon our contemporary understanding of art. Szondi laid a ground for the elaboration of such a literary hermeneutics, a ground upon which one might well build further. He tested its methodological procedures on paradigms of the hermetic lyric and thereby brought to light the interdependence of criticism and hermeneutics. But he also illuminated the somewhat obscure initial stages of literary hermeneutics when he emphasized those moments in the general tradition of hermeneutics in which, since Chladenius, interpreters of a particular text became conscious of its aesthetic rather than theological or juridical character and began to apply a specific method of aesthetic exegesis to it.

Hermeneutics displays three orientations: understanding, exegesis, and application; or, to cite the didactically proven pietistic triad, the *subtilitas intelligendi, explicandi, applicandi.* In the literary hermeneutics Szondi left behind—which he himself certainly would have considered unfinished—the second orientation stands thoroughly in the foreground of interest. In taking up his project we should explore the extent to which the unique and independent character of literary hermeneutics is to be sought in the first hermeneutic act, the *subtilitas intelligendi;* and, further, how it partakes of the third hermeneutic act, the *subtilitas applicandi* that crowned the *subtilitas explicandi* for theological as well as for juridical hermeneutics. How valid for literary hermeneutics is Hans Georg Gadamer's claim that "application is as integral a component of the hermeneutic procedure as understanding and exegesis are"?[7] Fundamental questions like that have remained controversial even though literary hermeneutics has begun to solve some of its specific problems concerning the constitution, effect, and exegesis of aesthetically structured texts.[8] Thus in the foreground of my interest stands the attempt to clarify two issues through continual reference to the neighboring hermeneutics: first, what insight into the primary operation of understanding can be earned precisely from literary hermeneutics' aesthetic object; and second, to what extent may understanding in the aesthetic attitude go beyond pure artistic pleasure and reflective exegesis to its own application—be this in aesthetic identification or in aesthetic judgment.

In order to recognize what kinds of understanding, exegesis, and application are unique to a text with an aesthetic character, it seems to me necessary to distinguish among three procedures of interpretation and to reflect methodologically upon what tends to remain undifferentiated in the philological practice of exegesis. There the basis for understanding is sought in the reconstruction of the historical context—of the original intention of the author or work—and is introduced into the interpretation, which thus scarcely distinguishes any longer between the acts of understanding and those of exegesis, and thereby lets receptive understanding be absorbed into reflective interpretation. But if we wished to link the understanding of a text, despite the temporal distance between author and reader, to its aesthetic reception, we would do well to separate the horizon of an initial, aesthetically-perceptive reading from that of a second, retrospectively-exegetical reading and even from a third, historical reading which places the text within the horizon of its alterity and difference vis-à-vis our experience. This historical reading can begin with the reconstruction of the horizon of expectations into which the text entered at the time of its appearance for its contemporary reader. But such a reading will fully accord with the unity demanded of the hermeneutic triad only when the historical distance between the text and the present is worked out once again, and when the tradition of readings which paved the way for the latest application is clarified.

The problem of separating three horizons of interpretation in the hermeneutic process is most easily solved methodologically when one conceives of and describes the three hermeneutic acts phenomenologically as successive readings of the same text, wherein each time the preceding reading becomes the horizon of pre-understanding for the following one. The "horizontal" structure of all understanding emerges with particular clarity from the reception of a poetic text. It is therefore unfortunate that structuralist poetics has largely ignored this horizontal structure, although it has for the most part concerned itself with questions of the constitution of aesthetic texts. Whatever can be known in the completed texture of the text, in the closed whole of its structure, as a signifying function of language or as aesthetic equivalence, always already presupposes something anticipatorily understood *(ein vorgängig Verstandenes)*. In order to understand how the poetic text, thanks to its aesthetic character, allows us first or anticipatorily to understand something, we cannot start with the question of the significance of the particular within the fulfilled form of the whole; rather, our analysis must follow the signification as it is still open in the process of perception which the text, like a musical score, traces out for the reader. The investigation of the aesthetic character—which is unique to the poetic text in distinction to the theological, the juridical, or also the philosophic text—must follow the orientation provided for aesthetic perception through the structure of the text, the suggestion of the rhythm, the gradual fulfillment of the form. With the poetic text, aesthetic understanding is hermeneutically bound to the horizon of expectations of the first reading. The exegesis in the second (and every further) reading also remains referred to this horizon, as long as the interpreter claims to concretize a signification of the text, and does not want to exercise the license of allegoresis—that is, to grant a meaning to the text that is originally foreign to it; a meaning that cannot be attributed to the text without ignoring its poetic form. The exegesis of a poetic text always presupposes aesthetic perception as its pre-understanding; it can only concretize significations that appeared—or could have appeared—as possible to the interpreter within the horizon of his preceding reading.

Gadamer's dictum, that "Understanding means understanding something as an answer,"[9] must therefore be restricted, with respect to the poetic text, as applying only to the secondary act of exegetical understanding—insofar as this act concretizes a specific signification as the answer to a question—but not the primary act of perceptual understanding. With this formulation, I gladly concede that in aesthetic perception an understanding is also always at work[10]—only precisely not that understanding that must explicitly question the text in order to understand it as an answer; rather, the understanding is an implicit understanding of the spectacle of the world that opens itself to the reader in the aesthetic perception. The aesthetic *Gestalt* of a poem does not first disclose itself to perceptual understanding as an answer; rather, to speak with Husserl, "the eidetic reduction is spontaneously accomplished in the aesthetic experience."[11] Thus, the separation of reflective exegesis from the perceptual understanding of a poetic text is not as artificial as it first appeared. Such a separation is made possible through the evidently horizontal structure of the experience of rereading.

Every reader is familiar with the experience in which the meaning of a poem discloses itself only as he looks back upon it in the course of a rereading. It is then that the experience of the first reading becomes the horizon of the second: what the reader took in in the progressive horizon of aesthetic perception becomes capable of being articulated in the retrospective horizon of the exegesis. If one adds that the exegesis itself can become the foundation for an application—more specifically, that a text from the past can be interpreted in order to disclose anew its significance for the contemporary situation—then it becomes clear that the triadic unity of understanding, exegesis, and application, as that triad occurs in the hermeneutic process, corresponds perfectly to the three horizons of thematic, exegetical, and motivational relevance—the reciprocal relationships between which determine, according to A. Schütz, the constitution of subjective experience of the life-world.[12]

In developing a concept of interpretation that seeks to distinguish the three acts of the hermeneutic process, I can take up, and develop further, insights that Michael Riffaterre, Wolfgang Iser, and Roland Barthes have introduced into the analysis of procedures of reception. Riffaterre analyzes the course of the reception of a poem as a reciprocal play of anticipation and correction that is conditioned through categories of equivalence: tension, surprise, disappointment, irony, and the comic. Common to these categories is an "overdetermination" which forces attention through each correction of subsequent expectations, thus steering the course of the reader's reception and thereby progressively rendering more unequivocal the meaning of the text to be explicated. In my experience, Riffaterre's categories are more appropriate to narrative texts than to lyric ones. What is awakened by the reading of a poem is not so much "tension" or "suspense" *(Spannung auf den Fortgang)* as it is the expectation of "lyric consistency"—the expectation that the lyric movement will allow an initially hidden connection to become comprehensible verse by verse, and will ultimately allow a new perspective on the world to arise from out of all the evocations. Accordingly, the positive category of satisfied expectation should be aligned with the negative categories of surprise and disappointment of Riffaterre, even though he discusses satisfied expectation only pejoratively, as if it were synonymous with the effect of the cliché.[13] Finally, his model of the reception of a poem presupposes an ideal reader (or "superreader") who must command not only the sum of today's available literary-historical knowledge, but also the ability consciously to register every aesthetic impression and to refer it back to an effective structure *(Wirkungstruktur)* of the text. Thus the exegetical competency overshadows the analysis of perceptual understanding.

If Riffaterre, under the dominant category of overdetermination, renders the process of reception *nolens volens* unequivocal, Iser, in *The Act of Reading,* once again brings the aesthetic character of fictional texts to the fore under the dominant category of indeterminacy (and further determinability).[14] What remains for me is to describe the course of reception in the first, perceptual reading as the experience of receiving progressively compelling aesthetical evidence which, as the pre-given horizon of the second, exegetical reading, at once opens and limits the field of play for possible concretizations.

The change of horizons between the first and the second reading can be described as follows. The reader performs, verse by verse, the "score" of the text through continual anticipation *(Vorgriff)* of the possible whole of its form and meaning. He thus becomes aware of the fulfilled form of the poem, but not yet of its equally fulfilled signification, let alone of its "whole meaning." Whoever acknowledges the hermeneutic premise—that the whole meaning of a lyric work is no longer to be understood as a substance, as a timelessly pre-given meaning *(zeitlos vorgegebener Sinn),* but rather as a proposed meaning *(aufgegebener Sinn)*—awaits the insight from the reader that, in the act of exegetical understanding, he can only concretize one among all possible significations of the poem, the particular relevance of which for him must not preclude openmindedness toward other significations. From the fulfilled form the reader will then retrospectively seek and establish the still-unfulfilled signification through a new reading, in returning from the end to the beginning, from the whole to the particular. The initial obstacles to understanding have emerged as the questions left open by the first reading. In answering those questions, the labor of interpretation can be expected to turn the particular elements of signification—in certain respects still indeterminate—into a fulfilled whole of meaning comparable to the fulfilled whole of form that emerged from the first reading. That this whole of signification can be found only through a selective adopting of perspectives—

but cannot be arrived at through an ostensibly objective description—follows them from the hermeneutic premise of partiality. That premise, however, mandates consideration of the historical horizon which conditioned the work's genesis and effect and which now limits the present reader's exegesis. The determination of that horizon is the task of a third, historical reading.

This third step is the one most familiar to historical-philological hermeneutics, insofar as it concerns the interpretation of a work within the premises of its time and its genesis. But the traditional hermeneut sees the historically-reconstructive reading as the very first step, to which historicism even attaches the injunction that the interpreter must disregard himself and his standpoint in order to be able to take in the "objective meaning" of the text that much more purely. The objectivistic illusions of this scientific ideal are today transparent to almost everyone, but under its spell, the hermeneutics of classical and modern philology was accustomed to grant priority to historical understanding over aesthetic appreciation (something rarely attempted at all). This tradition thereby failed to recognize that the aesthetic character of its texts must be employed as a hermeneutic premise since that aesthetic character alone makes possible—as a hermeneutic bridge denied to other disciplines—the historical understanding of art across temporal distance. Conversely, however, aesthetic understanding and exegesis remain dependent on the controlling function of historically-reconstructive reading. Such reading prevents the text of the past from being naively assimilated to the present's prejudices and expectations of meaning, and through the explicit separation of past and present horizons, it enables the poetic text to emerge in its alterity. The investigation of "otherness"—the peculiar distance within the presentness of the literary work—demands a reconstructive reading that can begin by seeking the questions (for the most part inexplicit) to which the text in its time was the answer. But the historical interpreter of a literary text should realize that the text "answers" such formal expectations of meaning as the literary tradition traced out before its appearance and such questions of meaning as could have posed themselves in the historical life-world of its first readers. The reconstruction of the original horizon of expectations would meanwhile relapse into historicism if the historical exegesis could not eventually serve to turn the question, "What did the text say?" into the question "What does the text say to me and what do I say to the text?" Like theological and juridical hermeneutics, literary hermeneutics may well move from understanding through exegesis to application; and even if its application does not lead to practical action, it does satisfy the no less legitimate interest of measuring and broadening the horizon of one's own experience through the experience of the Other in the course of literary communication with the past.

Roland Barthes's analysis of the reception of a Poe story illustrates the consequences of the failure to separate the three hermeneutic horizons.[15] The strength of Barthes's analysis lies in its demonstration of how the structuralist description of the narrative principle—which explains the text as a variant of a pre-given model—can be carried over into the textual analysis of *significance* which allows the text to be understood as a process, as an ongoing production of meaning or, more precisely, of possibilities of meaning ("les formes, les codes, selon lesquels des sens sont possibles").[16] Its weakness lies in its naive fusion of horizons: the reading is to be, according to its own intention, immediate and ahistorical ("nous prendrons le texte tel qu'il est, tel que nous le lisons. . . ."),[17] and yet it only exists through a "superreader" who brings a comprehensive knowledge of the nineteenth century to bear and who in the course of the reception concentrates on the passages where cultural and linguistic codes can be identified or associated. One cannot speak here of an intertwining of interpretation with the process of aesthetic perception, for the latter—as the "çode des actants" in connection with the "code ou champ symbolique"—can itself only be one code among others (the "code scientifique, rhétorique, chronologique, de la destination," etc.)[18] Thus a reading arises that is neither historical nor aesthetic, but rather is as subjective as it is impressionistic; at the same time, this reading is to ground the theory that each individual text is a web of texts—the endless play of a free-floating intertextuality in "the struggle of men and signs."[19]

Yet literary hermeneutics—which Barthes not accidentally views as being an "enigmatic code"—is certainly no longer interested in interpreting the text as the revelation of a single truth concealed within it.[20] Opposing the theory of the *texte pluriel* and its presentation of "intertextuality" as an unlimited, arbitrary production of possibilities of meaning and of no less arbitrary interpretations, literary hermeneutics today offers the hypothesis that the historically-progressing concretization of the meaning of literary works follows a certain "logic." This "logic" precipitates in the formation and transformation of the aesthetic canon and by all means allows, in the change of interpretive horizons, for a distinction between arbitrary exegeses and those available to consensus, between exegeses that are merely original and those from which shared norms can be derived. The *fundamentum in re* that supports this hypothesis can only lie in the aesthetic character of texts, which, as a regulative principle, makes it possible for a series of interpretations for a literary text to differ in their exegeses and still remain compatible with respect to the concretized meaning. In this regard I can recall the attempt at a pluralistic interpretation of Apollinaire's poem "L'arbre," which was undertaken at the second colloquium of the *Poetik und Hermeneutik* group. True enough, the particular distance from the poem adopted by different readers allowed different aesthetic perceptions to arise, and each specific concretization of the significance necessarily had to ignore other, no less consonant exegeses. But the surprising discovery that the individual interpretations did not, despite their differences, contradict one another led to the conclusion that even this "pluralistic text" itself can give, within the horizon of the first reading, a unifying aesthetic orientation to perceptual understanding.[21]

One may certainly object that a modern poem after Baudelaire will furnish such evidence of a compelling whole not with the first reading, but rather only upon rereading. *Mutatis mutandis,* a poem from an older tradition or from another culture often opens itself up to aesthetic understanding only after historical understanding has cleared away barriers to reception, thereby making possible an aesthetic perception of the previously unenjoyable text. These objections are indeed my own,[22] and I can use them for clarifying a final specific point.

The priority of aesthetic perception in the triad of literary hermeneutics requires the *horizon* rather than the temporal priority of the first reading. This horizon of perceptual understanding may well be acquired upon rereading a text or with the help of historical understanding. Aesthetic perception is no universal code with timeless validity. Like all aesthetic experience, it is closely related to historical experience. Therefore the aesthetic character of poetic texts from the Western tradition can only contribute heuristic starting points for the interpretation of texts from other cultures. By means of the three achievements of the hermeneutic process, literary interpretation must compensate for the fact that aesthetic perception itself is subject to historical change. In doing so it can win, beyond aesthetic understanding, the opportunity to broaden historical knowledge, as well as perhaps to develop, through its unconstrained kind of application, a corrective to other applications that are subject to situational pressure for decision and action.

NOTES

1. Throughout this essay, Jauss exploits a distinction existing in German between *Interpretation* and *Auslegung* (and their verbal and adjectival forms), employing the former as a general, collective term for the activity of reading and trying to understand a text, the latter as a more narrow term for the specific exegesis or explication of a text. I have rendered *Interpretation* as "interpretation," and *Auslegung* as "exegesis." The German *Deutung*, which occurs only a few times, has also been translated as "interpretation." (Tr.)

2. To be sure, in the foreword to his *Linguistics and Literary History* (Princeton: Princeton University Press, 1948), Leo Spitzer sought to explain his stylistic method via the hermeneutic circle. But the im-

plicit theory of his interpretative praxis—as unsystematic as it is inimitable—by far exceeds his marginal hermeneutic reflexion, as best emerges from the appreciation by Jean Starobinski, in *L'oeil vivant, II: La relation critique* (Paris: Gallimard, 1970), pp. 34–81.

3. "The old style of interpretation was insistent, but respectful; it erected another meaning on top of the literal one. The modern style of interpretation excavates, destroys; it digs 'behind' the text, to find a sub-text which is the true one," in *Against Interpretation and Other Essays* (New York: Farrar, Straus, 1966), p. 6. [Jauss's use of the term *opera aperta* refers to Umberto Eco's analysis of the "open" structure of the modern work of art in *Opera aperta* (Milan: Bompiani, 1976). (Tr.)]

4. "Bemerkungen zur Forschungslage der literarischen Hermeneutik," in *Einführung in die literarische Hermeneutik* (Frankfurt a.M.: Suhrkamp, 1975), p. 404.

5. Ibid., p. 25; in English, "Introduction to Literary Hermeneutics," in *New Literary History* 10, no. 1 (Autumn 1978): 27.

6. Ibid., p. 13; English: 20.

7. *Wahrheit und Methode: Grundzüge einer philosophischen Hermeneutik* (Tübingen: Mohr, 1960), p. 291; in English, *Truth and Method* (New York: Seabury, 1975), p. 275.

8. As representative instances, see: Wolfgang Iser, *Der Akt des Lesens* (Munich: Fink, 1976); in English, *The Act of Reading* (Baltimore: The Johns Hopkins University Press, 1978); U. Japp, *Hermeneutik: Der theoretische Diskurs, die Literatur und die Konstruktion ihres Zusammenhangs in den philologischen Wissenschaften* (Munich: Fink, 1977); Paul Ricoeur, "Die Schrift als Problem der Literaturkritik und der philosophischen Hermeneutik," in *Sprache und Welterfahrung*, J. Zimmermann, ed. (Munich: 1978), pp. 67–88; see also (semiotically, not hermeneutically, oriented) Jurij Lotman, *Die Struktur literarischer Texte* (Munich: Fink, 1972).

9. In relation to *Wahrheit und Methode*, p. 291 (English, p. 274): "Exegesis is not a supplementary (*nachträglich*) act accidentally being added to understanding; rather, understanding is always exegesis, and exegesis is therefore the explicit form of understanding."

10. In a still unpublished lecture on literary hermeneutics, delivered at Dubrovnik, Yugoslavia, in 1978.

11. Cited by Gadamer in a still unpublished lecture on literary hermeneutics, delivered at Dubrovnik, Yugoslavia, in 1978.

12. *Das Problem der Relevanz* (Frankfurt a.M.: Suhrkamp, 1971); in English, *Reflections on the Problem of Relevance*, Richard M. Zaner, ed. (New Haven: Yale University Press, 1970).

13. *Essais de stylistique structurale* (Paris: Flammarion, 1971), p. 340.

14. See note 8.

15. "Analyse textuelle d'un conte d'Edgar Poe," in *Sémiotique nar-*

rative et textuelle, Claude Chabrol, ed. (Paris: Larousse, 1973), pp. 29–54.

16. Ibid., p. 30.
17. Ibid., p. 32.
18. Ibid., p. 51.
19. Ibid., pp. 30, 52.
20. Ibid., p. 30.
21. *Immanente Asthetik, ästhetische Reflexion: Lyrik als Paradigma der Moderne,* ed. Wolfgang Iser. Vol. 2 of *Poetik und Hermeneutik* (Munich: Fink, 1966), pp. 461–84, esp. pp. 473 and 480: "For a concrete interpretation, and for a judgment of the quality of the poem, it is not sufficient to provide its structural principle and to describe Apollinaire's poetic technique. A series of ambiguities is not yet a compelling whole. If this whole, on the grounds of the technique with which it is constructed, calls for ever more interpretation, then the latter is nonetheless neither arbitrary in its details, nor free of a fundamental orientation that is enforced through the structure of the text. The first reading provides this forceful character (*dieses Zwingende*) through the suggestion of the rhythm. The interpretation must engage this medium in which the poem moves" (Dieter Henrich).
22. On this, see my *Alterität und Modernität der mittelalterlichen Literatur* (Munich: Fink, 1977), esp. pp. 10 ff.

3

Criticism as Evaluation

The Name and Nature of Criticism

Monroe C. Beardsley

To say what literary criticism is is not to take inventory of the diverse activities that literary critics engage in. The question invites an elucidation of roles and responsibilities rather than a sociological inquiry. (If this obvious remark sounds patronizing, consider it my self-reminder: I hereby resolve to be wary of a confusion that still seems to claim its victims.) Or if, for convenience, but not without risk, we permit ourselves occasional reference to what "the critic" does, we must bear in mind that we are speaking of an idealized critic, therefore normatively in part: the question is which of the critic's tasks are central and basic, in that others are ancillary and dependent, and which are distinctive and obligatory, in that literary critics, by their nature and nurture, are best equipped to perform them and, though plainly desirable, they are apparently not assigned to anyone else. On the other hand, of course, there must be some intelligible connection between what the ideal critic does and what real critics do.

We cannot of course prohibit the tempting extension of the term "literary criticism" to all discourse about literary works, but we can deplore it. There are too many important distinctions that need to be marked, and too few handy terms to mark them clearly and conveniently; and, I think, we have a better use for this particular term. One principle for classifying discourse about literary works appeals to a pragmatic distinction: to whom is the discourse primarily addressed? (I have to say "primarily," because there may be others listening in or overhearing, even with profit.) First, there is discourse of an impersonal sort, addressed to persons in general, or at least to persons *qua* members of a social group. In this category I place literary history, reader-psychology, writer-sociology, and other kinds of scientific or quasiscientific discourse. Even if, as some would argue, such impersonal discourse never rises to the genuine universality at which it characteristically aims and to which it sometimes pretends, but rather tacitly circumscribes its audience with restrictions of class or race, still it is not directed to someone in virtue of a social role, or tied to a social practice. Second, there is discourse primarily addressed to the literary artist, designed to help or guide in the making of literary works. When such advice, solicited or unsolicited, takes the form of specific recommendations for improvement of a particular work, it may be called *counseling;* when it takes the form of training in generalized skills to be brought into play in the making of literary works, it may be called *coaching*—or, more technically, art education. Third, there is discourse primarily addressed to readers, or potential readers, designed to help them find what is worth attention and arrive at a reasonable estimate of its worth. When such advice takes the form of training in generalized skills required for understanding and enjoying literature, it may be a form of *aesthetic education;* when it is concerned with a particular work, it may be *criticism*.

Although such a line of thought may not be quite as exciting as the more far-out tales that are told these days about the nature of literary criticism, it seems reasonable to me to think of literary criticism as a species of criticism in general—a mode of discourse that is pervasive in our serious activities and essential to rationality in the conduct of life. To live is to make choices, and to live in a fully human way involves trying to make rational choices, i.e., choosing for good reasons. This, in turn, calls for judgment of what is better or worse in some field of alternatives, and for understanding what makes one thing better or worse than another.[1] Although such remarks are platitudinous, their point is too seldom considered in discussions of literary criticism, I think. Wherever there is a recognizable *kind* of object or event, and ground for taking an interest in things of that kind, we are confronted with the need to evaluate or appraise. And poems are, in this highly abstract respect, not different from refrigerators, senators, constitutional amendments, tennis players, corporations, and cats.

Interesting questions arise about the limits of such criticizable classes. Francis Sparshott, for example, ties the concept of criticism to that of performance, and says that it is always a performance that is criticized.

> There are critics of paintings but not of sunsets; there are music critics, but no birdsong critics. I do not say there could not be; but in fact there are not. . . . One may indeed "criticize" the weather on a rainy day, but this becomes more than a mere adverse comment only in so far as the weather is tacitly regarded as a performance of Jupiter Pluvius.[2]

I shall not pause to discuss Sparshott's thesis, but it is plausible enough to deserve denial. And its plausibility depends on thinking of criticizing as counseling: for it is only of things fashioned by rational creatures that we can sensibly make recommendations, like "I advise eliminating stanzas three and four" or "Perfect! Let it stand; don't change a thing!"

Granted that mere adverse comments (or complimentary ones) are not in themselves criticisms; we shall see in a moment, however, that it is not the assumption that the weather is the result of a deliberate action that turns adverse comments on the weather into criticism, but something different. If there are no sunset critics, persons who specialize in this field of judgment, the reasons are adequate: they are partly economic, since under our system it would be hard to make a living that way, and they are partly aesthetic, since the class of sunsets does not offer the scope for criticism that the class of paintings does.[3] As for birdsong critics, they do exist, though they are a rare species. A reader of Charles Hartshorne's definitive work will find birdsong criticism of a highly competent sort.[4]

Of course criticism of poetry is very different from criticism of refrigerators or of senators. But what it shares with them is a concern to *explain* why the thing criticized is as good or as poor as it is, is good or bad in just the way it is. It consists in discovering—in both the sense of coming to know and in the older sense of showing or making manifest to others—how selected features contribute toward making the thing good of its kind or detract from its goodness. These features are merits and defects—grounds of praise or dispraise. As Hume said, "No criticism can be instructive, which descends not to particulars, and is not full of examples and illustrations."[5] It is fault-finding and merit-marking that make criticism an informative, a discriminating, an illuminating, and indeed a difficult task—something a bit more than the mere expression of approval or disapproval. If I may use the term *analytical appraisal* for this active concern with desirable and undesirable features, then I am claiming that analytical appraisal is the characteristic and essential element of criticism, in any of its fields of application.

Though we are engaged, not in criticism, but in metacriticism, Hume's strictures may apply to some degree, so I pluck one from a sheaf of examples, namely, Irving Howe writing on William Faulkner some years ago in *The New Republic:*

> *Requiem for a Nun* contains some exquisite rhapsodic interludes, but in the central sections, *so clearly meant to be dramatic,* it falls into inert statement. *The Fable,* which may come to hold a place in Faulkner's work somewhat analogous to *Pierre* in Melville's, is a book *noble in conception* but incoherent and hollow in execution [emphasis mine].[6]

First, I hope it will be agreed that this is criticism, fragmentary as it may be. It is not *a* criticism, in the sense of an adequate *critique* of any of these novels. It does not contain explicit and careful judgments of any novels as a whole, though even from this brief passage one gathers that Howe thinks that *Requiem for a Nun* is better than *The Fable*. The particularities, though few, are instances of analytical appraisal. Setting aside the intentionalist phrases which I have shamed with italics, we can extract certain assertions: (1) that *Requiem for a Nun* is somewhat commendable is explained (in part) by the fact that it contains some "exquisite rhapsodic interludes"; (2) that it is not really excellent is explained (in part) by the fact that in central sections it falls into "inert statement" and thus lacks dramatic intensity; (3) that *The Fable* is a poor novel is explained (in part) by its incoherence and hollowness. Of course we could press our demand for further analytical appraisal: I want to know, with instances, just what sorts of inertness, incoherence, and hollowness are present, and which details of the works explain these properties. But as far as it goes, the passage makes sense as criticism. What it gives us—the mark of criticism—is what might be called "normative explanation": that is, it tells us (however incompletely) why the work is good or poor, in what ways it is good or poor.

We have noted some kinds of things that can be criticized—and the passage from Irving Howe has, in my opinion, parallels in passages we might write about refrigerators, senators, etc., except that, of course, the flaws and assets (so to speak) would be of different sorts. Now we must also note that there are different types of criticism and that, for each kind of thing, there is likely to be one type of criticism most appropriate to it, although many kinds of things can be subjected to more than one type of criticism.

The criticism we find in the passage from Howe betrays its type (though without being explicit) by the concepts it employs: rhapsody, drama, incoherence. It is *aesthetic criticism*, because it reflects and is guided by an interest in the sort of experience that can be obtained from reading these novels. For present purposes, I hope, we need not strain for a more precise and accurate characterization of aesthetic criticism than this: that it seeks to grasp and expose features of the work that either enhance or diminish the work's power to give a reader an experience that is desirable on account of its character. In this way aesthetic criticism is distinguished from the numerous alternative types of criticism: moral, political, economic, environmental, technological, medical, and so forth. The attempt to sort criticism in this way leads to many philosophical problems,[7] but here it must suffice to be sketchy. We can distinguish different interests we take in something, or interests we take in different aspects of the same thing—say, in the taste of food as distinct from its nutritional value. The different types of criticism reflect these diverse interests or points of view. Not all of them can be applied to a novel by Faulkner, I suppose: could we judge it in terms of its environmental impact, its contribution to traffic safety, or its medical efficacy? But we can certainly bring aesthetic criticism to bear upon it, and since it is a literary work of art, this type of criticism can hardly be dismissed as inappropriate. Not that I wish to minimize the hard philosophical problems lurking in the vicinity—indeed, part of my aim is to emphasize them, because I think we would have much better answers to the question "What is criticism?" if those who essay to answer the question had the patience and the wit to take these problems seriously. The concept of art and the concept of the aesthetic are by no means simply related, nor is their relation free from sharp controversy. But even if neither is definable in terms of the other, and even if the classes of artworks and of aesthetically interesting things do not coincide, there is a rather intimate tie between them. So one tempting answer to our opening question is just this: literary criticism is the aesthetic criticism of literary works.

This proposal can hardly be challenged as too broad, even if we allow a wide range of experiences that can be assumed to be worth having on account of their noteworthy qualities. But it may well be thought too narrow by those who find in the case of literature one of those perhaps rare, but logically possible, classes of things that have equal (or nearly equal) rights—or obligations—to be subjected to criticism of two distinct types. An ancient issue now turns up again and demands attention. Suppose we are interested in a literary work for what we can learn from it—for the knowledge or understanding it gives us—about ourselves or our world. An interest in learning is not to be dispraised or discouraged, nor is there any obvious absurdity in seeking truth even from works of fiction. Truths and insights are of many sorts, and we may include among them *moral* wisdom, where it can be had. Let us say that to judge a literary work (or anything else, for that matter) in terms of its capacity to teach us something we didn't know or to give us, or help us obtain, some form of truth, is to subject it to *cognitive criticism.*

Take, as an example, another passage from the essay by Irving Howe—occasioned by the publication of the third and last volume, *The Mansion,* in Faulkner's Snopes trilogy. Citing an incident in the novel in which Cla'ence Snopes is ridiculed out of a congressional campaign by those who arrange for him to be mistaken by some dogs for their favorite thicket, Howe remarks that

> in the context of the trilogy the incident is damaging, since it suggests that the threat of Snopesism can easily be defeated by the country shrewdness of a Ratliff—an assumption which all the preceding matter has led us gravely to doubt and which, if we do credit it, must now persuade us that the danger embodied by the Snopeses need not be taken as seriously as the whole weight of the trilogy has seemed to argue. [P. 18]

There is aesthetic criticism here, in the accusation of logical incompatibility between two implied theses—if this incompatibility can make our experience of the whole trilogy less coherent. But the main thrust of the criticism seems clearly cognitive: the insight which most of the work gives us into the nature of evil, in its virulent Snopesean form, is said to be blurred or weakened by the insertion of the anecdote, so that from the cognitive point of view the novel would be better without it. (It is of course no part of *my* purpose to endorse Howe's criticism; whether justified or not, it will serve as an example.)

As this example shows, much critical discussion of the intellectual or ideological content of literary works can be subsumed under aesthetic criticism, whose real point is to consider the work with respect to the experience it can give, and does not presume that (say) Faulkner's ideas about evil are either true or false, profound or shallow, illuminating or misleading. But as the example also shows, there can be cognitive criticism of literature that is independent of aesthetic considerations, and it is in the special nature of literature, among all the arts, that cognitive criticism is always pertinent—it is never out of order to ask how good a work is as a bearer of knowledge or a source of insight, and what features of the work help to give it, to strengthen or to weaken, this cognitive capacity. Certainly a substantial part of the discourse of literary critics consists of cognitive criticism. And there is an honorable tradition that places teaching side by side with delighting as an end of literary creating. So a case can be made for broadening the proposal made above: perhaps we should say that literary criticism is the aesthetic or cognitive criticism of literary works.

Despite my solemn resolution earlier not to mix up persons and their roles, some consideration of critics as well as of criticism may cast light on the problem we now face: whether to adopt the broader or the narrower account of literary criticism. The broader account does not compel us, but it does encourage us, to assign both aesthetic and cognitive criticism to the same person. And this dual assignment makes sense as far as one of the two basic tasks of cognitive criticism goes: to find out as exactly as possible just what the literary work actually contains in the way of cognitive content, of philosophical, religious, ethical, political, or other implicit theses. There is generally no difficulty in getting a rough idea, but what is interesting and important is the precise and subtle implication. Just what does the spotted-horse episode in *The Hamlet* say, by suggestion, about the kind of evil personified in Flem Snopes? What is the narrator's implicit judgment of the mule-in-the-yard episode of *The Town?* This task calls for the talents and skills of the aesthetic critic: those which the literary critic by bent and practice is fitted for. But the second task of cognitive criticism is to make some judgment of the truth or cognitive worth of the theses, once fully grasped. If Faulkner's trilogy says something about evil, or leads us to look at evil in certain ways, the question is whether we have encountered a fresh and illuminating view or a false and distorted view of life, or of human nature. I don't suppose that literary critics, as such, are specially trained to deal with the philosophical or theological problems of evil—or with other doctrines that may turn up in the works they study. Of course one might happen to know a great deal about these things, and be capable of sound and penetrating judgment about them; but being a good aesthetic critic does not in itself guarantee that one is a good cognitive critic.

Still, these are practical problems about assigning roles and obtaining responsible performance in those roles: our concern has to be more abstract. In so far as all literary works are aesthetically criticizable, but some are not cognitively criticizable because they contain no implicit general reflections about human nature or society or the universe, it seems that aesthetic criticism has a certain priority in literary criticism. And in so far as sound cognitive criticism of literary works presupposes that some aesthetic criticism has been done, that the work has been understood, aesthetic criticism seems again to be the more fundamental kind. A critic who gives us aesthetic criticism of a literary work is recognizably doing his job, even if he is unable or unwilling to give us any cognitive criticism; but one who discourses on literary works and *never* gives us aesthetic criticism, but is solely concerned with the truth or falsity, verifiability or unverifiability, probability or improbability, of their implicit ideas, may be performing a very useful social function, but it is that of a philosopher or social commentator, or preacher, or politician. I do not deny—in fact I strongly believe—that literature must be cognitively criticized, or a crucial part of its worth is lost. But it seems to me a clear and appropriate use of the term "literary criticism" to reserve it for the aesthetic criticism of literature—or, with a harmless extension, of literature and of other discourses that may lend themselves to this approach.

Besides cognitive criticism of course, there are many other activities in which a real live critic may justifiably and usefully engage. He may write about a work in a way that helps to make it more accessible and intelligible to readers—especially if it is radically new and off-putting, and can be somewhat domesticated (though it is no service to carry this very far) by being interpreted and by being placed in the context of literary history. The critic may enrich the potentialities of a particular work, say a novel by Faulkner, by showing how larger patterns of meaning arise when it is seen in relation to other works by the same writer. He may get attention for a deserving but neglected work (provided he doesn't end up by distracting attention from it) by providing selected information about the writer's life and the psychological and social circumstances of the writing. He may talk about individual works in ways that help to strengthen and support the institution of literature, to keep alive and well the *idea* of literature as a vital element in human life and culture. This last is a responsibility that always remains, whether it is consciously felt or not.

But I think we can see that these activities are secondary; they are not what makes the critic a critic, though they may be part of what makes him or her a *good* critic. What underlies all these activities, and is essential to the nature of literary criticism, is that peculiarly direct and intimate relation to literary works, in which they are considered with judiciousness and sympathy from the aesthetic point of view.

NOTES

1. Cf. my article "What Are Critics For?" *Susquehanna University Studies* 10 (1978): 239–53.
2. *The Concept of Criticism* (Oxford: Clarendon Press, 1967), p. 40.
3. But there is an old W. Steig cartoon in which one viewer of a sunset (apparently a painter) remarks to another, "Too much purple."
4. *Born to Sing: An Interpretation and World Survey of Bird Song* (Bloomington: Indiana University Press, 1973).
5. "On Simplicity and Refinement in Writing," in *Essays: Moral, Political, and Literary* (Oxford: Oxford University Press, 1963).

6. "Faulkner: End of a Road," *The New Republic*, 7 December 1959, pp. 17–21.

7. See my papers "The Aesthetic Point of View," *Metaphilosophy* 1 (1970): 39–58; and "In Defense of Aesthetic Value," *Proceedings and Addresses of the American Philosophical Association* 52 (August 1979): 723–49.

Criticulture: Or, Why We Need at Least Three Criticisms at the Present Time

Wayne C. Booth

> Literary criticism is not, and never has been, a single discipline, to which successive writers have made partial and never wholly satisfactory contributions, but rather a collection of distinct and more or less incommensurable "frameworks" or "languages," within any one of which a question like that of poetic structure necessarily takes on a different meaning and receives a different kind of answer from the meaning it has and the kind of answer it is properly given in any of the rival critical languages.
>
> R. S. Crane

What *is* criticism? To ask the question implies that I should surely be able to find an answer to it, somewhere. Perhaps I could simply suggest that the best answer is given in *Critical Understanding*—a complicated, hard-worked answer that surely should satisfy everyone once and for all.* But even before the first review appears, I know what the chances are of that. Well, then, perhaps I could just say that the present collection of essays will provide an ostensive definition, a nicely

*Wayne C. Booth, *Critical Understanding: The Powers and Limits of Pluralism* (Chicago: The University of Chicago Press, 1979).

pluralistic one: here is what criticism is, all right. But what is that? The trouble is not only that some of these essays may attempt to cancel out all the others; taken as a group they exclude much that would have been included if some other list of critics had been invited to the orgy.

What *is* criticism, then? Criticism *is* nothing determinate, no one thing, no collection of things. In the abstract, as some *thing* to be grasped either as now present or as some future goal, criticism simply isn't. Though we are naturally led to think of the term as referring to some collective identity, as the term "mammal" refers to all creatures that suckle their young, this term fails to do that. There is not even what Wittgenstein calls a family resemblance among all the practices pursued in its name. A term that is used to refer to theory of literature, literary history, speculation about society's goals, ethnomethodology, anthropology, philosophical psychology, book reviewing and promotion, psychoanalysis of linguistic usage, semiotics, political propaganda, theology, sociology of knowledge, hermeneutics, and theory of rhetoric—such a concept is no concept at all but a mess.

We are thus wasting our time if we try to decide which of our many accounts of our literary experience, some of them contradicting some others, deserve to be called criticism. But we are not wasting our time if we try to decide which of them can serve in our culture to ensure the continued appreciation of past artistic and critical achievements and the creation of new ones. Instead of trying to answer the unanswerable question of our title, then, suppose we work at an answerable one: At the present time, what are *some* of the important tasks that might increase, however slightly, the chances that the understanding, appreciation, and creation of serious art will survive?

As soon as we reshape the question in this form, we thrust ourselves decisively into kinds of talk that are laden—to some people's discomfort—with value judgments. Whether there are critical goals that might be value-free—for example pursuit of a positive knowledge about how genres interrelate, or how the creative process works, or what the nature of language is—our reshaping of the question forces us into a practical or pragmatic task, the preservation and stimulation of certain kinds of valued objects. Obviously one cannot talk in this way, a way chosen from among many ways of talking, without trying to distinguish the works worth preserving from those that are not.

We need not say that the word "criticism" should be reserved exclusively for talking about the good and bad in the things offered to us as art. But we are driven to acknowledge that such talk is needed: unless we decide that all art works and all "artistic" activities are equally worthy, we must embrace the task that all critics before our own time have performed without demur. Whether they have called their work criticism or not, they have sought ways of talking about why some works are worth preserving and some are not.

What, then, might be some functions of an openly evaluative criticism at the present time? Without repeating here my recent arguments that our critical purposes and methods can never be reduced to one or three or any other determinate number, I should like to urge, without space for adequate argument, the importance of three relatively neglected tasks.

ETHICAL CRITICISM

The first task is one that would traditionally have been taken for granted. Johnson, Coleridge, and Arnold would all have been shocked to learn that a time would come when critics refused to make discriminations between good and bad works of art on any grounds other than technical skill. It was not merely the etymology of the word "critic" that led them to judge the ethical and social value of poems. It was to them self-evident that art can harm or heal, that whatever is precious is always in danger of being lost, and that any culture that would expand its treasures must know how to distinguish treasure from tinsel. Some few critics today would share this view, but too many have given up any attempt to show why one well-wrought urn deserves to be placed upon an altar while another may be tossed aside.

It is not that we have no defenses of poetry. It is that most of them are too general, written as if everything we can call "art" or "artistic" belonged to some sacrosanct noble caste. We are flooded with efforts to defend the humanities-in-general—defenses of poesie that show, using ancient arguments advanced as new, that the arts and their study are essential to the human soul.

Given the rarity, perhaps the total nonexistence, of enemies who attack all poetry or all art, it is surely surprising that so much of what we write sounds as if the entire enterprise were under fire and must be defended totally, without distinction. We write as if "the humanities" were a single entity to be attacked, defended, or called into question as a whole.

Yet as soon as I think about the actual works of art produced now and in previous times, I notice at once that I have no interest whatever in defending all of them, or even all that are created with great skill. Who would want to defend everything that goes on now in the name of the arts or the humanities? Is there anyone who will stand before the drugstore book rack—or even the fiction shelf in the college "bookstore"—and fight to the death about the importance to the spirit of man of all the paperbacks on display? Well, the answer seems to be yes. At least we have seen many instances of humanistic "experts" testifying to the redeeming social or literary value of works whose authors could not make the slightest claim to any motive other than ripping off a gullible public.

My point is not that we should join the would-be censors. It is that the humanities-in-general neither need a defense—"they" are supported by a vast commercial and educational apparatus that insures some kind of continued activity—nor deserve one. The humanities-in-general include both the finest and the basest that people can produce. And the most pressing need of criticism today is for ways of talking about those differences.

What I mean can be shown by thinking about how scientists talk about themselves. No physicist would think of trying to defend his vocation by defending everything that pretends to give knowledge of physical reality. In fact much of what scientists say to the public in their own behalf is in the form of discriminating "normal" or "genuine" science from the fraudulent. The scientist does not want to be confused with the Christian Scientist or the Scientologist, the astronomer cares about divorcing himself from astrology, the medical researcher attacks what he believes are quacks. Our defenses of "the humanities" or "the arts," on the other hand, resist discriminations; in form they resemble what we would have if some physical scientist wrote a defense of "Talking about the Universe," or if a doctor wrote a defense of "All the Profferred Cures in the World." Scientists and doctors try to show how they differ from others who travel in their name, while we defend everyone who ever puts pen to paper with a declared "artistic" aim.

But obviously a defense in general of what is produced these days in the name of art must be an absurd defense; any business executive or government official or Parent-Teachers president knows without a second thought that it is an absurd defense. What the noncritic knows, in a confused kind of knowledge that can easily lead to terrible errors of judgment, is that judgment is necessary among the works of artists; that some "works of the spirit" will kill the spirit and some will enhance it; that there are kinds of "artistic" cleverness that are vile; that some motives for producing and consuming art works are life-enhancing and some are base.

The noncritical public, knowing these things, is not likely to respond to us when we make our general defenses of poetry. They are much more likely to grasp blindly for criteria that they might apply to protect themselves and their children from the trash that seems to threaten a suffocation worse than threatens the San Bernardino hills. "This book has the word 'fuck' in it: burn it." "That book contains communistic ideas: ban it." "This novel reveals a pessimistic view of life; protect my children from it." "That play shows characters for whom sex is everything—and a degraded sex at that. Run it out of town."

We are accustomed, we professional critics, to scoff at such folks, but we forget, as we scoff, that they are no more absurd than those who, with equal lack of thought about what they see before them, embrace anything and everything that travels under the name of art.

If I am right that we have two absurdities here—a public who think they can discover and impose value judgments without half trying, and a professoriate who talk as if you can't discriminate among ethical or moral judgments of art no matter how hard you try—one obvious task for criticism today is to work in the middle ground between the two absurdities. We might try to restore and improve the ancient art of discussing why some "well-made," "clever," "profound," "unified," "self-deconstructing," or even "beautiful" works are superior to others that earn these and similar terms of praise.

It will not be enough to show that works are or are not put together well, though discriminations of craft will always be part of our job. The essential need is for that most difficult of all human performances: a reasoned appraisal, an "assaying," of the relative worth of diverse created "worlds," or "visions," or "orders," or "value systems." The metaphoric languages we choose may be borrowed from many different ethical, political, or religious domains, and the standards we appeal to will obviously be plural and controversial.

Just how controversial and threatening a territory I am asking us to occupy can be seen by looking at the work of those who are now already there: the many indicters and deplorers of "male chauvinist" or "racist" or "liberal" or "reactionary" or "immoral" or "bourgeois traditionalist" literature. Only the last of these is now thoroughly buttressed with a thriving theoretical literature. For the most part we have an abundance of angry denunciation, offered either by people who have no training in criticism (and thus are free to say what they *feel,* without much argument), or by those who feel guilty because their training in "criticism" has taught them that what they want to say about literature cannot be anything more than a bleat of "personal" or "subjective" preference. One other group of uneasy violators of neutralism should be mentioned as our potential allies: a surprising number of literary biographers find themselves talking of the "moral worlds" or "philosophical visions" of their subjects—and thus inevitably of the inferiority of other possible worlds: for example, *The Moral Basis of Fielding's Art* (Martin C. Battestin, 1959); *The Moral Art of Dickens* (Barbara Hardy, 1970); *Ethical Perspective in the Novels of Thomas Hardy*, (Virginia R. Hyman, 1975); *The Moral Imagination of Joseph Conrad* (Serajul Islam Choudhury, 1975); or *The Moral Vision of Oscar Wilde* (Philip K. Cohen, 1978). They may, like Battestin, choose to defend an author's morality ("For all its uproarious good humor, *Joseph Andrews* is ultimately a moral book.") or they may, like Barbara Hardy, explicitly repudiate the task of "preferential judgment" of one author as opposed to another. But all of them in fact at least imply that in illuminating the moral or ethical universe of their author they are defending his work; and most of them make distinctions among the better and worse passages or works of their chosen figures.

The controversial reception of John Gardner's recent *On Moral Fiction* was not simply the result of its being a slovenly, slapdash work. Even if Gardner were the kind of author who stoops to giving reasons for his beliefs, his subject would have ensured a hostile response from many current critics. His project was essentially unfashionable: a barefaced claim that literary works can properly be subjected to moral judgments. But Gardner's was the first widely read book in a long time that dared to label *this* book as immoral, *that* one as moral, and the effect of shock did not depend on either the capriciousness or the general "conservatism" of his judgments.

I might summarize my first plea, then, like this: let us not be misled by the John Gardners who reduce ethical criticism to applying labels. What they are attempting—namely, restoration of a criticism that grants literary works their true importance to souls and societies by appraising their distinctive powers for good or ill—is the most important, and also the most difficult, of all human achievements except the creating of significant art works themselves.

Most works that attempt ethical judgment tend to treat classes of works so generally that they leave us puzzled about how the authors might distinguish a good work from a bad.

Are all works that reveal signs of male chauvinism equally bad? Are all of Fielding's works equally "moral"? Is the racism of Shakespeare and Conrad indistinguishable from the racism of Céline, and that from the racism of Mickey Spillane? Too seldom do we receive any hint of how we might decide such questions. Just as the older academic moral critics like Babbitt, Leavis, and Winters tended to apply their standards wholesale, and without adequate explanation of how they were derived and defended, so the defenders of these new programs tend to imply that a decision to embrace a particular code is in itself the major step; all else will follow if we can just recognize what is permissible and what is not.

The first task for criticism in our time, then, is not the further production of theoretical pleas for this or that kind of criticism, but the more difficult practice of detailed argument about why this work is or is not praiseworthy. Is *Hamlet* really "male chauvinist"? If so, what does that tell us about its value for us? Precisely how is Chinua Achebe wrong or right in his powerful and detailed argument that *Heart of Darkness* is racist? Precisely how are all those novelists who are indicted by John Gardner wicked, if they are?

If we attempted to work on particular judgments—to work on them as hard as Matthew Arnold, say, worked in deciding, on ethical grounds, that his "Empedocles on Etna" should not be included in his collected *Poems*—we would not need to seek flat judgments of *imprimatur* or "to the Index!" Instead we could talk about works as invitations to live engagement with ethically active readers, readers who are potentially capable of resisting ethical harm from anything, no matter how bad it might be for other readers. And in that discovery and its articulation in particular cases, we would look as closely at ethical qualities as we have been taught to look at linguistic forms, and we would in fact be teaching ourselves to live with literary works without either worshipping them or underrating their inescapable effects, for good or ill, on the lives we lead.

POLITICAL CRITICISM

It is impossible to draw a sharp line between the ethical and political values of a poem. No good feminist critic, setting out to appraise Henry Miller's works, would find it easy to separate the judgment that they are ethically contemptible—that is, that they depend upon and tend to promote a peculiarly vicious brand of male chauvinism—from a political judgment that such works both reflect against our society and reinforce what is wrong with it. But there is a useful difference between talking of what is good for souls and of what is good for societies, and I would therefore plead for a second kind of criticism, a social or political criticism that would relate literary values to political and social forces and needs.

The Marxists have always advocated such criticism, but their practice has, with few exceptions, been as simplistic as Gardner's practice of ethical criticism. Why we have had so few social critics as perceptive as Lukács and Raymond Williams; why there are so few histories relating literary genres critically (not just descriptively) to social and political judgments; why authors who attempt them so often produce tracts of little critical value; why there are so few books of this kind worth comparing to the recent *Love and Marriage: Literature and its Social Contexts* by Laurence Lerner; and why these are somewhat different questions from the question of why we have so little good criticism of any kind—all these are questions worth asking, even if we cannot hope for very precise answers.

If space allowed, I would propose here some specific examples of "works needed." But I can suggest only one: a serious study of how the increasing pressure of mass sales, produced in part by new conglomerate publishers with no interest in books as books, have affected the quality of American writing in the past three decades or so. Such a study would require immense labor, collecting and interpreting correspondence among authors, agents, and editors. Its unpredictable results would inevitably be controversial, since whoever undertook it would be forced both to judge whether a particular editorial suggestion or requirement was for the better or worse, and to argue openly for political judgments. It would run great risks of overgeneralization, biased interpretation, and—since it would be politically "engaged" in some sense—it would offend many powers or would-be powers. But it would be criticism, criticism both of our culture and of its works, shoddy or sublime.

THE HIGHER JOURNALISM

The third task, and to me the most important, is usually placed only as a footnote to criticism, if it enters discussion at all. To talk of the critic today as educator of taste carries a taint of arrogance that few are willing to risk. But the task of mediating between authors and readers is no less important, perhaps more important, than it was when "men of letters" flourished. Every culture must fear the disappearance of an audience capable of recognizing the best art its artists can produce. Nothing kills the rage for perfection quite so surely as a public that hails muddlers as masters.

Now of course there are never enough sensitive connoisseurs of an art to satisfy the artists themselves, and it is no doubt true that too many artists have excused their own failures by blaming "the public." But everyone knows that the public for serious art is fragmented, and our artists feel themselves increasingly isolated from those who, by their critical responses, might confirm their sense of vocation and drive them to attempt better and better works. If you talk with serious novelists, when they are not driven into idiocies by appearing before mass audiences, you hear from them one gloomy refrain: Where are my *readers*? Where are those reader-friends who will care enough and know enough and attend long enough to discover my art?

At the moment America has a score or so, perhaps more like a hundred or so, of really fine fiction writers. Presumably most of them manage to publish whatever they think publishable, though even the best of them are likely to run into trouble with the third book if the first ones have sold only the number of copies—five to ten thousand, say—that in any earlier period would have established a reputation. But with few exceptions, they can be sure that only a small band of devotees knows of their existence. The devotees of Austin M. Wright (now seeking a publisher for his third novel—quite possibly in vain) do not know about the works of Wright Morris, whose followers in turn do not know of Cynthia Ozick, whose readers in turn do not know of Jayne Anne Phillips. Though each season produces its *Ragtime* or *The World According to Garp* or *The Executioner's Song*, books "read by everybody," their readers will not know—nor will most reviewers give them any way to find out—whether those best-sellers have any qualities that deserve sustained attention. In fact, even the "best-sellers" tend to be read by factions, not by what I am calling a "critical culture." The readers of Didion do not read Marilyn French, the fans of *Fear of Flying* would not be caught dead reading *Scruples*.

This fragmentation of American critical culture is of course not entirely new, and we all know that it has many causes, only some of which are amenable to anything a critic might do. But I suspect that we have not recognized the degree to which we are, in our roles as critics, contributing to it: (1) some of us openly claim that rational argument is impossible about artistic judgment (implying that the reader who loves *Love Story* or thrills to *Jaws* or *Valley of the Dolls* can have no motive for attending to any claim that they are shoddy); (2) some of us imply by the way we write that knowledge is reserved for a precious few, whose taste, like their vocabulary, is forever inaccessible to all but true initiates; (3) some of us spend our spirit in a waste of shame praising lust in action, defending the popular arts indiscriminately and slashing at "elitism," as if every difficult author were equally suspect and every popular titillator who appeals to "the pit" another Shakespeare.

Meanwhile the discriminations that alone can reward the true artists, whether difficult or popular, and lead the poor ones to take up a less arduous metier, are left to the marketplace, and the marketplace becomes less and less discriminating as publishing becomes more and more like any other business that seeks a quick kill.

What might a critic do, for example, about the simple fact that most novelists rightly feel abused by the hasty reviews they receive, and yet never find themselves treated to a serious second look? Authors who are not hacks—that is, authors whose offerings to the world are of a kind that they would themselves respect if another author made the offering—"serious artists" find, after spending from one to twenty years on a novel, that reviewers generally spend at most a day or so on it; the reviewers are uncomprehending, whether they praise or blame, and yet the reviews are the last that authors hear of their work, in print. Unless they happen to become subjects for academic criticism—unless they happen to be taken up by the quarterlies—authors may wait a lifetime without ever finding even one critic-friend who will sit down with a book and savor it, reading and rereading until the full quality emerges, then writing and rewriting words of praise that will help build a critical culture able to see what has been made.

What we need is a public practice of the kind of thing that goes on in the best colleges—and not only in the classroom: steady criticizing of first readings by second, a habitual public criticism of first impressions, with each reader's carelessness and biases subjected to that kind of communal refinement which finally justifies criticism itself.

But where, in our journals, do we find any analogue for this process? The weeklies and monthlies do not, for the most part, discuss a book more than once: that hasty first review. The quarterlies do not, for the most part, deign to mention what the weekly reviewers had to say. Their critics are too busy with a standard short list of problems—intentionality, aesthetic distance, narrativity, textuality, referentiality, pluralism—or an even shorter list of established works and authors "worth criticizing." Even when a critic stoops to serious discussion of the unestablished, the disestablished, or the underrated, the reviewer will not read the discussion: he is off bleeding other victims, tearing through other books without a suspicion of the culturecide he is committing.

Would it be too much to ask of us that we try to invent forms of critical *exchange*, ways in which critical reflection might feed into the reviewing process? Is it inconceivable that *The New York Times Book Review*, say, should have a weekly column "Mistakes Our Reviewers Made A Year Ago"—a column of revaluations in which misreadings of last year's reviewers would be exposed? Is it not likely that if *The Saturday Review* or *The Atlantic Monthly* carried a column in which reviewers were exposed for the bad reading they performed the year before, the quality of reviewers' reading would rise? At least they should be tempted to read the books they review from cover to cover, if they knew that there might be, as today there generally are not, serious consequences for literary mutilation. At the other extreme of the gap between "critic" and "reviewer," would it be too much to ask of *The Georgia Review* and *Critical Inquiry* and *Diacritics* that they include some attempts to grapple with the relation of what critics talk about there to what goes on in weekly reviewing? Can it really be true that the readers of the weeklies would have no interest in discussion of characteristic booboos of their reviewers and of the probable reasons for overpraise or condemnation?

My plea is, then, for critics who will risk their reputations as profound theorizers by attempting the fine and difficult art of literary journalism. It would no doubt be disastrous if every critic heeded my call and tried to write home-truths-in-a-plain-style. But there is no inherent reason why most of the concepts debated in the critical journals cannot be rendered active on the cultural scene. Should we, for example, continue our debates about "aesthetic distance" and "irony" and our arguments for an opaque textuality without applying them to those easy inferences, drawn in great numbers weekly, about the author's beliefs and actions as seen in what characters and narrators do or say? Can no critic write about genre theory in a way that would help reviewers correct their absurd confusions of pomegranates and pomeranians as they try to make every "novel" conform to some common mold?

We have no way of knowing whether we can in the slightest degree reduce the present gap between an increasingly esoteric (and highly paid) band of professional critics, and an increasingly ignorant (and poorly paid) band of vulgarians. It may well be that social and commercial forces (of the kind that political criticism must grapple with) are so powerfully against the creation of a critical culture that nothing anyone can do will make a difference. We know that the great "men of letters" of our immediate past—critics like Edmund Wilson—grew increasingly disillusioned about the future of their kind. It is hard even to imagine what a revival of the kind might be, or where it might be "housed" and "fed." In the universities? Let no one think that the kind of journalism I am suggesting will earn tenure at the "better universities" these days. Attached to the journals? No one could possibly make a living from commercial reviewing today, let alone from the *haute vulgarization* I am suggesting.

Only one possibility remains: critics who *have* "a living" and the freedom that goes with it, critics with academic salaries, must find ways to talk not just to each other about theoretical questions but to general readers about the practice of criticism. If it is true that certain characteristic deflections of taste are committed by our reviewing, publishing, and advertising practices, is it beyond belief that literary critics could talk about those deflections in a way that would interest those who are most victimized by them, the readers of the journals?

In arguing that we need more and better ethical and political criticism, and more efforts to build a broad critical culture, I do not mean to deny the importance of other kinds of criticism. There can never be too much good criticism—criticism of the kinds that cherish the arts and teach us how to live in and through them. What I have said does, however, imply that much of what is called criticism these days is so trivial or imitative or destructive of our enterprises that we'd be better off without it. My plea is essentially pluralistic, but it is not a relativism that welcomes all comers equally. I could easily compile a hit-list of kinds of criticism that are *un*needed at the present time: (1) explications of verbal intricacy designed to show, one more time, that literary works are complex unities or complex incoherencies: unities transcending multeity, as in the old New Criticism, or incoherent multeities underlying seeming unity, as in the New New; (2) essays demonstrating that one more work, regardless of what it is, illustrates the truth that the enterprise of writing is, or is not, self-contained; (3) essays killing off realistic fiction, or reviving it—one more time; (4) essays proving, once and for all, that true poetry reveals the highest truths; or (5) essays showing that true poetry has no use for truth at all; (6) essays demonstrating that the words on the page are inert until some reader brings them to life; or (7) that the words on the page are NOT inert; (8) essays proving that some previous mode of criticism is now outmoded, or (9) that the essayist has now discovered the one critical mode that will save literature and criticism; . . . .

In short, let us have less proving of propositions that, given the premises of the agument, are self-proving. Our critical journals—I know this not only from working as an editor of *Critical Inquiry*—are flooded with works that will, even taken at their highest estimate, teach the world only what it already knows; given certain unproved general assumptions and a certain special way of thinking oneself from assumption to conclusion, such-and-such conclusions about art and life follow.

What we can never have too much of is a criticism that teaches us the subtle arts of appraisal. Such arts can never be confined to a single list; they will always be controversial. But in learning to practice them we find our best hope of building some sort of bridge between our theories and our various publics, inside and outside the universities. The final hope of any critic ought to be that what he writes might somehow sustain both the artists as they try to turn talents into something greater than talent, and the "appreciators of art"—we have no general word for them—who would enhance their lives in and through art. We have an immense number of talented artists in all the arts. We have a larger number of people ostensibly practicing "criticism," and being paid to do so, than any other culture in history. And we have a society with millions of consumers of art. What we do not have, as we limp toward a new century, is a critical culture.

Art without Critics and Critics without Readers *or* Pantagruel versus The Incredible Hulk

Mary Pratt

A collection of essays titled *What Is Criticism?* aims less at answering the title question than at displaying a range of responses to it. For there is no defining criticism, at least not in any detailed terms, because criticism does not exist in any absolute or stable fashion. As a social activity conducted by and within some living community, criticism always goes on in some specific context, with respect to some specific body of art, some specific grouping of artists, audiences, and critics, some specific social and institutional structure. Its concerns and methods vary along all these lines. What I propose to discuss here are some aspects of contemporary critical practice in the United States, and some possibilities for change.

The issues I particularly wish to raise were underscored for me recently by a dinner conversation with a group of friends. To fill in a lull, someone dutifully asked whether anyone had read any good books lately. Instead of the usual blandnesses, the question triggered a storm of complaints. Everyone loved to read, but no one could remember when she had last read a

For much helpful advice, discussion, and general inspiration on this paper, I would like to extend my thanks to Jean Franco, Kathleen Newman, Rina Benmayor, and all the members of the Tabloid collective.

book worth the reading or worth passing on. The cries of disgust gave way to a blow-by-blow critique of current paperback best sellers, Michener's *Chesapeake*, M. M. Kaye's *Far Pavilions*, Howard Fast's *Immigrants* series, Judith Krantz's *Scruples*, Trevanian's *Shibumi*, and so on. The adjectives that most recurred were "shallow" and "repetitive." As I was the one academic critic present, the discussion raised some professional questions for me. My friends—a systems analyst, a child-care worker, a switchboard operator, and a social worker—represented an enormous reading public, the millions of readers of so-called popular fiction (affectionately known to the initiated as "trash"). Where, I wondered, was the criticism that would impress the dissatisfaction of that readership upon the people producing for it? Where was the criticism that would reliably connect that readership with works they would find worth the reading (if there were any)? And where was the criticism that would make sense of these books themselves, of the responses they evoked, of the changes apparently taking place within their genre? Our literary predicament pointed up these two peculiarities about contemporary American culture: first, most of the art produced goes virtually without criticism, and second, something we academic critics perhaps more keenly feel, most of the criticism produced goes virtually unread. It is these two facts, and the relation between them, that I propose to explore in the next few pages.

Peculiarity number one, that most art goes unaccompanied by a criticism, refers not just to paperback novels, but to the vast artistic production generally lumped under the label "mass culture" or "mass art,"[1] especially television, Hollywood film, and popular fiction. These are the main forms in which art is experienced in this culture; however, they are certainly not the main forms with which criticism deals. In fact, they are almost entirely excluded from the concerns of academic criticism, though their critical consideration is deemed appropriate in the limited context of reviewing (of which more in a moment). Peculiarity number two, that most criticism goes virtually unread, refers, of course, to the vast critical production taking place in colleges and universities. Quantitatively speaking, most criticism by far is now produced by professors of literature and addressed to other professors of literature. Moreover, as critics of the profession relentlessly point out, the production of criticism within the closed circle has far outstripped the capacity to absorb what is published. Thus, if professors of literature form a relatively small potential audience for criticism, the actual audience for any given critical piece is likely to be downright minuscule.

As is often observed, the absorption of criticism by the university is a fairly recent development, having come about mainly in this century as part of the general retreat of elite culture from so-called mass culture. The move into academe further solidified and institutionalized the breach between elite art and mass art, but, more pertinent here, it also institutionalized an alignment of criticism with elite art. Side by side the two took up residence in departments of literature and philology, while no organized criticism developed around the burgeoning nonelite art forms. With the reexamination of academic institutions and intellectual life which was part of the upheaval of the late 1960s and early 1970s, this distribution of critical resources was called into question, and at least some academic critics directed attention to at least some sectors of mass art. (Film seems to have been a particular beneficiary here.) The expansion of scope has not continued, however, and some developments, such as the reestablishment of Western Civilization requirements, suggest a return to an exclusive focus on elite culture in the university. In this context, it is necessary to reaffirm the importance of efforts to extend criticism outside the traditional elite canon, and to overcome limitations arising from its university-bound organization.

It is not just a matter of incorporating mass art into the purview of the university. It is also a matter of establishing criticism within the sphere of mass art. For the criticism of any art form has to operate in the spheres where that art form is received and, where relevant, produced. For elite art, that sphere is schools, especially the university, where most of the reception of elite art takes place, as well as a good proportion of what production there is. Obviously the university houses only a tiny portion of the recipients of mass art forms, and even fewer of its producers. In the absence of organized critical study, discussion and understanding of those art forms rarely gets beyond immediate response to individual works, and generalized accusations of impoverishment and wasted resources. Without the historical perspective produced by a critical tradition, changes in these art forms go unnoticed or uninterpreted, often producing bafflement and scapegoating, but little in the way of critical understanding. The dinner conversation I referred to earlier is one example, but the clearest case of a gap in criticism at the moment is television, a medium whose very invention took place after criticism's move into the university, and whose only critical tradition is the Nielsen ratings, doubtless the crudest critical tool ever conceived. In recent years, a gap has been opening between TV programmers and viewers right where criticism ought to be. Far from being bound to each other in a mindless consumer orgy, the television viewing audience and programming establishment have by now (Fall 1979) so fallen out of touch with each other that a crisis of sorts has been acknowledged.[2] Public dissatisfaction with programming is widespread and profound. Complaints, lawsuits, and boycotts multiply, while TV watching stunningly shows its first decrease. The networks respond with a frenzy of wasteful production, trying out series after series, pilot after pilot, special after special, in hopes that something will click. Viewers seem able to communicate only what they don't want to watch, not what they do; networks seem unable to explain their successes and failures except individually and in terms of scheduling, weather, raw chance, or perhaps the price of oil. On the one hand there are audiences who have a taste for novelty that gets more and more difficult to satisfy, yet who are sufficiently involved with the medium that they continue to watch even when deeply dissatisfied by what they see. On the other hand there are production forces locked into a "lowest common denominator" principle (make works that are accessible to the greatest number of people) that is insensitive to diversity in the society, and locked into commercial compromises that restrict what subject matters can even be broached. But on neither side do we find means of making social, cultural, or artistic sense of what is going on. Similar circumstances seem to obtain in Hollywood film and paperback fiction as well. In the responses to both these media we likewise find widespread complaints of repetitiveness, rigid use of formula, a general narrowing or closure, and in both we find audience defections, to older or foreign films, to nonfiction literature, or to other cultural activities altogether. My aim here is not to diagnose or explain these developments, but rather to point out that there are enormously complex cultural goings-on here to be explained, and a lack of resources dedicated to explaining them.

To speak about extending criticism outside the academy and the elite art canon is not to talk simply about "applying" some predefined criticism to some additional body of art. There is no separating what criticism is "applied to" from the way it is applied, the way its priorities are defined, the way it is conceived and carried out, the roles it plays in the society. And there is no separating these from the way art itself functions in the society. These interdependencies are amply illustrated by the one variety of criticism which survives in the realm of mass culture, namely reviewing. When reviewing is juxtaposed to academic criticism, the first observation is usually that the former's business is evaluation and the latter's interpretation or analysis. This distinction is inaccurate, however, referring only to the function that superficially motivates the discourse in each case. Both kinds of criticism do both things. The interpretive functions of reviewing are to some extent hidden, however, by the fact that reviewing is up to its ears in what academic criticism resolutely tries to turn its back on, namely commercialism and the treatment of art as a commodity. The standard stance for present day reviewers is that of the consumer reporter, assisting the potential customer in deciding which works to spend time and money on. The focal point of the review is the recommendation to the consumer, the body of the text standing ostensibly as explanation and defense of the recommendation. The commercial ideal is for works of art to be consumed one after another like potato chips, to become obsolete as soon as a single exposure has taken place. This is the way they are dealt with by reviewing, one at a time as they first appear. Reviewers are not motivated to offer significant generalizations, let alone to concern themselves with theory.[3] Reviews are rarely the primary focus of the publications in which they appear, and must take their cues as to length, level of sophistication, and choice of subject from those items (news, fashion, pornography) which do make up the primary focus. Their relationship to the entertainment industry, which usually produces both the works under review and those doing the reviewing, puts reviewers under pressure to approach art primarily as diversion or escape (like the prominent TV producer who recently mused that "in the primary school of life, television is recess"). Finally, the review itself is a commodity, and the cash concerns of both reviewer and publication give rise to immediate constraints at every level.

Nevertheless, just as it is a mistake to think of mass art as purely manipulative and purely escapist, so it is a mistake to think of reviewing as purely a device of consumerism. It performs cultural tasks that are central to criticism. Reviewing plays an important role in the critical process of working out community consensus of judgment and interpretation of art—which is why people read and discuss reviews after having taken in the work, or even when they don't intend to take it in. A preoccupation with entertainment value obviously does not preclude serious consideration of art. Entertainment and leisure are serious matters, increasingly so as fewer and fewer people have their spare time and money taken up by family-connected work. And precisely because of its presence in the midst of the marketplace, reviewing does mediate directly between producers and receivers of mass art, forming a privileged and consequential line of communication from the latter to the former—which is why reviews are published and read after a one-time event like a concert.

It is worth adding here that, partly in response to developments in the mass arts like those mentioned above, reviewing is a genre whose vitality is increasing at present. Reviewing sections are now part of all magazines and newspapers that can afford them and (especially as books, movies and concerts get more expensive) people are reading and discussing reviews more than ever. Elaborate reviewing channels are now being wormed out of television. Each fall now brings a greater flurry of critical scrutiny of the new season of shows. In addition to *TV Guide*, which has grown grouchier and more analytical over the years, there are TV review columns in most large newspapers and magazines and (something apparently new this fall) review slots added to local TV news programs. Interviews and articles contemplating the crisis in television are multiplying. Even CBS, in an expensive face-saving gesture, has introduced a lavish monthly program in which it travels the country interviewing viewers who have written to complain about particular CBS shows. In sum, though there is no question of reviewing alone giving rise to an adequate mass culture criticism, we should not overlook it, nor the fact that it performs some vital functions that academic criticism has given up.

If reviewing is shaped by journalism and consumerism, academic criticism is shaped by the university and by its association with elite art. The point of the move into the university was to insulate both criticism and elite art from the direct control of the marketplace, and thus to create a point of resistance to commercialization and commodification of culture. This strategy has in some measure succeeded, but not without contradiction. Within the university, the establishment of published criticism as the measure determining job security, salary, and professional worth has commodified criticism anyway (though at a slight remove from money, since teaching is ostensibly the work for which we are paid). We think of criticism as working towards consensus via polemic, and of the university as fostering the free unfolding of this process. Yet some institutional pressures work in the opposite direction. The equation of publishing with prestige institutionalizes a need for the proliferation of criticism, and gives every critic a stake in the idea of criticism's inexhaustibility, the potential infinity of interpretation, the need for as great a plurality as possible. And if at times we panic, when, as Geoffrey Hartman says, "on looking into the intellectual heavens we see chaos: a plurality, perhaps infinity of competing hypotheses and mind-wearying speculations," ways are nevertheless found to legitimize what Hartman calls our "freedom to fall upwards,"[4] by viewing it as criticism's greatest richness, or as a theoretical necessity, or as a practical one forced upon us by the complexity of the works themselves. The need for proliferation has had the beneficial effect of encouraging some expansion of subject matter, including ventures into minor genres and into the realm of mass art. But it has also fostered overspecialization and complacency rather than consensus-oriented debate. Certainly Wayne Booth's recent characterization of criticism as a "melee" threatening to become "a free-for-all prizefight among blindfolded sluggers swinging at the air"[5] rather overdramatizes what goes on in the arcadian pastures of our scholarly journals, though he is right about the blindfolds.

The particularly striking aspect of the academic context, however, is that the strategy for insulating elite art and criticism from commodification has tended to isolate them from just about everything else that goes on outside the university, and thus tended to foster a view of "culture" as something existing apart from social life.[6] When elite culture is the only culture recognized by criticism, the escape from commercialism leads only to an equally impoverished isolationism. For elite culture has little participation in the ongoing life of society. It lives only in schools; it is always consciously, institutionally learned, always, as Philip Fisher says, "something to be entered from the outside."[7] It is not easy to see either this art or its criticism as social practices with any bearing beyond themselves. For this reason, it is important that these not be the only art and the only criticism recognized in the academy. Focus on the elite canon identifies criticism chiefly with the literature of the past, as commentary long after the fact of composition. The tendency then is to see criticism's main task as that of mediating contemporary reception of past works, while the concept of a criticism that also participates in ongoing, cotemporaneous artistic production recedes from view.

The tendency to sever culture from social life has consequences not just for critics and criticism, but for the whole society, especially since it comes at a time when criticis are also teachers, and when the democratization of postsecondary education has given the university direct intervention in the lives of more people than ever before. Most critics originally encountered elite culture "from the outside," and this is perforce the way we present it to our students, "under conditions," as Fisher says, "that compel a sacrificial act of severing social experience—tacit, felt connections between thought, order, personal experience, and memory—from known, read, cultural experience."[8] The sacrificial act obviously also includes a severing of knowledge and experience of art, at least in its mass forms. Moreover, the pedagogical context assumes that even this sacrificial act is not enough, that full understanding is only for professional specialists, while the lay person can master only rudiments. Too often, culture is dealt out like vitamins, to correct deficiencies only the doctor really understands. As with other professions, part of the message we pass on is that the client/patient should never feel able to do without our specialized guidance. How different is the idea of a criticism that functions as a complement to the artistic knowledge and experience of a group. How few academic critics do their work in a context in which artist, audience, and critic are cotemporaneous members of the same community, each with stakes in, and a say in, how art is practiced in that community. This is not of course to say that critics should abandon Pantagruel and learn to love the Incredible Hulk; it is to say only that elite art should not and need not be the unique focus of academic criticism. It is a matter of increasing the critic's roles, not of eliminating any of them.

Change is immensely difficult, however, because most of us have internalized values that legitimize the severing of culture from social life, values like "critical distance," which can make it easier, for example, to deal with contemporary works of other cultures than with those of one's own. The university context contributes here, by making criticism an outright bedfellow of the more prestigious and powerful sciences, whose standards are the institutional norm. The supposed nonsocial character of scientific knowledge and activity suggests an approved model for criticism; critical stances develop on analogy with that of the scientist observing biological phenomena (text as organism) or psychological phenomena (reader as experimental subject). Description and explanation become the explicit goals, along with theoretical speculation, and evaluation becomes implicit. Professional jargons are developed to separate the knowledge produced from the realm of shared or shareable community knowledge. The relationship to science is not unequivocal, however. Its contradictoriness is revealed in one of contemporary criticism's most distinguishing features, its obsession with its own validity. This obsession reveals at one and the same time the internalization of scientific values and the recognition of their limitations. Hence the doubly defensive stance typical of much modern criticism, against the pressure of the sciences within the university, and the pressure of mass art outside it.

Another powerful strategy reinforcing the isolation of criticism is the commonplace assumption that what the critic does is determined by the works of art themselves. It is often tacitly assumed that works "invite" criticism, that the best works invite the best criticism, and the worst works invite none at all. This amounts to an assumption that what the critic does is somehow naturally rather than socially governed,[9] an assumption that works well in conjunction with an even greater constraint, the concept of "mass art" itself. For this is the label that communicates to us all that that art which is part of daily, unspecialized social experience is not art or culture at all, is beneath criticism, beneath interpretation, beneath taking seriously. Ironically, to the extent that academic criticism implies or even disseminates such a view, it supports the very commercial interests it elsewhere undertakes to resist. Raymond Williams's comments on the mass media in general are pertinent here:

> The bourgeois concept of 'mass communications' and the tied radical concept of 'mass manipulation' are alike inadequate to the true sociology of these central and varying institutions. . . . What both bourgeois and radical-empiricist cultural theory have achieved is the social *neutralization* of such institutions: the concept of the 'mass' replacing and neutralizing specific class structures; the concept of 'manipulation' (an operative strategy in capitalist advertising and politics) replacing and neutralizing the complex interactions of control, selection, incorporation, and the phases of social consciousness which correspond to real social situations and relations. . . . The complex sociology of actual audiences, and of the real conditions of reception and response in these highly variable systems (the cinema audience, the newspaper readership, and the television audience being highly distinct social structures), is overlaid by bourgeois norms of 'cultural producers' and 'the mass public,' with the additional effect that the complex sociology of these producers, as managers and agents within capitalist systems, is itself not developed.[10]

Though Williams is here speaking chiefly of sociology, his remarks readily extend to other concerns of criticism as well. The concepts of mass art and mass culture oversimplify or "overlay," as Williams puts it, a highly complex range of cultural activities about which we know very little, in comparison with the knowledge and understanding we have achieved of elite art. Our understanding of elite art too suffers from this gap, for we tend to overlook its continual interplay with mass art forms. I refer not only to the erudite ancestors of the Incredible Hulk, but also to the fact that the Hulk is perfectly likely to engender allusions of his own in a high art novel or a sculpture exhibit. He and Pantagruel, put in the same room, will not devour each other. They will simply compare notes.

NOTES

1. As I shall be discussing later on, "mass culture" and "mass art" are blanket terms that grossly oversimplify a wide range of cultural

activity. I use them here reluctantly, and as a reminder of where there is work to be done.

2. For recent discussion of this crisis from within the industry, see *Television Quarterly* 16, no. 2 (Summer 1979).

3. It is interesting to note that many of these observations about reviewing do not apply to the *New York Review* and publications like it which, though not operating out of the university, do operate within the sphere of elite or high art and find their main audience in the academy.

4. "Literary Criticism and its Discontents," *Critical Inquiry* 3 (1976): 211.

5. *Critical Understanding: The Powers and Limits of Pluralism* (Chicago: University of Chicago Press, 1979), pp. 6–7.

6. I am indebted here and in what follows to Philip Fisher's article, "Questions of English," *College English* 40, no 7: 727–39.

7. Ibid., 734.

8. Ibid.

9. It is not my intention here to deny that what critics do may vary according to the works involved, nor to claim that all the critic's roles will be equally pertinent all the time.

10. *Marxism and Literature* (Oxford: Oxford University Press, 1977), pp. 136–37.

The Social Relations of Criticism

Richard Ohmann

On publication of *What Is Literature?*, to which this volume is a sequel, I was mildly surprised that only a single contributor had alluded to a book that came out thirty years before, with the same title. I admire Sartre's *What Is Literature?*, and I want to begin this essay by making amends for our omission—mine and that of other contributors. For Sartre devotes an aside to critics and criticism:

> It must be borne in mind that most critics are men who have not had much luck and who, just about the time they were growing desperate, found a quiet little job as cemetery watchmen. . . . The dead are there; the only thing they have done is write. . . . The trouble makers have disappeared; all that remains are the little coffins that are stacked on shelves along the walls like urns in a columbarium. The critic lives badly; his wife does not appreciate him as she ought to; his children are ungrateful; the first of the month is hard on him. But it is always possible for him to enter his library, take down a book from the shelf, and open it. It gives off a slight odor of the cellar, and a strange operation begins which he has decided to call reading.

In reading, the critic enters into a kind of "possession" by a book "written by a dead man about dead things," a book which "no longer has any place on earth," which does not interest us directly, and whose feelings have "passed on to the status of exemplary feelings and, in a word, of *values*." Sartre's critic considers with equal distance the racism of Gobineau and the humanitarianism of Rousseau (between whom he would have had to choose if he had been their contemporary), because both Gobineau and Rousseau are "profoundly and deliciously wrong, and in the same way: they are dead." Enjoying thus the "well-known superiority of live dogs to dead lions," the critic reduces what were their burning causes and urgencies to "messages" about themselves, often contradicted by their lives. When nothing remains of them but

> these capital truths, "that man is neither good nor bad," "that there is a great deal of suffering in human life," "that genius is only great patience," this melancholy cuisine will have achieved its purpose, and the reader, as he lays down the book, will be able to cry out with a tranquil soul, "All this is only literature."[1]

You may judge for yourself whether or not the philosopher is unfair to us. Either way, you will probably want to comment that Sartre's critic occupies a different situation from the one in which we write our criticism: apparently he earns his meagre living from it, for one thing; if we had to do that we should find the first of the month a bitter moment indeed. I begin with Sartre, though, because he looks at criticism as the activity of people in particular circumstances, whose criticism responds to those circumstances as well as to literature. Like Raymond Williams, he sees criticism as "a practice, in active and complex relations with the situation and conditions of the practice, and, necessarily, with all other practices."[2] I wish to do likewise, mainly stating the obvious, because sometimes the obvious gets confounded in enigmas of our own making.

Let me insist right away: any enigma that inheres in the question "What is (literary) criticism?" must be partly of our own making. (By "we," I mean those in this society who profess literature and write about it.) I say this because although Williams adequately shows that "criticism" has become a "very difficult word" (p. 74), it is not a difficult word in our own professional use. Criticism is the formal writing and talking about literature that people like us do. One may wish, for some purpose, to extend the use of the term to cover what the reviewer in today's *Globe* writes about the new novel, or what we say about literature in casual conversation, or anyone's response of any sort to literature. Or one may wish for different purposes to restrict the concept of criticism so that it excludes judgment or interpretation or some other kind of writing. But I believe most will agree that if we examine the way we use the term for easy and natural converse among ourselves, rather than to argue for a different usage and a different criticism, we mean the articles in *Novel* and *Modern Fiction Studies* and do not mean the review in the *Globe* or this morning's argument in class about the ghosts in *The Turn of the Screw* or the applause at the end of the play last night; and we do mean the highly judgmental writings of Winters and Leavis along with Brooks's explications.

So where is the problem? Well, for one thing, the "what" in "What is criticism?" squints; in fact, it has triple vision. The question can mean: what are the various operations that critics carry on—what exactly goes on in critical discourse? That empirical question is difficult, and worth answering in careful detail. But it is no enigma. Nor is there a puzzle in the question read as I have read it in the previous paragraph, where "what" is taken to ask for the extension of the term, its domain. The enigma rises up when we take the "what" as a request to identify the *essence* of criticism, that privileged feature that makes some activities and texts really criticism and others defective criticism or not criticism at all.

Bewitchment. As if one were to ask "What is cooking?" and be satisfied neither with an account of what the word means nor with a descriptive analysis of the various things cooks do nor with an enumeration of the products of cooking, but insisted on knowing in addition what cooking *really* is—so as to prove triumphantly, perhaps, that boiling vegetables ("à l'Anglaise") is not cooking at all, or is a travesty of cooking, or is third-rate cooking. Taken this way, the question is an invitation to honor some cooks and excommunicate others. That may be worth doing, but not by the misleading and heavily ideological strategy of trying to derive a value from a fact—"What and how should we cook?" from "What is cooking?"

Now there may be polemical essays titled "What Is Cooking?" which are gathered from time to time in controversial books. But I doubt it, and not just because we all know that, minimally, to cook food is to heat it. (After all, we all know that criticism is, minimally, formal writing and talking about literature.) I think we have a controversy about what criticism is and not about what cooking is partly because the social relations that surround cooking are fairly obvious and those that surround criticism are opaque. Writing about intellectuals, Gramsci noted the futile effort to find a single feature that characterizes all their activities and distinguishes those activities from the activities of other groups. The error, he said, was to look for such a criterion "in the intrinsic nature of intellectual activities, rather than in the ensemble of the system of relations in which these activities . . . have their place. . . . "[3] The same, I think, holds for criticism and critics. I want to examine now the network of relations that surround criticism, putting to work a few basic marxian concepts.

Cooking, done at home, has a clear use value. Done in a restaurant or other institution where one pays to eat, it has that and an exchange value as well. Cooking, in relation to what has been cooked, is a commodity. In or out of the market, cooking is unmistakably a form of production, and in the market it is the usual sort of commodity. These elementary categories don't embrace criticism so readily. For whom does a work of criticism have a use value? Certainly for some other critics, who use it to inform their teaching and also to "keep up" with their field and to help them produce criticism of their own. It is as if cooking were mainly of use to other cooks, as an aid to further cooking and to instruction in cooking. In addition, criticism has use value for students, but mainly because they have been told to read it by a teacher-critic or because they have been required to write some criticism of their own in a course. This is not to say that critics and students never enjoy criticism or that nobody ever reads it in a disinterested way, but only that as we seek the use value of criticism we find ourselves circling, for the most part, within a chain of uses created by critics themselves.

It might seem easier to pin down the exchange value of criticism. At least some critical essays return a modest fee to their authors, and critical books yield royalties. Yet these payments do not generally flow from the free expression of needs through the market and from the corresponding search for profit on the part of publishers. Most of the few journals that pay for criticism are subsidized by universities or "angels," as are the university presses which print most critical books. And even with subsidy, the latter would not be able to survive except for sales to libraries at exorbitant prices, again made possible by university budgets. The few critical books that do remain available in paper covers year after year, and presumably earn their publishers a profit, do so mainly because of sales to other critics or to students required to buy the books for courses or to graduate students apprenticing themselves in the profession. With exchange value as with use value there seems to be no escaping a circle inscribed by critics themselves and by the institutions where they work. In any event, we are talking of a very small market which is largely an artifact of those who produce for it.[4] And does anyone doubt that the overwhelming majority of critical efforts, without even counting those of students, bring no return at all? Criticism is a strange kind of production, within capitalism, and barely a commodity at all.

In the central situations of criticism—a paper presented at a conference or published in a journal—critics are themselves producers, purveyors, and consumers. Criticism has little value of either the economic or the personal sort apart from our own needs and the needs we impose on students and librarians.[5] To go one step farther, what critics most urgently need is to *produce* criticism, not consume it. This seems true whether you take us singly or collectively. Singly, as everyone knows, we want to write it in order to prove our degree-worthiness, to get jobs, to gain promotions and tenure, to earn professional status—and also, of course, to win admiration, to gain self-respect, to have the pleasure of discovery, to celebrate literature, to enjoy argumentative combat, to hold converse with others who have similar interests, and so on. I leave it to you to decide which set of needs is most formative. Collectively we need to produce criticism and create the journals that print it and the ceremonies of its presentation, in order to confirm our standing as a profession. For a group of workers will not be recognized as professionals and granted the special benefits that go with that status unless they stand guard over and constantly augment a body of knowledge.[6] Criticism is not the entire body of knowledge that certifies this profession, but it is the largest one, and for twenty-five years or more it has been the privileged one. Critics need criticism in order to hold their place in the university.

But criticism is more than a reason for our exemption from the worst rigors of the capitalist labor market. When we do it we also *exercise* and *express* our professional freedom. In the lingo of our guild, we distinguish between our jobs and our "work." "How's your work going?" usually means your criticism or scholarship or other research, not your teaching. ("I haven't had time for my own work all semester.") Criticism is our work, but not our job. Our job is teaching. Its product is education, manifested as grades, credits, degrees. In our jobs we are directly answerable to our employers. It's a long way from the secretarial pool or the assembly line to the university classroom; nonetheless, we too sell our labor power to our bosses, and they set the broad terms upon which we yield up our labor—the courses, schedule, rules of instruction. Unlike most nonprofessional workers, we retain authority over some important areas of planning in our jobs, but the ground rules of teaching are beyond our control. A split between conception and execution exists for us—and of course our control diminishes in times of retrenchment like the present. We are not, technically, exploited, since no capitalist appropriates the surplus value from our labor and no university makes a profit. But we do surrender the product of our labor to our employers, who exact pay from the students or—with diminishing effectiveness, to be sure—from the State. The kinship many of us increasingly feel with other workers has its ground in alienation, no less real for being relatively benign.

But our "work" as critics, precisely because it does not produce a commodity that our employers appropriate, and in fact rarely produces a commodity at all, is not alienated labor. True, many critics must do this labor to survive, but in that respect we are not different from free-lance writers or self-employed physicians. We manage the labor process of criticism, from conception through the more challenging parts of execution. Then we hand over the detail work—typing, copy-editing, typesetting, proofreading, printing, binding, mailing—to others. Furthermore, the product belongs to us. Copyright symbolizes this fact, as does the recording of publications and delivered papers on our *vitae*. The critic's name is affixed to the product for good. He or she has performed an act of original creation through what can only be characterized, at this level of analysis, as unalienated labor. So in the practice of criticism, critics come closer than most people ever do to freedom from the usual conditions of labor in capitalist society.[7]

This sounds attractive, so attractive that I should think it would provoke a skeptical question: why is criticism not entirely satisfying to those who practice and consume it? Why doesn't criticism appear to us as an area of freedom—both a free exercise of our creative labor and a freely chosen collaboration with others in the exchange and development of ideas? I offer two answers to this question, both of which point to the same kind of structural defect in our freedom.

First, it is not quite true that we do criticism outside the system of exploitation. The university and college managements that employ us make indirect use of criticism and all other research they sponsor, though they do not strictly appropriate these products or sell them for profit. Management demands research in order to keep up the "quality" of the faculty and of the institution. That's to say that the university claims its rank among institutions mainly by citing the research that its faculty carries out, even otherwise useless research like criticism. Research supports its Cartter rating, and all the more informal measures of repute, such as the flow of promising graduate students, the marketability of those students when they gain Ph.D.'s and the university's position in the bidding for those same students later on, when some of them gain distinction as researchers. This rating system and its values permeate higher education, operating with diminished force "down" through the prestigious colleges, the lesser universities, and the state and municipal colleges. Community colleges and some others may neither reward nor demand research: that fact both reflects and establishes their position at the bottom of the hierarchy.

Management uses the status attained through our research to attract money: gifts from individuals and corporations, grants from foundations and the federal government, and routine funding by states and municipalities—and, in addition to these forms of the social surplus, the tuition that students and their parents pay. Rank turns into money which in turn confirms rank. For students themselves, the rank of their college or university translates into one or another position in the competition for jobs, and for unequally distributed benefits such as income, wealth, prestige, and power. This is just to restate the familiar truth that higher education plays a part in reproducing the class system. Research, including criticism, is one of the media through which class is transmitted. So whatever the aims of the critic, she or he participates through criticism in the processes of competition and of class, as well as of exploitation. I think we feel at all times the pressure of these social relations, and the tension between them and the free, collaborative exercise of creative labor.

The second reason that the practice of criticism does not measure up to its ideal can be traced through the history of criticism. As Williams points out in *Keywords,* a main modern sense of "criticism" is *judgment.* As the reception of literature became more isolated, from the seventeenth century on, the reader assumed a position something like that of a consumer, and some readers were able to claim authority as judges. The very idea of judgment implies a division into two groups of people: those qualified by taste, sensibility, or cultivation (later by formal training) to judge, and those disqualified by youth, ignorance, barbarism, or dullness. Furthermore, it implies the existence of external standards by which works are to be judged. Of course there are no such standards: there are only the social processes through which some people are able to win hegemony for their responses. To posit standards is always to engage in an ideological maneuver, to generalize the interests and values of one class or group and present them as the interests and values of all. To the extent that critical practice still disguises response as judgment, critics must feel some insecurity about the concealed power relations that accompany the move from "I like it" to "It is a great work."

It might seem that in the last hundred years, as criticism has become linked to a profession and to the professional emphasis on rigor, method, and objectivity, the class relations of judgment would have drained out of it. And indeed, one now encounters much less explicit judgment in critical practice than formerly; the judgment of works has receded into the background, retained mainly in the form of a tacit and corporate professional judgment as to which works are worth reading, teaching, and criticizing. Judgment is embodied in whatever agreement exists about the canon.

But at the same time and for the same reason—professionalization—that critics have come to judge less, criticism itself has come under judgment more frequently, more formally, and more consequentially. Professionals with the power to grant or deny advancement—graduate professors, editors of journals, referees, reviewers, etc.—judge criticism at every stage of a career, and on their judgments depends the passage through college to graduate school to first job to reappointment to tenure and to final promotion. Beyond that, there is the lifelong race to *distinguish* oneself in the judgment of other professionals. Small wonder that the process has led to some rather arcane intellectual gymnastics, to an idea of criticism as itself an art in competition with literature, to post-this and neo-that, to journals intelligible only to a handful of initiates.

Many will feel that along the way criticism has become an activity in which we exercise our freedom only to be judged and ranked according to what we produce, and in which we can establish our worth only by invidious comparison with others. In this way, and in its tendency to make knowledge inaccessible and private rather than collaborative, the social relations internal to criticism duplicate those very social relations of the larger society from which we try to escape by creating a space for unalienated labor. Nor is this surprising, since the existence of such space contributes to the continuance of just those social relations.

NOTES

1. Jean-Paul Sartre, *What Is Literature?*, trans. Bernard Frechtman (New York: Washington Square Press, 1966), pp. 17–22.

2. Raymond Williams, *Keywords: A Vocabulary of Culture and Society* (New York: Oxford University Press, 1976), p. 76.

3. Antonio Gramsci, *Selections from the Prison Notebooks,* ed. and trans. Quinton Hoare and Geoffrey Nowell Smith (London: Lawrence and Wishart, 1971), p. 8.

4. It may seem at first that the same could be said of the market for vaginal deodorants and power-driven leaf-blowers. But those who stimulate or create the needs for *these* commodities are not the producers; they are marketers who do so by means of advertising.

5. I recall muttering with colleagues about a survey done by the Great Books people from Chicago in the early 1960s: What were the most important books of this century? Not a work of criticism appeared among the top hundred.

6. I developed this argument at length in chapter 9 of *English in America* (New York: Oxford University Press, 1976).

7. Another vaguely remembered survey, this one just a few years ago, asked a variety of workers how they would spend the extra two hours of an hypothetical twenty-six-hour day. Professors led all other groups in answering that they would use the extra two hours for work. I don't imagine they meant grading exams.

A Search for Subjective Truth

Martin Esslin

"Criticism" is one of those terms so beset by confusion between various different common and scholarly usages that they defy definition: there is the "critic" who reviews books or plays in the daily press, the "academic critic" who writes learned books; there are the associations of the adjective "critical" and the verb "to criticize" which imply the finding of faults to the point of utter rejection; and then there are the usages of the term in philosophy, also with quite a number of different connotations.

There is nothing one can do about such a state of affairs. One has to live with it and resign oneself to the facts that neither the term, nor the field it refers to, is capable of exact definition and that the sense in which it is used will always be vaguely delimited and will have to be inferred from the context in which the word occurs and from which one must decide whether one is confronted with the "higher" or with the "everyday" use of the term, the "scholarly" or the "journalistic," the neutral or the pejorative.

But I for one feel that even in the "higher," scholarly context the usual dictionary definition, on the lines of "the explanation and analysis of works of art or literature," is already too exact and specific. The term after all is, quite legitimately, applicable to such a variety of different, albeit related, activities, that even such a definition seems to narrow it down too much. There are many different types of questions to which the answers might be regarded as instances of a critical activity:

> What do you think of this picture (poem, novel, book, symphony)?
> What is it about?
> How does it affect you?
> How does it achieve its effect?
> Why do you like (or dislike) it?
> Do you advise me to see (read, hear) it?
> What should I look for in it to derive pleasure or profit from it?
> How does it relate to other works in its field?
> What can I learn from it to help me excel in the same art form?

All these—and many other questions—will evoke answers that fall under the general heading of critical discourse. Hence I would confine myself to saying that "criticism" (in its "higher" and more specialized connotation) can not aspire to a more specific definition than "discourse on art," literary criticism to no more than "discourse on literature." And that still leaves open the related and even wider question of how we ought to define "art" and "literature."

"Discourse on literature": such a humble definition, however, does not, in my view, at all lower the status of the activity to which it refers. For to talk well on a subject like literature is anything but easy: it requires a multitude of skills, much intellectual discipline, wide knowledge, insight, discernment, subtle powers of expression, sensitivity and sensibility, the ability to relate things and to see hidden connections between them, a keen eye for the essential features of the matters under discussion, cool detachment as well as passionate intensity of feeling, the empathy to experience emotion from within, as well as the coolness to stand back and see the order behind an apparently chaotic proliferation of forms. All this and a host of other talents, accomplishments, and specialized skills.

Inevitably value judgments will have to be involved in such

discourse: to talk about the more significant objects rather than the less significant ones, to concentrate on those which are the best examples of the skills involved is obviously the most sensible course. Yet it is my conviction that the undue emphasis on the evaluative function of criticism has done much to divert it from its most important tasks and to distort its image and has tended generally to bring it into disrepute. Such an overemphasis on the evaluative function of criticism has led, above all, to much unjustified arrogance among critics; to the assumption, on the part of many, that they were—and are—officiating at some prodigious Last Judgment (*Judex ergo cum sedebit*) with the power to consign some unfortunates to Hell and to elevate a few chosen to Paradise. It requires considerable strength of character to resist the temptation to assume such a position of great power (which has always been wholly unjustified) and the even more insidious temptation to suppose that one's judgments are made on the basis of absolute standards. For if the analogy is to hold water, "judging" works or authors implies the existence of a set of laws, written or unwritten, which can be applied with rigor and exactness. It is this analogy—wholly false, in my opinion—which has led to the search for rules, immutable laws, in literary criticism.

In periods in which the laws of conduct were regarded as having been divinely revealed through scripture, analogously the literary judges went by authority: Aristotle was assigned the function of suppyling the revealed truth. In a more scientific, positivist age, the quest has shifted to an attempt to discover laws of criticism in analogy to the discovery of the laws of nature by the natural sciences. That analogy, it seems to me, is equally fallacious and even more harmful.

Of course there are points at which criticism and science overlap: in a discussion of painting, the chemistry of pigments or physiology of seeing might occasionally be relevantly invoked. In a discussion about drama in the cinema, the mechanics of film-making are manifestly not without significance; and similarly, in dealing with the novel one might well bring the psychology of characters into the discussion from a "scientific" point of view (if indeed psychology is a true science).

But this kind of borrowing is a far cry from the assumption, which underlies so much misguided criticism, that there could ever be such a thing as a truly scientific framework for our "discourse on art." For science is concerned with establishing objective truths, verifiable facts, immutable causalities. But the arts, above all literature, are concerned with *subjective* truths, *subjective* experience and the subjective causality which creates a different, *subjective* reaction to the same object, in different individuals. There can, thus, be no absolutes in criticism.

Does that mean that there is no generally accepted body of knowledge in this field, no generally established standards? By no means: but these generally accepted standards, these widely held convictions merely have the status of a *consensus,* not of an absolute truth. It is quite possible to find, say, a poem which will generally be regarded as execrably bad, *nemine contradicente.* Nevertheless it is perfectly possible that, circumstances being changed, different points of view having gained acceptance, the same poem will be regarded quite differently: as an exquisite example of a previous epoch's "bad taste," for example, or as so terrible as to be again wonderfully funny and amusing. That may be an extreme example. But is the fact that Shakespeare was long regarded as being bad because in breach of established rules of dramatic construction and in need of "correction" and improvement any less extravagant?

The *consensus* in question is of two kinds: about minimum standards of *craft,* on the one hand, minimum standards of *taste* on the other. The craft aspect, what I. A. Richards called the field of "technical criticism," seems most straightforward. The publisher's reader who rejects a novel because it is "technically inadequate" operates in this field, and, on the whole, the degree of accuracy and reliability in such judgments is high. There seem to be even verifiable criteria here: the exposition of a play may be inadequate or too clumsy; the descriptions in a novel too longwinded, repetitive, and boring; the construction of a plot too illogical. But beware: there are no absolutes of craft either. What seemed the perfect expositions in the well-made plays of Scribe or Sardou nowadays tend to appear intolerably overexplicit. Under the influence of the more economical dramatic techniques of the cinema and television our skill in decoding expositions has generally improved, we have become "quicker in the uptake." Even the masterly expositions of Ibsen are now, in some cases, overexplicit to our taste. So much for the view, still held in not a few places, that at least the "psychology of perception" which deals with the human mind's ability to digest information could form the basis for at least some truly scientific foundations for "aesthetics." One has only to think of the corresponding views in music on the physiological basis for our perception of harmonies, to see how far from absolute such scientific foundations for artistic matters can prove to be.

When, in my capacity as head of the BBC Radio Drama department, I had editorial responsibility for accepting or rejecting plays out of the one to two hundred manuscripts sent in every week, I was reasonably certain that the ones I turned down were verifiably not worth doing, were certainly below acceptable standards; I remained, nevertheless, equally certain that their unacceptability, their verifiable badness, was so only within the context of prevailing tastes, prevailing expectations, prevailing conventions. Those conventions, that consensus, I was equally well aware, are in constant flux, subject to constant almost imperceptible change. But one has only to look at the bulk of old films, read the best-sellers or even some of the "classics" of yesteryear, to realize how radical that change is over longer periods.

An awareness of the absence of standards of judgment independent of local, cultural, historical, social, and other specific circumstances, and hence of the impossibility of applying absolute criteria of any kind, does not mean that we cannot reason about works of art within an ordered logical framework: we must merely be aware of the relativity of that framework itself. In other words: if the convention concerned demands an inner consistency, if there are canons of taste or plausibility or harmony or seemliness applicable to the artifact in question, it is possible to discuss it within that convention, provided always that the limited validity of such a framework is implicitly recognized, and at least occasionally made explicit.

If there are no absolute standards of judgment, similarly there are no absolute standards of critical methodology. Here too the analogy with science must be recognized as fallacious and as a source of error. There is not, nor can there be, one all-embracing method of criticism, simply because there is no objective truth to be uncovered; there is instead a multiplicity of motivations and intentions in the discourse about art, springing from a wide variety of interests that underlie the desire to enter into the discourse.

Historically, at least in Western culture, criticism can be traced back to origins within the schools of rhetoric, whose main concern was to evolve a set of principles according to which effective public speaking—and later verbal communication in general—could be taught. Empirically, and within their own cultural and special circumstances, the rules evolved were highly effective. The idea that supreme excellence in at least some literary areas could be *taught* (which was correct only to a very limited extent, and applicable only to the basic mechanics of the construction of speeches or poems) still lingers on to this day, as the last remnant of the various treatises on public speaking and *artes poeticae* from Horace to the Renaissance and beyond. The implication that it might be possible through analysis of the creative process which underlies some great masterpiece to find a way by which similar masterpieces might be produced at will still haunts, albeit unspoken and perhaps even wholly unconscious, a great deal of contemporary criticism. In fact, rules derived *a posteriori* from the analysis of admitted masterpieces and elevated into *a priori* criteria and rules to which all subsequent works must confirm tend to become veritable beds of Procrustes inhibiting the organic development of literature.

The search for the infallible method by which masterpieces can be produced is but one of the many differing intentions behind critical activity. There is also the search for fuller knowledge about the personality and psychology of creative individuals; the discussion of literary works as historical and sociological source material; the quest for confirmation of political theories and arguments (as in "Marxist" aesthetics); or the analysis of texts as structures of signs and symbols.

Each of these differing intentions—and there are no doubt many others—gives rise to a multitude of differing methodologies and techniques by which texts are approached, analyzed, explained and discussed. Each of these, in my view, is valid, so long as it is recognized that each deals with a different aspect of a wide and multifarious subject matter and can yield results only in relation to the intentions that originally motivated its formation. But are not the originators of the differing schools or methods of criticism and their followers convinced that theirs is the only truly valid approach? *Should* they not so be convinced? There lies one of the paradoxes behind the whole activity of criticism as discourse about literature: Discourse implies a plurality of viewpoints, dialogue, discussion, a dialectic. It is of the nature of a dialectical process that there must be differing opinions, passionately held and argued, confronting each other. That, after all, is the assumption underlying such well-proven dialectical systems as political democracy or the Anglo-Saxon judicial procedure, based as they are on a contest between antagonistic viewpoints. Hence it is important that those who contribute to the dialectical process which is, in my view, the very essence of the critical activity, should believe in the absolute truth, the supreme rightness, of their own ideas. Yet, as in the democratic or judicial process, it would be wise if the antagonists also knew at the back of their minds that the passionately held truth of their own beliefs is of a special kind: subjective and temporary at best, simply because absolutes in this field of human endeavor are a logical impossibility. Is it possible for the same mind to hold two such seemingly contradictory convictions simultaneously? Just think of the writer who strives with total commitment to create an "immortal masterpiece" and yet knows that immortality may at best mean survival for a few hundred, perhaps a thousand years; think of the lover who passionately believes that his beloved is the best, most beautiful individual ever to have trod the earth; he knows, simultaneously, full well that this belief is a subjective one and valid only for himself and for that moment. Indeed, he knows that it would be monstrous if it were otherwise: for if it were literally true he would be faced with competition from the rest of male mankind.

The same is true in the field of literature as in the other arts: if such a thing as the perfect masterpiece, the absolutely valid critical principle for the production of masterpieces, could exist, the activity of literature itself would come to a halt. All further endeavor would be pointless. In fact, there can be no end-points and no absolutes in an area concerned with subjective experience. The experience of each individual changes his reaction to his next experience. The experience of each generation modifies the experience of the following generation. Their reaction is a reaction to their predecessors' reactions: in such a dialectical process there can be no end-points. Each journey may reach its destination, but each destination is merely the starting point of a new journey. The movement of traveling toward the destination is the essential element, not the destination. Stopping at the destination, that is, reaching a rigid, fixed result, an immutable principle, an infallible method, would be tantamount to coming to a full stop; it would mean fossilization and death. There are precedents for such fossilization in the history of literature and of criticism.

Thus the movement or progress of the arts—and that of discourse about the arts, criticism, within them—is not concerned with reaching objectives, achieving lasting results. It is the process, the movement itself, which is the essence of the matter. The objectives of the moment are important merely insofar as they keep the movement going. The critical activity, which is concerned with formulating such objectives, is an essential ingredient in that process; hence it may be vital that the individuals who contribute to the formulation of those objectives should passionately believe in their absolute value.

Seen as a dialectical process—as discourse, debate, exchange of reactions, impressions, views—resulting from widely varying interests and intentions, criticism clearly is a *collective* endeavor which will at best produce a *consensus*, sometimes long-lasting, sometimes short-lived, about individual works, problems, techniques or values. The debate takes place both on a synchronic level, among contemporaries, and diachronically, from period to period. This latter process seems to me to be of decisive significance: in reacting to a work from a previous epoch, each generation confronts not only the work itself but the impact of the critical consensus of previous epochs, crystallized in the received opinion about it which is, in the case of works of enduring importance, in turn the product of the dialectical clash of a number of differing reactions through time. Each work comes to us surrounded and enveloped by the critical reactions it has evoked and which have adhered to it. This is another reason why absolutes in criticism are a logical impossibility: for the work of art and the reaction it has evoked become fused, inextricably linked. We cannot see a work of the past independent of the critical reaction that surrounds it, and in reacting to the work itself we cannot but also react to its reputation, its previous critical interpretation. Attempts to look at works from the past with virgin eyes and in disregard of all previous opinions and preconceptions (which attempts are made again and again) are foredoomed to failure: can the scholar who tries to see a Shakespearean sonnet, say, without *any* preconception really achieve that blessed state of blankness? I doubt it. And if he could, would he then not be excluding the preconceptions which Shakespeare's contemporaries who actually did read that sonnet with completely virgin eyes, had in their minds—and thus get a result wholly different from that truly virgin reaction? And if he argued that, precisely, that was what he wanted to achieve, would that result then not be merely an extreme reaction to previous reactions, merely another step in a continuous dialectical process? In other words: it may be possible to jump out of a moving train, but we cannot jump out of the process of history; there is no Archimedic point from which we can step out of the world itself.

That we cannot perceive a work of literature of the past without the critical discourse which has accumulated around it is merely another aspect of the basic nature of literature itself as a form of communication: there can be no perceived object without a perceiver, and the nature of the perceiver determines the mode in which the object is perceived. Hence there cannot be a work of art as a "thing in itself," hence all discourse about works of art must contain a subjective element. The critical consensus around a past work of art thus becomes part of its perception in the mind of new perceivers and modifies their perception. It is thus through criticism, through the talk which it has provoked, the opinions it has elicited, that a work of art achieves continuing validity, becomes a classic.

Indeed, one of the principal social functions of criticism—and one of immense significance for the identity, the self-perception of whole civilizations—is, it seems to me, the institutionalization of the relatively restricted number of literary works which constitute the canonical books of a culture and thus decisively determine its character and ethos. The works concerned are simply those around which the greatest volume of critical opinion, the most powerful critical consensus has accumulated. These are the relatively few works of literature (poems, plays, novels) which have entered into the educational process of the culture, a knowledge of which—at least among the opinion-forming elite—is taken for granted. The emergence of such a canon of books is an objective and verifiable fact. But it too is not an absolute, for the canon itself is in constant flux, with new works being added from year to year, others being superseded and dropping away.

Be that as it may, the importance of this process, and of literature itself, for the society concerned is manifest: ideas, values, attitudes will to a very considerable extent be determined by the texts that form the backbone of the educational system of a civilization. But it is the critical process which produces this canon. If the poets are the unacknowledged legislators of the world, the critics are the electoral college that puts them into power.

The crystallization of collective experience is one of the valuable end-products of the dialectical process of discourse about the arts; another equally important one at the other end of the spectrum is the formation and enrichment of individual sensitivities. If the arts in general, and literature in particular, are concerned with communicating the intellectual and emotional experience of outstanding individuals, and doing so with the maximum degree of skill, the maximum degree of (subjective) *truth*, clearly an exposure to the arts and to literature will contribute to enlarging the capacity, on the part of the individual exposed to the artifacts in question, to experience life, to profit from the experience of other individuals before him. It is through discourse about these artifacts, through exchanging opinions about them, having them discussed, analyzed, and explained that each individual can train and develop his own sensibilities, increase his discernment in perceiving the finer points of skill involved in their creation and school his capacity for emotional experience through empathy and imaginative involvement, and enlarge the scope of his intellectual capacity through the insights to be derived from the more complex and subtle forms of human communication.

Criticism provides the *techniques* for such discourse and the multiplicity of views and viewpoints that constitute that discourse itself. Moreover it helps, through such discourse, to school, guide, and stimulate the creative individuals who are destined to contribute further artifacts to form the basis of further continuing discourse. This latter constitutes a third major function of criticism: the dialogue between the communicator and the recipient of the communication. The artist who works solely for his own satisfaction is, on the whole, a pious myth. The artist who claims that he creates merely for his own closet is merely too timid or insecure to risk the communication he has worked for. Most artists are hungry for reaction. Hence reaction is of immense importance to the artist, in whatever field he may be active. It is the critic who articulates this reaction. He allows the artist to gauge the extent to which he has actually succeeded in communicating what he intended to convey (which, however, may not be the message valued most in the long run and by later generations; but for the artist, here and now, the possibility of learning how well he succeeded in his intention becomes a vital ingredient in his next effort). Even uncomprehending or insensitive criticism is thus of value to the artist: at least he knows where he failed to make an impact and on what kinds of individuals. He may dismiss those who did not respond as stupid or insensitive and concentrate on "the happy few" as Stendhal did; in any case his mind will have been clarified, his intentions consolidated.

Art as well as literature deals in subjective truths; so does criticism. Literary criticism differs from other forms of criticism in that it uses the same medium as the artifacts about which it indulges in discourse. Criticism of painting is discourse about painting; literary criticism is discourse about discourse and is thus itself a branch of literature. It cannot be a science, but it certainly should be art. One of the most detrimental consequences of the idea that literary criticism could be made into an exact science is the concomitant assumption that it can be as badly and insensitively written as some scientific treatises, that it need not be beautiful as long as it is true. But can it contain true appreciation of matters requiring sensitivity and taste and the ability to respond to complex and sensitive discourse if it displays its own lack of sensitivity and its inability to perceive the subtleties of discourse? Can we trust an unmusical listener's opinion about music?

Ill-written literary criticism thus contains its own corrective, eliminates itself. It is, after all, precisely the fusion of form and content, the fact that *how* something is said deeply affects and determines the nature of *what* is said, which distinguishes literature from other forms of verbal communication. (Here we are back where we began, for in defining criticism as discourse about literature, I avoided a definition of literature. Well, here we are close to one aspect of such a definition, one view to be thrown into the dialectical process which will endlessly revolve around that question.) The form of an utterance has much to communicate about the mind from which it proceeds, its motivations, its perceptiveness, its emotional intensity. It may be true that to be a good critic of drama or of the novel one need not be a dramatist or novelist (although practical experience in those fields certainly is not without value), for there is a different talent involved in talking about one's perception of an object from that required to create such an object. But in the case of criticism what is involved is precisely the talent to talk about an object, a talent which produces an object which is discourse about an object. How can we respect the sensitivity of the perceiver if the way he expresses his experience displays insensitivity?

Criticism thus appears as a self-correcting activity: unacceptable performance eliminates itself by displaying its unacceptability to the perceiver. But, of course, that again is not a matter of objective, but merely one of subjective truth. In other words, what *I* regard as badly written, insensitively organized, "unmusical" critical writing loses all credibility in *my* eyes. Yet in expressing my opinion about it, in rejecting it, I am still keeping it within the critical process, the dialectics of the discourse which results, precisely, from the clash of such subjective perceptions, and which constitutes the continuing process of literary criticism.

4

Criticism as Communication

Criticism and Its Institutional Situations

Herbert Lindenberger

1

The question posed by the title of this volume is open enough to entice a range of responses. Those with a cherished method or ideology to propagate can readily translate the question to mean "What should criticism be?"; and if they wish to bolster their arguments with historical precedents, they can give the question either a conservative or a radical twist. The conservative might inquire, "What has great criticism been in the past and what, in view of its recent lapses, can we do to restore it to its rightful and traditional place?"; whereas the radical might ask, "Why has the criticism of the past, with its outmoded conception of the role of the critic, of interpretation, of the very nature of literature, proved inadequate for us today?"

On the other hand, one can attempt an approach more descriptive than prescriptive in intent. Fully aware though I am that one's ideological commitments reveal themselves in even

I wish to acknowledge my gratitude to the members of my 1979 NEH Summer Seminar, "Major Modern Critical Texts," whose lively discussions helped me immensely in the preparation of this paper.

the most nonprescriptive modes of inquiry, I have opted for an approach that keeps my own commitments relatively hidden from view. Therefore, instead of interpreting the copula of the title to mean "should be," I shall translate it into functional terms: "What is the function of criticism?" But if one remembers Arnold's and Eliot's essays entitled the "Function of Criticism," one recognizes that the singular all too easily invites the critic to prescribe what he takes to be the proper function of criticism at the present time. In hopes of avoiding any such pronouncements, I shall shift to the plural and ask simply, "What functions can we discern among those utterances we label literary criticism?" How, for instance—if I may anticipate some later stages of my argument—is a critical utterance a response to the way the critic's role is defined in a particular social milieu or national tradition? How does the style in which a statement is expressed itself make a statement? How do critical statements achieve the authority they need to be taken seriously by their readers?

Rather than confront these questions head-on, I shall start by examining three short passages from well-known critical essays of this century. The statements come from different critical traditions—different languages, in fact. They are also spaced at least two decades apart. About the only thing they unmistakably have in common is that they purport to comment on a few lines from famous literary works. They could all, in short, qualify for a place in an anthology of literary criticism.

My first example comes from Viktor Shklovsky's essay on *Tristram Shandy*, specifically his comments on the narrator's statement of "having got, as you perceive, almost into the middle of my fourth volume—and no farther than to my first day's life." Shklovsky writes:

> But when you begin to examine the structure of the book, you see first of all that the disorder is intentional, that the work possesses its own poetics. There is a kind of order in it, as in a picture by Picasso. Everything in the book is displaced, everything is transposed. The dedication occurs on page 25, contrary

> to the three basic requirements of content, form, and place. Nor is the Preface in its usual position.[1]

Without a knowledge of Shklovsky and his circle, the reader might take these lines and most of the essay from which they are drawn simply as a description of the narrative techniques present in Sterne's novel—what, within the Anglo-American tradition, we are accustomed to call "practical criticism." Yet the essay's opening line clearly warns us that despite the detailed analysis that follows, Shklovsky is using the novel to build a larger theory of fiction: "In this essay I do not propose to analyze Sterne's novel, but only to use it as an illustration of the general laws of plot."[2] If we note the reference to Picasso, we become aware of a deliberate analogy between *Shandy* and the work of a modern painter who, at the time the essay was written (1921), was still a controversial figure. Shklovsky has chosen to analyze a classical novel in order not simply to devise a theory of narrative, but also to provide a defense of modernism. If we look beyond the words of the passage, we learn that Shklovsky and his group were closely allied with the Russian Futurists, that the "disorder" he locates in the classical text under analysis is, in effect, analogous to the disorder that contemporary readers perceived in such writers as Mayakovsky and Khlebnikov. The intentions guiding Shklovsky's essay can be defined not only by those kinds of writing it attempts to defend, but also by those against which it sets itself in opposition. One can cite at least three types of critical discourse for which Shklovsky, with his stress on the formal properties of a text, provides an alternative model: first, the positivistic literary history dominant at the time in Russian universities; second, the impressionistic style of the Russian Symbolist poets and critics whom the Futurists were trying to displace; and third, the antiformal social bias that has remained a central strain in Russian criticism from Belinsky through Soviet aesthetic policy. Finally, one can infer still another bias behind Shklovsky's essay: in analyzing narrative displacements to discover the "general laws of plot," he utilizes the complexities of a long narrative somewhat as a linguist would utilize his analysis of a sentence to make generalizations about the nature of language.

My second example, from Robert Penn Warren's "Pure and Impure Poetry," comments on several lines spoken by Mercutio in *Romeo and Juliet:*

> 'twould anger him
> To raise a spirit in his mistress's circle
> Of some strange nature, letting it there stand
> Till she had laid it and conjured it down.
>
> Mercutio has made a joke, a bawdy joke. That is bad enough, but worse, he has made his joke witty, and worst of all, intellectually complicated in its form. Realism, wit, intellectual complication—these are the enemies of the garden purity.[3]

The "garden purity" Warren evokes with obvious disdain refers to two short love lyrics, one by Shelley, the other by Tennyson, which he had analyzed in a strongly deprecating way earlier in his essay. The passage from Shakespeare exemplifies what he calls "impure" poetry against the "pure" poetry toward which the nineteenth century strove. Writing in the early 1940s, Warren thus addresses himself to readers who have not yet abandoned their inherited taste for romantic poetry. "That is bad enough," he says and mimics that conservative critical stance which would refuse a place for bawdiness within poetic language. Yet our recognition of his mimicry works to draw us into complicity with him against those who force us to assent unthinkingly to Victorian values. Warren assumes the rhetorical stance of the public critic, a stance that has been a part of Anglo-American criticism since Dryden; his role is both that of arbiter of taste and propagator of moral values, which are here defined by the phrase "realism, wit, intellectual complication"—words that straddle the ethical and the stylistic realms of discourse. These values are of course those inherent in the poetry of Warren and his friends and, indeed, in the whole strain of post-Symbolist poetry that descends from T. S. Eliot. The modernism that Warren's essay defends, with its stress on intellectual complexity, has decidedly different emphases from the "disorder" that Shklovsky celebrates: there are of course multiple modernisms, and a wide gulf separates Fugitives from Futurists. Yet like Shklovsky's essay, Warren's implicitly attacks rival modes of critical writing—in Warren's case both the standard academic literary history that unreflectively accepted an outmoded notion of the English literary canon and an impressionist mode that not only shared this same outmoded notion but also cultivated a prose style imitative of the pure poetry it was advocating.

My last example comes from Jacques Derrida's commentary on Rousseau's admission of his masturbatory habits. Citing a passage from the *Confessions* on Rousseau's terror at meeting a fellow masturbator ("The recollection of this incident cured me of it [this vice] for a long time"), Derrida comments:

> For a long time? Rousseau will never stop having recourse to, and accusing himself of, this onanism that permits one to be himself affected by providing himself with presences, by summoning absent beauties. In his eyes it will remain the model of vice and perversion. Affecting oneself by another presence, one *corrupts* oneself [makes oneself other] by oneself [*on s'altère soi-même*].[4]

The skeptical, sarcastic tone of the question with which Derrida's comments begin ("Pour longtemps?") reveals a far different attitude toward the text under consideration than the two earlier examples I cited. Unlike Shklovsky he does not treat the text as an object merely to be described or analyzed; and unlike Warren, he does not approach the text as something primarily to be judged. Rather, he engages actively and openly with it: his own various terms for this engagement—*decomposing, decentering, deconstructing*—have in fact become part of the common critical parlance. By establishing a dialogue (of an often violent sort) with Rousseau, Derrida signals the reader that his own utterance occupies a status not different in kind from the text it purports to discuss. If Shklovsky speaks as an analyst of form and Warren as a moralist and arbiter of taste, Derrida presents himself as a philosopher, the last, as his work implies, in a line (within which Rousseau provides a crucial instance) that extends back to

Plato. In his verbal complexity, above all his wordplay, he separates himself decisively from the straightforwardness and lucidity of presentation traditional to academic writing in pre-1968 France, and at the same time he advertises his link with the German philosophical tradition. The translator's need to supply two meanings for "on s'altère soi-même" is symptomatic of the punning characteristic within this tradition and, as with Hegel, Nietzsche, and Heidegger, it is predictable that one side of the pun (in this instance the notion of corrupting) is of a distinctly materialistic or negative nature. One discerns something provocative in Derrida's stress on an activity such as masturbation to illustrate his own major philosophical theme, namely the attempts of great thinkers of the past to delude themselves with false presences (Warren's exposure of Shakespearean bawdiness seems tame by comparison). In its provocativeness and in its attempt to undermine past systems of thought the passage is of a piece with the kind of writing—for example the open-ended structures of Sollers and Borges—admired by Derrida and the *Tel Quel* group of the 1960s.

2

I have deliberately chosen three critical texts that vary sharply in the role they assign the critic (not to speak of the author or reader), in the types of writing they implicitly defend, and in the earlier critical modes they reject or with which they identify. Any common denominator one might think up to describe features within all three texts would, I suspect, sound too banal to be useful. Difficult though it may be to discover significant features they hold in common, one can at least subject the institutional situations out of which they arose to a common method of description. I shall not attempt a systematic institutional analysis as a contemporary sociologist might do,[5] though I believe that literary criticism since the Enlightenment would lend itself to this type of inquiry. Nor do I use the work *institutional* in quite the same way as Frank Kermode, who, in his recent book *The Genesis of Secrecy*, explores the process whereby new ideas and modes of mental operation become accommodated to (or rejected by) the intellectual community.[6]

My emphasis, unlike Kermode's, is not so much on the process by which critical utterances move toward acceptability, but on the interactions between a critic (whether dissident or orthodox) and his surrounding contexts. Thus, I see the rhetorical style of the three passages above as intimately related to each critic's response to a particular institutional situation—his alignments and feuds with other critics and writers, his consciousness of the rhetorical stance with which he can persuade or provoke (sometimes both at once), the particular public whose attention and loyalty he craves. Every critical statement can be described as a response to certain pressures and demands the critic feels obliged to meet. The critic working within an already sanctified academic framework strives to meet what he deems "professional standards"—often without realizing that these are subject to change with a minimum of notice. Even the scholar whose colleagues recognize him as hopelessly out of date can be responsive to real pressures and demands, though these are often simply the biases and methods implanted in his conscience by his teachers many years before.

The institutional framework surrounding critical utterances is often most readily discernible among those groups which, at any given moment, we dub the avant-garde; through the rhetorical extravagance with which they attempt to alter our perceptions of authors, works, and of what constitutes literature itself, the complicated alignments of friends and enemies are laid bare for anybody interested in the sociology of literary study. In America today, at a time when the critical voices of the European avant-garde are sounded everywhere, those who seek to defend earlier critical modes have adopted a polemic that sometimes emulates avant-garde extravagance. A recent book tellingly entitled *The Failure of Criticism* uses the words *sacred, redemptive,* and *life-enhancing* as alternatives to the values the author sees emanating from the ideology of modernism.[7] At times of considerable critical ferment such as the present, the polemical satisfactions enjoyed by those who brand their enemies as out of date are easily matched by those who label incoming movements as "modish," "trendy," or whatever the most fashionable terms for the fashionable are at a given historical moment.

It would be comforting to think that at least certain activities within that large domain constituting literary study would remain immune to the pressures of changing institutional situations. Certainly the preparation of a critical edition would seem to be one of these activities. Yet if one observes how major writers have been served by successive editors, one notes that both the scholarly commentary and the editorial principles guiding the presentations of the texts themselves can be linked to particular historical frameworks. For example, the pioneering Hellingrath edition of Hölderlin, initiated before the First World War, embodies the ideology of the Stefan George circle, to which Hölderlin owes his revival and to which Hellingrath belonged; typographically the poems have the bold and simple appearance of George's own poems, while the commentary is suffused with the locutions characteristic of the George group.[8] The Stuttgart Hölderlin edition, completed after the Second World War, shows a distinctly nationalist bias (the late hymns are grouped under the title "Die vaterländischen Gesänge"), and the strict division of final versions from earlier drafts and fragments reveals that conception of the individual poem as an autonomous entity which prevailed at the time. The current Frankfurt Hölderlin edition reflects the leftist bias dominant among German scholars in the late 1960s and 1970s; not only does it highlight Hölderlin's sympathies with the French Revolution, but through its presentation of early and later drafts in the order of composition it suggests a notion of poetry as process, characteristic of our own time.[9]

To cite an example from a different national tradition, the De Selincourt-Darbishire edition of Wordsworth, a product of the 1930s and 1940s, is governed by editorial principles quite antithetical to those of the new Cornell Wordsworth. The former edition privileges the final versions of Wordsworth's poems, a procedure quite in keeping with the editors' Victorian tastes and their unquestioning belief in an author's stated intentions. The new edition, by contrast, privileges the early versions of the poems, in most instances publishing these versions in full for the first time. These early versions, less formal and less consciously "poetic" than the final ones, are more in tune than the latter with such values of contemporary poetry as directness of perception and plain language, while the editorial disregard for the agèd Wordsworth's intentions consorts well with the suspicion in which we hold authorial authority these days.[10]

Since our critical predications often need to sound like eternal truths to assure a receptive response, it is rare for a critic to admit to the institutional contingencies that surround his statements. In his 1962 preface to *Theory of the Novel,* Georg Lukács carefully places his work in a set of diverse contexts that include the philosophical, political and literary—the neo-Hegelianism emerging in the years preceding the First World War, the depressing political atmosphere of the war years, during which he wrote the book, and the literary time-consciousness of a novelist such as Proust, whose work Lukács did not yet know while he was writing his treatise.[11] Since Lukács, by the time of his preface, was nearly a half century and several political turnings removed from his early masterpiece, examining it in perspective was probably a relatively painless, perhaps even an exhilarating task. By contrast, Erich Auerbach is exceptional among critics for explaining some of the circumstances surrounding his major work within the book itself. In the final chapter and epilogue of *Mimesis* he describes his isolation during the Second World War in Istanbul, where the lack of library facilities forced him to rely on primary texts and where he had ample opportunity to contemplate the disintegration of traditional European culture. Moreover, he makes an explicit connection between his own critical method, which relies on the suggestive power of short literary passages, and the method of a modernist writer such as Virginia Woolf, who, in the text he has himself just examined, invested a simple incident such as Mrs. Ramsay's knitting a brown stocking with the most considerable significance.[12]

Once a critic becomes sufficiently established to command a

public and occupy a definable place within the intellectual spectrum, the image that he and his readers carry of his own career becomes an integral part of his institutional situation. The vicissitudes that mark such careers are especially evident in certain documents that might be called the critic's last will and testament, a genre including such otherwise diverse texts as Yvor Winters's *The Function of Criticism,* Murray Krieger's *Theory of Criticism* and Wayne Booth's *Critical Understanding.*[13] (Of course critics ordinarily do not stop writing, but live on to add a goodly number of codicils, of which this very volume doubtless contains some examples.) The books within this genre customarily restate and redefine the critic's earlier arguments in the face of new movements that threaten to render these arguments obsolete; the self-consciousness of the genre is reflected by one such recent volume containing thirty-six footnote references to, as well as several lengthy quotations from, the critic's own preceding writings.

Whereas critics often refer to their earlier work to defend the legitimacy of positions they see under attack, new and controversial critical movements utilize prestigious critics of the past to confer legitimacy on their own endeavors. The Russian Formalists, who demonstrated the usefulness of linguistics for literary analysis more than sixty years ago, have achieved an almost mythical status for critics of the last two decades. It is significant, however, that during the 1960s the Formalists were invoked in distinctly different ways by French Structuralists and German practitioners of *Rezeptionsästhetik.* Whereas the French used the Formalists primarily for the analysis of narrative structure and transformations, the Germans, interested as they were in reader expectations and the history of reception, stressed the notion of literary evolution that came down from Tynjanov through the Prague Circle. Whenever an earlier critical system is exploited by later critics, they quite naturally choose only what they deem appropriate to their own institutional situations. Yet one cannot overestimate the need that critics have always felt for legitimizing precedents. However much the Italian sixteenth-century theorists twisted Aristotle to suit their own purposes, the authority he conferred made their own authority possible. In more recent times we have characteristically invoked Kant to back up any arguments we might make about the autonomy of the aesthetic sphere; or Coleridge when we want to defend poetry as an active form of knowledge; or Heidegger when we need to cite a Continental model for criticism as a form of imaginative writing. The fashion prevailing at any given time dictates one's choice of precedents. Among the examples I used earlier, Shklovsky, especially his concept of defamiliarization, has been cited in recent years by a multitude of critics representing many persuasions. By the same token, contemporary critics are not likely to cite Warren or any of his colleagues from the now quite unfashionable New Criticism. Derrida, I might add, is still so controversial that he is cited variously as a liberator or as a diabolical force.

Contemporaneous critical movements based on what seem essentially similar principles assume quite distinctive forms within different national settings. For instance, the American New Criticism has often been compared with that phase of German criticism called the *werkimmanent* or intrinsic method that flourished during the 1950s. Certainly both critical movements share some common assumptions, above all a respect for the autonomy of the individual work and a belief in the value of close reading. Yet anybody reading a typical Anglo-American or German essay of the period might well be more aware of differences than similarities, for the two movements developed within quite different institutional situations. The German essay, for instance, is likely not to stress irony or intellectual complication, for the poetic model that German critics of the time followed was lyric poetry of the age of Goethe and not the metaphysical lyric that stands behind the New Criticism. Moreover, the German essay usually establishes explicit links between the poem under analysis with a standard period concept drawn from *Geistesgeschichte,* which maintained a hold on German scholarship to a degree that no earlier American academic method did on the New Criticism. Any German close reading of the time is also likely to seem more exhaustive and detailed than an American one, for German academic style, emanating from a system in which scholarship occupies a place distinct from the world where literary works are made and reviewed, is more rigorous and treatiselike than the essayistic style of the Americans, who could evoke the casualness of tone cultivated by the poet-critics who created the New Criticism.[14]

As I indicated while commenting on the three passages at the start of this essay, the stylistic garb with which a critical essay presents itself to the world is intrinsic to the message it is conveying to its readers. The rigor and exhaustiveness of German formalistic essays of the 1950s implicitly suggest an attitude toward the role of the critic and the nature of literature different from the more personal manner and the frequently moralistic coloring of Anglo-American criticism at the time. The hortatory, often apocalyptic tone of the famous avant-garde manifestos of our century suggests that the critic (usually assuming a dual role of poet and critic) can remake literature and, as often as not, remake the world. At an opposite extreme, the scientific discourse of the Soviet semioticians, exemplified by the formula Fm (CVemp) $\supset$ Fn (CVemp) to be found in Toporov's essay on Suetonius's use of omens,[15] not only reveals the linguistic and mathematical background of members of the group, but is doubtless also a subterfuge for the pursuit of formalist research within a culture that demands a traditional Marxist approach among those who set up shop as literary scholars.

As institutional situations change, so do the particular critical issues that consume much of the verbal energy of those caught within these situations. The issue about how to define boundaries between standard language and poetic language was central for the Russian Formalists and Prague Structuralists as well as for I. A. Richards and the New Critics. It is no longer a vital or interesting issue (like many today I used words as *vital* and *interesting* to replace what scholars at a more confident time would have called *right* and *appropriate).* The contemporary debate as to whether critical discourse is a type of art seems to me a quite different issue, one closely related to that other debate in recent American criticism as to whether or not interpretation can lay claim to truth value. Issues, of course, are never settled, despite the considerable argumentative prowess of many who debate them; it would be more accurate to say they are replaced by new issues that rise out of changing institutional situations. If I may choose a Russian Formalist precedent to lend authority to my own remarks, let me say that critical issues inevitably wear themselves out after a point, that they create an automatization of response among those who have had sufficient exposure to the terms in which the issues are presented. To cite a personal example, I confess I have become tired in recent months of hearing how readers rather than writers produce texts. Indeed, I recognize I am even beginning to tire of the word *text.* Since this word does not commit me to determine the artistic status of a work, I have found it a convenient means of bypassing a contemporary issue I do not care to confront. For later readers who pass this way, I suspect that the frequency with which the word appears may help define the institutional situation surrounding my contribution to this volume.

NOTES

1. *Russian Formalist Criticism: Four Essays,* trans. and ed. Lee T. Lemon and Marion J. Reis (Lincoln: University of Nebraska Press, 1965), p. 28. The translation has been emended by my colleague Edward J. Brown.
2. Ibid., p. 27.
3. "Pure and Impure Poetry," *Kenyon Review* 5 (1943): 231. The essay was originally delivered as a lecture at Princeton in 1942.
4. *Of Grammatology,* trans. Gayatri Chakravorty Spivak (Baltimore: Johns Hopkins University Press, 1976), p. 153. The original version was published in 1967.
5. See, for instance, Niklas Luhmann's application of institutional theory to the study, respectively, of legal proceedings and of religion, *Legitimation durch Verfahren* (Neuwied: Luchterhand, 1969) and *Funktion der Religion* (Frankfurt: Suhrkamp, 1977). For an application to literary study, see Wilhelm Vosskamp, "Gattungen als literarisch-

soziale Institutionen," in *Textsortenlehre-Gattungsgeschichte*, ed. Walter Hinck (Heidelberg: Quelle und Meyer, 1977), pp. 27–44.

6. *The Genesis of Secrecy: On the Interpretation of Narrative* (Cambridge: Harvard University Press, 1979). See also his article, "Institutional Control of Interpretation," *Salmagundi*, no. 43 (Winter, 1979): 72–86.

7. Eugene Goodheart, *The Failure of Criticism* (Cambridge: Harvard University Press, 1978), p. 151.

8. Note these phrases describing "Der blinde Sänger": ". . . ganz reif und ausgetragen, ganz abgelöst von der Person, ganz abgelöst vom Schmerz des Erlebnisses, ganz Kunstwerk geworden" in Hölderlin, *Sämtliche Werke*, ed. Norbert V. Hellingrath et al., 6 vols. (Berlin: Propyläen-Verlag, 1922–23), 4 (2nd ed., 1923): 297.

9. Some crucial differences between the Stuttgart and Frankfurt editions are evident in the treatment of lines 79–80 of "Heimkunft." The new edition presents Hölderlin's last version of these lines as "Blutlos. Aber der Schaz, der unter des heiligen Friedens / Bogen lieget," with the editorial commentary centering on an earlier Hölderlin letter expressing his hope for a peaceful form of revolution in Germany. See *Sämtliche Werke*, ed. D. E. Sattler et al., 4 vols. to date (Frankfurt: Verlag Roter Stern, 1975–), 6:314–15, 319. The Stuttgart edition presents the final version of these lines as "Aber das Beste, der Fund, der unter des heiligen Friedens / Bogen lieget," and includes the word "Blutlos" only among the variants, while the commentary centers on the literary and Biblical allusions behind the rainbow image and presents the Napoleonic Peace of Lunéville and not the Revolution as the appropriate historical background for these lines. See *Sämtliche Werke*, ed. Friedrich Beissner, 5 vols. (Stuttgart: Kohlhammer, 1946–52), II, i, 98 and II, ii, 624, 630.

10. For a more detailed description of the differences between the two editions, see my review-article of the *Home at Grasmere* volume of the Cornell Wordsworth, *Studies in Romanticism* 18, No. 2 (Summer 1979): 303–11.

11. *Theory of the Novel*, trans. Anna Bostock (Cambridge: MIT Press, 1971), pp. 11–23.

12. *Mimesis*, trans. Willard R. Trask (Princeton: Princeton University Press, 1953), pp. 548–57. For a more explicit retrospect written several years after the original publication of the book, see Auerbach's "Epilegomena zu Mimesis," *Romanische Forschungen* 65 (1953): 1–18.

13. *The Function of Criticism* (Denver: Alan Swallow, 1957), esp. pp. 9–78; *Theory of Criticism* (Baltimore: Johns Hopkins University Press, 1976); *Critical Understanding* (Chicago: University of Chicago Press, 1979).

14. The differences between American and German New Criticism

are manifest in such typical anthologies of the time as Ray B. West's *Essays in Modern Literary Criticism* (New York: Rinehart, 1952) and Benno von Wiese's *Die deutsche Lyrik: Form und Geschichte* (Düsseldorf: Bagel, 1957). The German tendency to tie historical constructs to formal analysis is evident in Wiese's subtitle.

15. V. N. Toporov, "The Semiotics of Prophecy in Suetonius," in *Soviet Semiotics*, ed. Daniel P. Lucid (Baltimore: Johns Hopkins University Press, 1977), p. 164.

On Feminist Criticism

Catharine R. Stimpson

My subject is not criticism, but a way of criticizing; not a complete series of acts, but an incomplete activity; not a corpus of work, but a corps of workers. It is "feminist criticism," a term that provokes surly suspicion, numb apathy, or passionate commitment. Feminist criticism is neither serene, nor monolithic. The needles of the compasses that its practitioners carry pivot and point in a number of directions.[1] Helping to prevent a nomadic anarchy is the fact that feminist critics share at least one tenet: they are subversive, even in revolt. I want now to describe some of that variety, and unity.

The origins of feminist criticism are scattered in the traces of the protests of women against the discrimination they have suffered in the domains of literacy and literature. After 1945, feminist criticism became a more systematic process, brought into being by such massive modernizing forces as the entrance of women, of all classes and races, into the public labor force and political processes; a partial secularization of society, which softened the power of traditional religions in the formation of identity and institutions; a greater belief in supplementary ideologies that praised equality and autonomy; and a democratization of education and culture that permitted women to participate in them more freely. Some may still think the linking of women and criticism, let alone feminism and criticism, oxymoronic, even moronic.[2] However, the figure of the New Woman—who takes pleasure in "intellectual talk," who expects to earn her own living, who studies for examinations—is far more familiar now than she was to the nineteenth century that generated her.[3] The New Woman is the feminist critic's immediate precursor and alter ego.

In part, feminism has been the political movement of, and for, the New Woman. Its growth since the 1960s has been, in actuality as well as name, inseparable from that of feminist criticism. Both are discontented with their civilization. Feminist critics can be activists as well. The movement has also encouraged women to behave as if each were a critic, capable of dissenting, dissecting, and becoming conscious of the strength of symbolic systems, ideologies, dogmas, and the casual text. A woman who might once have read a book rhetorically, be it a Hawthorne or a Harlequin romance, might now read it dialectically. She would be disturbed, not because the book questioned her assumptions, but because she was beginning to question its.[4] Feminism called for re-reading, re-writing, and "re-vision," a pun on "revision" and "re:vision." In addition, some theoreticians claimed, the most revolutionary politics had to do with statements and the state of language. In France, the group "Politique et psychanalyse" was convinced that

> . . . there can be no revolution without the disruption of the symbolic order—bourgeois language, the language of the old humanisms with their belief in a coherent subject—and that only by dislocating syntax, playing with the signifier, punning outrageously and constantly can the old language and the old order be subverted.[5]

Given such contexts, feminist criticism appeared outside of colleges and universities as well as within their more orthodox precincts. Original ideas and salient discourse emerged from artists, their model often Virginia Woolf; from rogue academics; and from small, independent groups. Within colleges and universities, the instability of the boundaries of criticism in general was helpful. As reading took on a new glamor; as authors became senders in a communicative act; as mythologies referred to soap-powders and detergents, not simply to the gods; as Marxist analysis in America became less taboo; and as manifestos called for a criticism that would be "more than the sanctioning of the existing order of cultural thought about art,"[6] the blasphemy of feminist criticism could not be in stubborn insistence upon change. It was, rather, in what might be changed, who might be changing, and why.

In the 1960s and early 1970s, a primary end of feminist criticism was endings: of men's cultural domination over women; of women's alienation from some of their cultural power, and powers. Feminist critics analyzed literary history, tradition, and custom as male prerogatives. They were hardly the first to sexualize letters. Linguistic yokings of the penis and the pen, of phallic discharges and the dissemination of the word, of the book and the maternal flesh, were the legacy to feminist critics, not their inventions. So was the appropriation of parturition as a metaphor for literary or artistic productivity.[7] However, feminist criticism saw such figures of speech, not as pretty rhetoric, not as male envy of female fecundity, but as signifiers of the assignment of cultural governance to men. The sense of women's marginality to culture was palpable. Absence and partial presence were not philosophical ideas, not fashionable analytic categories, but descriptions of female experience. Silence, invisibility, poverty, and enclosure were not just words, but markers and marks of the female condition.[8]

Feminist critics went on to add to their volatile compound of resentment, rage, history, and theory. They drew multiple overlays for Simone de Beauvoir's map, in *The Second Sex*, of the identities that men had imposed upon women through their mastery of language. Tainting such male fabrications, themselves acts of violence against existential ethics, were a false, flattering sentimentality and a genuine, disabling misogyny. Unsurprisingly, literary judgments about women writers reflected this misconduct. As two able editors of an anthology of feminist criticism wrote judiciously:

> The anger that our critics feel finds in their essays its proper target: not the literature itself but the misconceptions of past critics, the received evaluations about literature which, rooted in bias, have for too long passed for disinterested impartiality.[9]

Rarely, however, did the rejection of cultural deprivation and of much of what men had written about women lead to a rejection of the possibilities of culture and of writing. On the contrary, implicitly and explicitly, it embodied a longing for culture and for writing, a desire to take an active part in them. The grief of the feminist critic was that of a believer, not of the philistine.

Similarly hopeful, similarly moral, was her attitude toward other women. If they were "sometimes fearful, sometimes deadened," they were also "sometimes compassionate, original, vital, authentic, free."[10] If they had been sexually repressed and suppressed, the return of the repressed, after a stripping away of masks, would reveal joy, pleasure, vitality. If women had been driven mad, or diagnosed as mad, they were capable of lively sanity. If they had been silent, they could speak. If they wrote, they did not have to be "feminine," a signifier for the lyric, even the languid; for the frail, even the weak; for the unremarkable, even the dull. They could be cagy and radical, cunning and original, subtle and smart.

In great part, feminist criticism is without nostalgia. The received past and the canon might be cathartic. They might be liberating. More probably, they have also pressured women and their imaginations. However, the ideas about culture and about women that feminist critics have trusted have had their element of Utopianism. Feminist critics have construed the present as a path towards a more open, a richer, a humanly forged future. Many have gone on to ask how they might aid in that progressive process. They may find formalism a way of clarifying texts, but they believe that formalism without a larger goal is incomplete, perhaps even a form of passivity. They disagree less about whether or not criticism ought to join moral and political enterprises than about the specific nature of those enterprises.

Some speak of the worth of enhancing consciousness, of increasing the store of human dignity. Others ask forcefully for a literature and a criticism that help to alter inequitable arrangements between the sexes, between classes, and among races. Still others demand that critics link literature and women's liberation. One has written:

> Because of its origin in the women's liberation movement, feminist criticism values literature that is of some use to the movement. Prescriptive Criticism [*sic*], then, is best defined in terms of the ways in which literature can serve the cause of liberation. To earn feminist approval, literature must perform one or more of the following functions: (1) serve as a forum for women; (2) help to achieve cultural androgyny; (3) provide role-models; (4) promote sisterhood; and (5) augment consciousness-raising.[11]

The demand that criticism be a prescription puns on Socrates' comparison, in *The Phaedrus*, between medicine and rhetoric. If medicine examines the nature of the body, so rhetoric examines that of the soul, and then uses language and discipline to implant moral strength and skill. Still insufficiently examined is the possibility that prescriptions can breed iatrogenic illnesses, that cures can themselves infect, that laws might become a source of malfeasance. The androgyne, popular in the 1970s, was then quickly diagnosed as an illogical construct that was, ironically, apolitical. Predictably, the blending of criticism and politics was distrusted, and not simply because of feminist criticism's own understandable theoretical immaturities. Some thought it vulgar, trivial, socialized literature. Others assumed it would tyrannize reading and writing. Less from the power of such attacks, which were often sloppy, than from the arduous nature of the task, the full conjoining of feminist literary criticism and politics has yet to be done.

In the late 1960s, feminist critics also began self-consciously to fill an intellectual space that was apparently left between the corrosive skepticism of the cultural past and the laudable, if sometimes imprecise, wish to have culture nurture and transform the future. They started to excavate the terrain of a female cultural tradition whose creators were interesting because they were women, because they were productive, and because, like the feminist critics themselves, they were "concerned with assaulting *and* revising, deconstructing *and* reconstructing. . . . "[12] To chart that tradition, critics needed a certain semiological deftness. If women had been repressed, they must have consciously and unconsciously hidden some of their messages, particularly about sex and anger. The crypt of their lives and texts was, then, a province of cryptography. The critic also had to learn the spatial and psychic architecture of the domestic, which women had inhabited so pervasively. Taking on such jobs provoked a contagious enthusiasm. Two brilliant critics exuberantly used medical and mythic references to describe their project:

> Ideally, as Matthew Arnold knew, the criticism of literature should be the criticism of life. . . . For women . . . the rise of so-called "feminist" criticism has brought the ideal within the realm of the real, or at least the possible. . . . [W]omen's writing about literature by women has lately been marked by an exhilarated sense of the intense relevance of such work, a sense that here at last is a criticism whose function is creative as well as analytic, therapeutic as well as hermeneutic. . . . [T]he task of the feminist critic may be nothing less than the recreation of her own suppressed matrilineal genealogy, and thus the recovery of an entire lost female tradition, a tradition sunk like some aesthetic Atlantis beneath a flood of patriarchal exegeses.[13]

The restoration of the female and the doubting of the phallocentric have not been limited to feminist critics.[14] However, they have been the most diligent archaeologists and the most eloquent witnesses. Some of the work has been bibliographical and archival, the publishing and publicizing of older texts, forgotten authors. Some of it has been sociolinguistic, the describing of the speech patterns of women and men. Some of it has been historical, the scrupulous decipherment of cultural formations and of intertextualities. Some of it has been generic, the attempt to discern if special female conventions exist.[15]

Whatever the particular ambition in the general effort to bring women writers into a theoretical home, away from an imposed cultural exile, the subjective was appealing. As it has in other contemporary criticism, the "I" entered discourse and played upon the page. In the first paragraph alone of an introduction to an anthology (the form that concretely presents a reading of the female tradition), the editor used the first person singular five times.[16] Women's autobiographies, diaries, letters, and journals became favored genres. Though such attention was partly narcissistic, a self-involvement the more enjoyable because one's image was apparently newly reflected, it was also consistent with certain principles of feminist criticism. It valorized autonomy, the singular self that had so often been instructed to submit to a collective identity. It praised forms that had so often been held in contempt. It delighted in human details, in the recording of the everyday. For some, subjective writing was even a "female" response to "male" objectivity, that putative casting of a net of arid, abstract generalizations over the raw territories of life. As language became genderized, discourse split apart, dimorphically. A French writer, for example, said of her contemporaries:

> blank pages, gaps, borders, spaces and silence, holes in discourse: these women emphasize the aspect of feminine writing which is the most difficult to verbalize because it becomes compromised, rationalized, masculinized as it explains itself. . . .[17]

If inadvertently, Charlotte Brontë gave feminist critics a figure that might emblemize many of their theories, ambitions, and efforts. Indeed, women writers have often prefigured and shadowed feminist ideas. *Jane Eyre* tells of an abused girl who loves books. They are her escape, her fantasies, and a source of names that might validate experience. Jane happily reads *The History of British Birds*, *Pamela*, Goldsmith's *History of Rome*. A boy, John Reed, meant to inherit the books, takes them from her. A bully and a torment, he throws them at her and draws blood. Jane is then punished for John's violence. Her brain "in tumult," her heart "in insurrection," she resolves to escape from "insupportable oppression." Her circumstances force her to conceal consciously and suffocate unconsciously her rage, energy, and being. However, she is also tough, intelligent, morally alert. She has vision and fiber. She might become Bertha Mason, but she does not. She endures and triumphs. At the end, she is not only a reader and a listener, but a writer. She grasps language and gives her story to her reader, in the first person.

The rebellion against the masculinized hegemony of culture; the quest for a female subject, history, and texts, for the true picture of Charlotte Brontë and a Jane Eyre—these were necessarily, even proudly, entwined with an assessment of the difference between men and women. In America, that question was often secondary to the exploration of the differences among women themselves that race, class, and lesbianism had created, and to which feminist criticism had often been insufficiently sensitive.[18] Clearly, such multiple categories of difference reflected the politics of the 1960s and 1970s. Despite the seriousness of these concerns, the very logic of feminist criticism, its concern with the syllogisms of female and male, entailed the tricky, theoretical exploration of sexual difference.

Except in fun, no one will deny the existence of some sexual differences. Feminist critics disagree instead about cause, permanence, signs, and significance. Many Americans saw much of the difference as a matter of gender, a social construct; not of sex, a biological feature; the imposition of experience, not of ahistorical structures. Difference, then, was a tomb, a musty monument to temporal conditions. Such Americans were suspicious of psychoanalysis, which granted symbolic and regulatory power to the phallus and the ph/father. They used and queried structuralism, which had some formal aplomb but which violated their desire to raze, not raise, the primitive strength of a binary distinction between female and male. Their scholarship and theories were implicitly historical, the codification of complex efforts, the cause of which was to become largely obsolete.

Other Americans, and some French feminist critics, often

theoretically very sophisticated, considered such convictions superficial, even dangerous. They reasoned, though in disparate ways, that sexual difference revealed both experience and organizing, organized structures—of the body, the conscious mind, the unconscious, and of language. If women were at last to write *as women*, their texts would be an overwhelming, explosive revelation of the specialness and joy of the female subject. The unique qualities of the male subject, as *male* subject, might also be fully understood.[19] The difference between female and male need not be oppositional, though some have said it is. It need not be hierarchal, though many have behaved as if it is. It might simply be difference, which language would quicken into complete being. Indeed, as "écriture féminine" overthrew "littérature féminine," perhaps only language could do so. In 1975, the French novelist Christiane Rochefort, sardonic and caring, said:

> Has literature a sex? With dignity, I, and most of my sisters, we would answer: No.
>
> But. But. But, do we have the same experience? Do we have the same mental structures? The same obsessions? Death, for instance, is a specifically male obsession. As well as essential solitude.
>
> After all we don't belong to the same civilization.[20]

Feminist criticism began as a disruptive attack against cultures that had often cast women as the angelic upholders of the civilized or as monsters and breeders beyond its bounds. It has moved on towards more celebratory assertions. The rejection of the past has not decreed the denial of language's vibrancy or literature's vitality. Feminist criticism is unfinished, at once volatile and generative. Though language is now a dominant intellectual concern, many despair of it. Though texts have become a popular metaphor for human activity, many lament their disenthronement. Against such grief, feminist criticism renews, even in the passion of its rupture from the past, the energy of the word, the beauty and zeal of the voice.

NOTES

1. The metaphor of the compass alludes to Paul Hernadi, "Literary Theory: A Compass for Critics," *Critical Inquiry* 3, no. 2 (Winter 1976): 369–86. The present brief essay necessarily simplifies my subject and fails to refer to important books, articles, and critics. For some more comment, see my essay, "Ad/d Feminam: Women, Literature, and Society," in *Literature and Society: Selected Papers from the English Institute, 1978*, New Series, No. 3, edited, with a preface, by Edward W. Said (Baltimore: The Johns Hopkins University Press, 1980).

2. A beginning of a study of the contradictions between our received notions of women and of criticism is Susan Sniader Lanswer and Evelyn Torton Beck, "[Why] Are There No Great Women Critics? And What Difference Does It Make?", in *The Prism of Sex: Essays in the Sociology of Knowledge*, ed. Julia A. Sherman and Evelyn Torton Beck (Madison: University of Wisconsin Press, 1979), pp. 79–91.

3. I am quoting and paraphrasing George Gissing's 1893 description of his character Rhoda Nunn in *The Odd Woman* (New York: W.W. Norton and Co., Norton Library, 1971), p. 3.

4. Obviously, these terms are adapted from Stanley E. Fish, *Self-Consuming Artifacts: The Experience of Seventeenth-Century Literature* (Berkeley: University of California Press, 1972).

5. "Introduction III," *New French Feminisms: An Anthology*, edited and with introductions by Elaine Marks and Isabelle deCourtivron (Amherst: University of Massachusetts Press, 1979), pp. 32–33. The book is a superb introduction to the account of contemporary French feminist theory.

6. Donald B. Kuspit, "The Necessary Dialectical Critic," *Art Criticism* 1, no. 1 (Spring 1979): 15.

7. A witty, insufficiently recognized anatomy of these terms is Mary Ellmann, *Thinking About Women* (New York: Harcourt Brace Jovanovich, 1968).

8. Perhaps the most influential early statement on silence was Tillie Olsen's "Silences in Literature," given as a talk in 1962, published in 1965, and then republished in *Silences* (New York: Delacort Press/Seymour Lawrence, 1978), pp. 5–21.

9. Arlyn Diamond and Lee R. Edwards, "Foreword," *The Authority of Experience: Essays in Feminist Criticism* (Amherst: University of Massachusetts Press, 1977), p. xii.

10. I have taken the words, somewhat out of context, from Joan Goulianos, "Introduction," *By a Woman Writt: Literature from Six Centuries by and about Women* (Baltimore: Penguin Books, 1974, first published 1973), p. xix.

11. Cheri Register, "American Feminist Literary Criticism: A Bibli-

ographical Introduction," in *Feminist Literary Criticism: Explorations in Theory*, ed. Josephine Donovan (Lexington: University of Kentucky Press, 1975), pp. 18–19. Register's essay also ably surveys the state-of-the-art of feminist criticism in the early 1970s. *Signs: Journal of Women in Culture and Society*, which the University of Chicago Press publishes as a quarterly and which I edit, offers periodic reviews of feminist criticism and of the new scholarship about women in literature. See Elaine Showalter, "Review Essay: Literary Criticism," *Signs* 1, no. 2 (Winter 1975): 435–460; Annette Kolodny, "Review Essay: Literary Criticism," *Signs* 2, no. 2 (Winter 1976); 404–21; Sydney Janet Kaplan, "Review Essay: Literary Criticism," *Signs* 4, no. 3 (Spring 1979): 514–27.

12. Sandra M. Gilbert and Susan Gubar, *The Madwoman in the Attic* (New Haven: Yale University Press, 1979), p. 76.

13. Sandra Gilbert and Susan Gubar, "Review Essay: A Revisionary Company," *Novel: A Forum on Fiction* 10, no. 2 (Winter 1977): 158.

14. See, for example, Gayatri Chakravorty Spivak on Derrida's hymeneal fable in "Translator's Preface," Jacques Derrida, *Of Grammatology* (Baltimore: The Johns Hopkins University Press, 1976), p. lxvi.

15. The Feminist Press has reprinted several important texts. Among the best historical works are Ellen Moers, *Literary Women: The Great Writers* (Garden City, New York: Doubleday and Co., 1976), and Elaine Showalter, *A Literature of Their Own* (Princeton: Princeton University Press, 1977). Moers had been publishing articles about the scope, power, and anger of nineteenth-century women writers since the early 1960s. Unlike Moers, but like Emily Stripes Watts, *The Poetry of American Women from 1632 to 1945* (Austin: University of Texas Press, 1977), Showalter places the "great figures" in a context that includes the "lesser figures" as well. This is as much an attempt to show the common features of a synchronic women's tradition, with its diachronic movement, as a repudiation of the ranking of reputations, a hierarchy (or "higher-wocky" as a child once spelled it) of talent. For a sample of an attempt to isolate generic features, see the deliberately tentative Annette Kolodny essay, "Some Notes on Defining a 'Feminist Literary Criticism,'" *Critical Inquiry* 2, no. 1 (Autumn 1975): 75–92, and the responses that followed in *Critical Inquiry* 2, no. 4 (Summer 1976): 807–32.

16. Goulianos, p. xiii.

17. Xavière Gauthier, "Is There Such a Thing as Women's Writing?," trans. Marilyn A. August, in *New French Feminisms*, p. 164.

18. A symbolic debate has arisen over Charlotte Brontë's novel *Shirley* and over her ability to recognize class as well as sex issues. The most recent contribution is Helen Taylor, "Class and Gender in Charlotte Brontë's *Shirley*," *Feminist Review* 1 (1979); 83–93. See, too, Carol

Ohmann, "Historical Reality and 'Divine Appointment' in Charlotte Brontë's Fiction,"*Signs* 2, no. 4 (Summer 1977); 757–78.

19. In "The Masculine Mode," *Critical Inquiry* 5, no. 4 (Summer 1979), 621–33, Peter Schwenger suggests that a uniquely male writing focuses on the body, particularly on the penis, and seeks to express itself, paradoxically, in silence.

20. Christiane Rochefort, "Are Women Writers Still Monsters?," in *New French Feminisms*, p. 186.

Criticism as Transaction

Norman N. Holland

Who needs it? Criticism would seem to have little, if anything, to do with the way real people really enjoy books, although, obviously, it has a great deal to do with the way professors write about literature and with the things professors ask of advanced students who have the good (or bad) fortune to see works of art in the classroom. Indeed some academic critics write as though readers only read books for a teacher.

Yet in the world outside academia I read a book, see a movie, attend a play, or watch television in apparent innocence. Seemingly, I simply have an experience. What more should I need or want?

As the most commonsensical and most lordly of our critics says, in the remarks on Gray's "Elegy" with which he ends the *Lives of the English Poets:* "I rejoice to concur with the common reader; for by the common sense of readers uncorrupted with literary prejudices, after all the refinements of subtilty and the dogmatism of learning, must be finally decided all claims to poetical honours." Why then should criticism be any more than a straightforward chronicling of popular reactions over a period of time? If that.

Johnson tells us why in that very remark. "I *rejoice* to concur. . . ." It was not enough for him simply to enjoy Gray's "Elegy," and having read, to pass on. He *rejoices* that he can agree with the common sense of readers and so have poetical honors finally decided. He and we—some of us, anyway—want something more than that first, unadorned experience of literature. We want to award honors, to agree with others, or to decide. To satisfy these transpersonal hankerings, we become, and we heed, critics.

According to one model, then, we can say that all criticism *begins* with some pure, primary experience. The instant we try for something more, however, the instant we analyze, buttress, color, describe, explain, freeze, garnish or whatever, that first gut reaction, we become critics. Beauty, said Rilke, is *"nichts als des Schrecklichen Anfang, den wir noch grade ertragen."* The critic is someone who has had a narrow escape with that beginning of terror that we can scarcely bear, and now he wants to tell about it.

In this model, then, criticism is the act of analyzing the act that it is. As such, it leads us into an infinite regression. Criticism is having an experience and analyzing that experience. Analyzing an experience entails having an experience of analyzing. Hence, criticism is

1. having a primary experience
plus 2. analyzing that primary experience
plus 3. having the experience of analyzing that primary experience.

But if we are truly inflamed with the passion of criticism, we will not stop there. Any having of an experience seduces us into analyzing it. Therefore,

3. having the experience of analyzing that primary experience
leads to 4. analyzing the experience of analyzing that primary experience
leads to 5. having the experience of analyzing the experience of analyzing that primary experience, which

leads to 6. analyzing the experience of analyzing the experience of analyzing that primary experience, which
leads to 7. having the experience of . . .
and so on, ad infinitum.

It does not matter what the critic uses to analyze the primary experience: justification in "the text" (however that be defined); a claimed "meaning" or "content"; the values of a critical community; religious or moral tradition; linguistics; psychology; semiotics; or simply a commonsensical appeal to the responses of readers, like that of Dr. Johnson or the *Rezeptionsästhetiker*. The strategies are infinite for transforming one's gut reaction into something that crosses over from one person to others, something transpersonal. What is essential in criticism is not the particular strategy but the whole idea of transforming one's inward, personal, intimate gut reaction toward something external, something sharable by the Other.

In becoming a critic, then, one chooses others. If I am writing criticism in a formal way, I choose an audience to write to: most often (in academic criticism) one's fellow professors, occasionally writers and students; in reviewing, that chimera, the literate public. Yet even if I plan no formal writing, if I am simply "thinking critically," I ally myself with significant others from a tradition I accept and, in accepting, create. I may reach back for guidance no farther than Kenneth Burke or Northrop Frye. I may try to ally myself with Coleridge or Aristotle—as I began this essay by marshaling Johnson to my slightly iconoclastic thesis. And always, as a human being, I write to what Michel de M'Uzan has called *le public intérieur.*[1] I work for my mentors, my friends, my wife, my children, my parents. Yet all these I constitute: whatever their "real" being, I cast them in the roles provided by the drama of my own thought.

In the same way, I choose what I shall be critical about. As Stanley Fish argues in his essay for this volume, criticism does not simply account for the facts—it establishes what the facts can thereafter be said to be. I decide what the text shall include: the title, chapter division, modern meanings of words, an accretion of criticism, accidentals like spelling, punctuation, or position on the page, illustrations, and the like. Most of all, I foreground some parts and set others aside. And I decide what other matters I shall include in my criticism: sources, biography, history, psychology, the common sense of readers.

Similarly, the critical self chooses a self—a third part of any act of criticism. Murray M. Schwartz has cogently defined the critic as *"a reader who makes a difference by using himself to represent an other."*[2] In mingling my inward and personal experience of a poem with something external, belonging to an other, I both re-create and define myself. The language I use, the choices I make, come from and rebound upon a prior me.

From a psychological point of view, then, to be a critic, even just to "think critically" and so transpersonalize one's inner experience, means creating and entering a shared verbal space (a "potential space" like that conceptualized by D. W. Winnicott to describe the way a baby constitutes a mother and a mother a baby).[3]

Like any transitional space, the critic's relates a self and an other. The transitional space of criticism has two (at least) kinds of "others": the facts as the critic constitutes them from the real world of literature and the significant other persons to whom the critic relates himself. The transitional space of criticism is, moreover, a verbal space, made up of words chosen by the critic from text and extra-text and from (and to) significant other people. Words both constitute and are responsive to those others. "The central problem of the critic," writes Schwartz, "can be seen as one of making representation 'presentable,' that is, of communicating in a language that can be 'heard' by the audience he seeks."[4]

Infancy provides a model for criticism. So, as Schwartz points out, does psychoanalysis, for the transforming mode of criticism closely resembles another shared verbal space, that between psychoanalyst and analysand. Imagine the analysand on the couch, his voice rambling excitedly or lazily along, rushing or drifting almost ahead of thought, practically by itself, while back at the edge of awareness another part of his mind listens to that voice and thinks about what it has been and is saying. The analysand is having an experience and listening to himself have an experience at the same time. As a long tradition in American psychoanalysis would have it, out of his trust in the analyst, the patient has been able to split his conscious mind into an observing ego and a participating ego.

The participating ego regresses into the displaced and unresolved fantasies the analysand brings to the analyst from his earliest experiences of other humans.[5] At the same time, his observing ego works (in a "therapeutic alliance") with the observing ego of the analyst. They share a verbal space (like the critic's) in which the patient's free associations provide the text.

The patient, in the mode of participating ego, writes like an author. In the mode of observing ego, he acts as critic to those words, relating himself to that most significant other, the psychoanalyst. The analyst, in turn, represents significant others to the patient, the others whose values and perceptions he has long internalized and the other to whom he is speaking at that moment. As Schwartz puts the process, "Freud's dictum, 'Where it was, there shall I become,' should be understood . . . as an endless process of triangulation in which self and other each transform themselves through the medium that joins and separates them both."[6]

Criticism and psychoanalysis create verbal spaces in which we can externalize and transform inner experiences. Yet, in this model of criticism, there is first the raw experience. What is that? Modern theories of perception and cognition offer a transforming model of our constitutive processes, also. We build the world by playing it against schemata in our brains, nerves, and sense organs. Schemata for verticality or straightness or pitch or color come from inside us, either born to our bodies or learned through culture. We test the world against them and make sense (gain a satisfying response); or we find we can't make sense (feel cognitive dissatisfaction), and we take steps to change either the world or the schemata we are bringing to bear until we do make a satisfying sense of it. In other words, we constitute the world through a complex process of feedbacks. (You can feel the process happen by letting your eyes unfocus against a blank, textured wall and then bringing them back into focus.)

We work these loops hierarchically. A loop for detecting color, say, nests inside a loop for detecting edges, which nests inside a loop for detecting shapes, which nests inside a loop for detecting a three-dimensional object, which nests inside a loop for thinking about picking that object up—and all of them work within our own large sense of what suits us.[7]

Our world is thus neither "objective" nor "subjective"—that dichotomy is obsolete—but relational between subject and object. In the word some psychologists use for that relation, we "transact" the world. This is not to say the world is "not there," but that it is not there in the form in which we know it until we know it through the feedbacks we have for knowing things. And similarly for language: we constitute it through the linguistic abilities we bring to it.[8] Spoken or unspoken, knowledge is as interpersonal an act as love—or literary criticism.

To define and explore the transactive, transforming space in which we join subject to object, I use identity theory, the rethinking of psychoanalysis that proceeds from the concept of identity initiated by Heinz Lichtenstein.[9]

Identity theory provides a way of conceptualizing relations among a person, a writing (or anything other), and what surrounds them: language, social context, cultural codes, conventions of interpretation, other individuals, intellectual communities, and the like. The key premise is that one can understand the changes and continuities in an individual's relations to the world through a concept of identity as a theme and variations. One uses a theme to express the sameness in a given person's behavior, and variations to express the novelty. The core of identity, then, is the identity theme: a way of putting into words someone's characteristic style—the continuity and sameness I can see in a person's actions by looking for what persists against the background of change, just as I might state a theme for a piece of music or a Shakespearean play that runs through all its variations or figures. "Identity" then equals identity theme plus a personal history of variations the individual has played and is playing upon it. This concept of identity says we *can* understand the ways different people differently transact (constitute and reconstitute) the world or the words in it as functions of their identities. We *can* understand cultural transactions as taking place through individuals' identities. Or, at least, we can try, as with any perceptual transaction, to "make sense," to get a satisfying feedback to our identity-based hypotheses.[10]

Criticism, then, must also be a function of identity—the critic's identity as interpreted by the interpreter of the critic. The choices I make, the texts I choose and the way I define them, the other persons I write to or from, all can be read as variations on my identity theme. Similarly, the transformations I make, the transpersonal ideas I refer my literary experience to, you can understand as functions of my identity.

But what modern perceptual psychology and identity theory add is that the original experience our model presupposed is also a function of identity. There is no such thing as a "pure, primary experience," if by that we mean an experience untouched by transformations that derive from a cultural or biological heritage—the "other." In perception I draw on the body I inherited from others, and I see and hear and taste through the schemata I imbibed from my culture. Similarly, in analysis, one identity comprises both a participating, associating ego and an observing, analyzing ego—and my identity is "between" me and significant other persons. The analysand, the infant, the critic, each of us all the time constitute the verbal and nonverbal world around us through a continual triangulation in a potential space made by our bodies and our culture through our differing identities that hover between self and others. That triangulation makes up a "gut reaction" just as much as a reasoned critical argument.

As ever, the succession of critics' Shakespeares provides the clearest example. To Johnson and his predecessors, Shakespeare was contemporary theater: the relevant facts were what would "go" and the acting script (with only scholarly gestures toward some sacrosanct Quarto). Beginning with the bardolization of Shakespeare by the pre-Romantics, people treated his plays as chronicles of events that the text merely portrayed. The events were central, not the text. Hence the relevant facts became things like knowledge of eleventh-century Scotland or a wisdom about human "character." In the first half of our century, Shakespeareans treated the text as poetry, hence an end in itself: what mattered were themes and images and structures "in" that text. Most recently, critics are coming round to the plays as plays again (but not as the popular medium they were for the seventeenth and eighteenth centuries; the relevant facts are those a director would find important). There are, however, signs of a characteristically postmodern, self-reflexive Shakespeare, like a *nouveau roman*. The relevant facts become the contradictions and the callings of attention to the plays as fictions.

> How many ages hence
> Shall this our lofty scene be acted over
> In states unborn and accents yet unknown!

Each period, each critic, constitutes a Shakespeare and chooses, accordingly, what the relevant facts shall be.

The cultural decision precedes the very perception of the plays. Johnson did not see the plays as Bradley did, nor would it be possible for Bradley to see the plays as I do. Whatever gut reaction I have has already passed through a complex of personal and cultural schemata. I do not, first, see the plays innocently, then turn on my twentieth-century inheritance of a long tradition of Shakespearean criticism. I see the plays from the first with a certain "set" or expectation, just as Johnson or Bradley did (although, now, I include theirs with my own as inevitably as they could not have included mine).

The supposed infinite regression of having an experience and analyzing the experience and having an experience of analyzing the experience collapses. Like Zeno's paradoxes it arises simply from considering as discrete and sequential what can be better thought of as continuous and simultaneous. There is no "raw" experience followed by a cerebral analysis of it. There are experiences, some of which involve more deliberate thinking than others, but all are equally functions of identity. We are not dealing with two stages any more than with "subjective" and "objective." We experience the world through continuous feedback loops.

The supposed paradox of our first model for criticism, experience followed by analysis, yields to another, larger paradox. I am myself dual, existing within myself and within the community that knows me, shimmering between an irreducible one and an infinity of different inferences about me. I sense an essential me—a primary identity within—that shapes my experience, although it is preverbal and unknowable. It becomes knowable only as you see in me a persisting, unchanging style. You can see, for example, how the form of this essay grows out of my tendency to seek ever wider, larger, more general themes, and you can articulate this essential me, this identity theme, as precisely as you choose to. Yet it is not me. It is between you and me, part of the relation you are establishing with me, part of your act of constituting me.

Freud commented (in the opening chapter of *Civilization and Its Discontents*) that "Our present ego-feeling is . . . only a shrunken residue of a much more inclusive—indeed, an all-embracing—feeling which corresponded to a more intimate bond between the ego and the world about it." Freud meant the infant's sense of union with an infinitely larger mother who has not yet become "other," a feeling re-created in mystical states or love. Many psychoanalysts since Freud, however, have found his hypothesis more universally applicable. Reality itself succeeds to the mother's role, especially human reality. As Erik Erikson has so eloquently demonstrated, we are born—we are conceived, even—into a community of other, expecting human beings. The paradox of my existence is that I am sole and whole—yet dual. I feel self-contained, yet I am de-centered, dis-placed, merged into others outside myself. Indeed, this merger is a precondition to my very existence as a biological entity: I could not otherwise have survived. Nor can I be heard otherwise. Nor can I otherwise hear—my very eyes and ears draw on transpersonal schemata.

Hence my duality as a human being creates my duality as a critic. I have an experience that is wholly and uniquely my own. Yet I feel the need to—and I *necessarily* do—set that experience in a community of others. What is criticism, then? It is a human activity whose appeal to the doer and to his audience is the *deliberate* blending of the personal into the transpersonal. Criticism is a heightened way we know and act out the dual, displaced—if you like, deconstructed—nature of all human experience, its being not only private and personal but also public and communal. Criticism is something we do with literature in which we consciously act out what we do in life. The paradigm of human consciousness, criticism is also therefore the paradigm of human community. In my othering as a critic I re-create the othering I live in as a human being. What is personal I make transpersonal, but what is transpersonal begins with the personal transactions of personal identity—which are, of course, transpersonal.

NOTES

1. Michel de M'Uzan, "Aperçues sur le processus de la création littéraire," *Revue française* de psychanalyse 29 (1965): 43–77.

2. Murray M. Schwartz, "Critic, Define Thyself," in *Psychoanalysis and the Question of the Text: Selected Papers from the English Institute, 1976–77,* n.s., no. 2, ed. Geoffrey H. Hartman (Baltimore: The Johns Hopkins University Press, 1978), p. 11.

3. D. W. Winnicott, *Playing and Reality* (London: Tavistock Publications, 1971), pp. 11 and 95–103. For an application of Winnicott's concepts "transitional object" and "potential space" to literature, see Murray M. Schwartz, "Where Is Literature?" *College English* 36 (1975): 756–65.

4. "Critic, Define Thyself," p. 12.

5. Elizabeth Zetzel and W. W. Meissner, *Basic Concepts of Psychoanalytic Psychiatry* (New York: Basic Books, 1973), pp. 292–96. Freud discusses splitting of the ego most generally in his own account of "ego-psychology," "Lecture 31. The Dissection of the Psychical Personality," *New Introductory Lectures in Psychoanalysis* (1933), in *The Standard Edition of the Complete Psychological Works of Sigmund Freud,* ed. James Strachey et al., 24 vols. (London: The Hogarth Press and The Institute of Psychoanalysis, 1974), 22:57–69.

6. "Critic, Define Thyself," p. 10.

7. This transactive view of perception is best summarized in Ulric Neisser's influential survey, *Cognitive Psychology,* (New York: Appleton-Century-Crofts, 1967). A more recent coverage of the field,

less in search, however, of an overarching principle, is Lloyd Kaufman's *Perception: The World Transformed* (New York: Oxford University Press, 1979). The hierarchical loop theory is convincingly worked out by William T. Powers in *Behavior: The Control of Perception* (Chicago: Aldine, 1973). Psychologists, by and large, have failed to take advantage of the possibilities of a feedback explanation for reasons developed by Powers in "Quantitative Analysis of Purposive Systems: Some Spadework at the Foundations of Scientific Psychology," *Psychological Review* 86 (1978): 417–35.

8. See my "What Can a Concept of Identity Add to Psycholinguistics?" in *Psychiatry and the Humanities*, ed. Joseph H. Smith, vol. 3, *Psychoanalysis and Language* (New Haven: Yale University Press), pp. 171–234; or "Identity: An Interrogation at the Border of Psychology," *Language and Style* 10 (1977): 199–209.

9. See Lichtenstein's collected essays, *The Dilemma of Human Identity* (New York: Jason Aronson, 1977), including the classic "Identity and Sexuality" (1961). Lichtenstein argues for a preverbal, ultimately unknowable "primary identity" imprinted in the infant by its responses to the unconscious needs of its mother prior to the differentiation of self and object around the eighth month of life. Identity theory as I use it here rests on a less taxing assumption: that one can infer an identity theme as described in the text, whether or not it be "in" the individual.

10. These concepts, premises, and axia, are stated more formally in my "A Transactive Account of Transactive Criticism," *Poetics* 7 (1978): 177–89.

On Whether Criticism Is Literature

Cary Nelson

What is criticism?[1] The question can neither be posed nor addressed innocently. To ask the question is to admit, indeed to have already admitted, that the answer is problematic, uncertain, open to disputation. The question itself therefore makes one countering response ineffective—that each of us knows what criticism is because the secure evidence of its practice is the only definition we need—by situating this response within the problematic it seeks to avoid. We can, of course, still object to discussing the issue, perhaps even repress it again, as the issue is often repressed in academic criticism; but within the larger community of critics those forms of rejection will be viewed, at least by some, precisely as evidence that critical activity merits analysis. Discussions of the question of criticism's status typically challenge the widespread notion that criticism can be a largely unreflective and straightforward form of discourse. Yet the question itself is, in turn, supported by an intellectual milieu that has recently sanctioned our positing it, that has made the problematics of criticism certainly a possible and perhaps even a necessary condition for critical discourse. Thus, while posing the question of criticism partly exposes and illuminates the institution of criticism, it also expresses that institution's present condition. The question "What is criticism?" is therefore exemplary for its ambivalence, for the institutional power it simultaneously opposes and represents.

As soon as we make critical writing an object of study, we grant a textual status that is inherently unstable to the products of the very institution designed to obtain and insure stability for other texts. Of course all texts subjected to interpretive pressure display some instability, but attention to criticism's verbal status makes the issue of textual instability into a general problematic. The result is more than just an intensified sense that critical language is ambiguous, for criticism's entire ontology can be threatened. Whether one finds such a problematizing viewpoint to be revivifying or unacceptable, it will tend to call into question not just particular critical texts but an entire discursive activity. The history of modern interpretation makes it relatively easy to credit works of literature with unresolvable ambiguity or obscurity, to treat them as generically mixed, or to consider their multiple and self-reflexive signification intrinsic to their achievement. But to admit that critical works of apparent value share such qualities is not only to alter our sense of those works but also to undermine all our idealized notions of critical discourse. Before admitting criticism has such a status, we might have been able to sustain an ideal of critical language as a transparent medium for description and demonstration, a graciously utilitarian medium that could be paraphrased without leaving behind a stylistic or psychological residue. Now that the question is with us, however, the illusion of criticism's innocently malleable discourse is forever lost, or at least we will ever be losing it anew. For our special condition now is not to have settled the question of criticism, but to be continually posing the question, indeed to experience ourselves as posed by the question. The question "What is criticism?" addresses not only a body of texts but also a practice, a practice that reflects an uncertain condition of self-knowledge. To write criticism today is to be grounded in and defined by that uncertainty.

The essential issue for criticism, both as text and as practice, is always its relation to literature. Although some have argued that recent criticism is once again becoming more like literature—more stylistically individuated, more ambitiously original and comprehensive in its vision, more demanding of its readers, more open itself to multiple interpretations—the distinction between criticism and literature still obtains.[2] Depending on one's ideological bias, criticism may seem either degraded or ennobled by its secondary status in relation to literary texts. Critics may respond to this status with reverence or aggression; they may solicit it and turn it into a self-chastening and self-purifying metaphysic, as have many—from the New Critics to Paul de Man—who take pleasure in a conception of close reading as a rigorous discipline; or they may defend themselves against it by their own acts of verbal creation, as have a great number of critics—from Walter Pater to Hugh Kenner—with markedly original writing styles; but the sense that criticism is a secondary activity remains inescapable. Yet the precise terms of this secondariness are uncertain, not only because it changes substantially in different critical practices, but also because it is regularly an area of uncertainty within individual practices. It is essentially unimportant whether the uneasy sense of being derivative, supplementary, or subservient always informs the experience of literature. Since neither the consciousness of the reader nor the actual perceptual process of reading is fully recoverable, speculation about them can contribute little to the study of criticism. The key problem is to recognize how the give and take between criticism and literature informs critical writing.

For both readers and writers of criticism, the relationship between criticism and literature, partly erased and partly underlined, is foregrounded in the experience of critical textuality. This relationship, in other words, is one of the main things we think about when we encounter a critical text; it is a way of entering into and ordering discourse that might otherwise be experienced in different ways. This particular foregrounding may not have been inevitable, but it now seems an unavoidable feature of critical discourse, one that reflects both the history of interpretation and the institutional training many critics have received. Although it is a distinctly selective foreground and hardly an innocuous one, since it blinds us to and perhaps protects us from other features of critical discourse, it cannot simply be rejected or ignored. It informs not only our assumptions about what is important in critical practice but also the style, organization, and ambitions of critical texts. A more reflective and theoretically oriented analysis of criticism can, however, make the relationship between criticism and literature a subject for discussion rather than an unquestioned area of consensus for critical practice. Yet it is an error to read criticism with the aim of reconstituting those interactions between the critic and the literary text that preceded critical writing, especially if we imagine that those prior interactions are reproduced in or have a direct causal relation to critical language. Even if we could be witness to the interactions between critics and the works of literature, we would discover those interactions to be substantially transformed in critical texts. Within critical discourse, we can certainly see characteristic responses to literature, but those patterns, which are grounded in the dynamics of critical writing, bear a relation to the experience of literature that is neither straightforward nor traceable.

A more appropriate subject for study is the way literature and literary language occur in and shape critical writing. Such study places us at the point of a definite change in the way we read critical prose and indeed in the way we can define the activity of criticism, for it makes the existence of literary texts, separate from critical texts, less important in the analysis of criticism. I want to suggest instead that criticism's own literary status constitutes critical discourse, even as it renders that discourse undecidable. Criticism's sense of its own literary status is therefore both formative, in that it energizes and structures critical discourse, and erosive, in that it is unresolvable and contradictory. Moreover, it is important to realize that the formative and erosive qualities of criticism's literary condition each produce both pleasure and anxiety. Juxtaposing the notions of constitution and undecidability may seem nearly paradoxical, since the first suggests formative process while the second suggests qualities that either preclude or dissolve formal possibilities, yet the interplay between the two terms can help point to the ambivalence central to all critical texts.

If we want to avoid simply offering prescriptive statements about what criticism should be—statements that are often symptomatic of an anxiety about what criticism has become—we have to begin with criticism's one irreducible condition—its own literariness.[3] If criticism is discourse about literature, it is also discourse that contains literature, whether by quotation, allusion, mimesis, or homology. No matter how relentessly critics work to purge their writing of its literary character, their subject matter will impart a literary quality to their prose. Of course a critic's own rhetoric will have metaphoric effects, just as his argument will exhibit a certain narrative drama, but even when these qualities are partially suppressed, or, as is often the case, when readers consent to ignore them, the literary subjects that critics discuss will permeate their own discourse. In its desire for intelligibility, for mastery over literature's metaphoricity, criticism will often try to escape from, transcend, or indict its own literary character. "Tropic," as Hayden White writes, "is the shadow from which all realistic discourse tries to flee."[4] Examples of this tendency are countless. They range from the cool, deliberately unrevealing language of a Jonathan Culler, who at once valorizes and distances himself from Roland Barthes as a more responsive and metaphorically playful critic, to the extreme efforts of an A. J. Greimas, who would found an abstract, logical language for criticism and then present it in a shattered form that guards his argument from a sense of narrative development. Yet metaphoricity is also criticism's unavoidable topic. However much it would deflect our attention from its own textuality, it will always be discourse about metaphoricity. Criticism must therefore solicit, evoke, inscribe within itself, the very literary language it tries to control.

It may be more useful, then, to consider criticism's relation to literature as a problem internal to critical texts, rather than as a relation between different texts. Once the critic begins writing, literature is a feature of his own discourse. The ambivalent pursuit of and struggle with its own literariness provides criticism with its generative tensions. Criticism's varied attempts to discover, express, or evade its own literary status produce continuing critical discourse. Criticism's literary status is thus a problem that individual critical texts try to work out; they are written in the service of its uncertainties. We might define criticism as a special form of discourse simultaneously preoccupied with and distanced from its own literary status. The varying tonalities of that distance—honorific, erotic, contemplative, alienated—create the texture and suggest the metaphysics of particular critical discourses. All criticism, however, shares the characteristic of continually tracing, retracing, and experiencing itself as being traced by, the distinction between literature and criticism.[5]

One could object to this by arguing that criticism written this way is actually not criticism at all but simply an awkwardly self-conscious form of literature—bad literature, as some would have it—thereby preserving for genuine criticism a less tainted ontology. One needs to show in response that such self-consciousness and generic uncertainty informs all critical writing, though the degree to which critics deal with it varies considerably. Establishing a special class of self-conscious writers will, moreover, create other problems for those wanting a rigid distinction between criticism and literature, a distinction that can block discussion of criticism's literary status. The resulting group of texts will include some previously thought to be primarily either literary or critical. Grouping them together will necessarily open the question of classification in the most risky context—works that tend emphatically to make the distinction undecidable, an undecidability that will then prove applicable to an increasingly wider range of texts. Hence arises a more important objection to my definition of criticism: that all writing, not just literature and criticism, is structured by its pursuit and avoidance of its sense of being a marginal supplement, a claim that would seem to collapse the distinction between literature and criticism. While that is a fair and productive point of view, it does not necessarily eliminate all generic distinctions within the world of discourse, though it does destabilize them. We can still make distinctions between different kinds of secondariness; indeed a full understanding of criticism's relation to literature requires that we do so.

Criticism's secondariness is grounded in a conviction about literature's power and originality. Within criticism, literature is an internalized otherness which is paradoxically at once a source of inspiration and a constraint on expression. Criticism is preoccupied with its incorporation of an otherness it seeks simultaneously to define and to assimilate; criticism wishes both to obliterate itself in this powerful otherness and to separate itself from it. These mixed purposes leave their traces in all critical texts; they animate as well the whole spectrum of critics' declared intentions, from René Wellek's insistence that evaluation is criticism's central task to Georges Poulet's desire to lose himself in the consciousness of the author he contemplates. Even criticism which denigrates particular works or authors—from Yvor Winters on T. S. Eliot to the average negative book review—assumes the actual and potential existence of such literary power elsewhere. Similarly, though we can construct arguments about intertextuality that undermine that sense of power, or that suggest it is overly codified and ritualized in critical thinking, a conviction about literature's power will nonetheless provide criticism with its structuring tension. This conviction orients criticism toward the literary textuality it regards or represses: criticism simultaneously honors and inscribes within itself a discourse it believes to be radically originary. Yet one of the effects of treating literary discourse as both self-generative and uniquely original in its own vision is to make it an elusive originative source within criticism. Literary discourse thus becomes an obliquely causative, unpredictably generous and oppressive force within criticism itself. Ironically, then, the sense of the otherness of literature, the belief in the inviolability of its power, is regularly called into question by criticism's various mimetic, historical, and interpretive strategies; however honorific they may claim to be, each of these strategies will appear to empower criticism with a knowledge of literature's originary force. What distinguishes criticism from other forms of writing, however, is the relentlessly schematic, binary basis of its self-consciousness. Criticism is structured by its guarded, sometimes unconscious exploration of whether it is or is not itself literature, an exploratory process whose results are continually denied. The undecidable difference between criticism and literature is criticism's special burden, though it is also criticism's mode of performative rigor, perhaps as well criticism's chief contribution to the humanities, and, for those, like Roland Barthes, who are willing to employ the resources of this problematic, criticism's form of play.

Though this should clarify the uneasy relation between criticism and literature, it will not entirely eliminate the argument that self-consciously literary criticism is basically a form of literature. Indeed, we have to consider that problem not only in broad, generic terms but also in terms of our particular historical context. As I stated at the outset, the question of what criticism is reflects its own historicity. We are all aware that criticism has been occupied with exploiting its own literariness at other points in its history: examples like Walter Pater and Oscar Wilde, the visionary and sometimes apocalyptic tradition in theories of American literature that runs from D. H. Lawrence and William Carlos Williams through Leslie Fiedler, as well as the history of manifestos written by poets, will suggest themselves immediately. Moreover, many are aware that the effort by academics to separate scholarly writing from the long and often self-consciously literary tradition of the essay is a relatively recent and perhaps illegitimate project, illegitimate, that is, at least in the sense that it can disguise that generic connection only by employing the conventions of an unspoken consensus among scholarly writers about how their prose will be read and discussed. In effect, critics collectively create an institution that validates particular notions of critical practice.[6] Both within academia and in the world of publishing, that institution exercises definite (though not identical or even always consistent) administrative and economic control over critical writers. Yet the less visible elements of the institution of criticism are equally important. It is in this almost intangible area—of criticism as an intellectual and ideological institution—that criticism calls itself into existence and valorizes itself as a certain kind of discourse. Of course the kinds of discourse valorized vary historically; this moment, moreover, hardly presents a homogenous image of what is permissible. Nonetheless, even now this discursive institution establishes both a zone of permission and a sense of what is taboo; thus, while it creates opportunities for discourse that would not otherwise exist, it also excludes opportunities it rejects. When functioning most effectively, the mechanisms for exclusion are invisible to participants in the institution: one of their main results is an unwritten agreement among critics not to discuss one another's work as though it were literature.

The history of how the institution of criticism conditions what can be perceived and expressed is difficult to unravel, since one is often dealing with areas of characteristic silence. Consequently, neither critics' stated intentions nor those implicit in their allegiance to a particular intellectual community will fully describe their reasons for writing. Limited by the extent of their self-knowledge, by the consensual codes of their peers, critics both willfully and unconsciously misrepresent their enterprise. Reactions to a topic like this one, the literary status of critical discourse, which is an area of particular instability now, will mix repression with moments of insight that often cannot be sustained. There are some critics on whom the topic cannot register at all. Others find it an affront. Some consider it obvious but irrelevant. More significant, however, is the recognition that even those who consider criticism to be a form of literature are often blind to the evidence for that judgment.

The nature of the current changes in the collective notion of criticism may be clarified by examining a process of change that is now almost complete. Only a few years ago it was not only easy but actually automatic for many American and European critics to view some forms of historically oriented criticism as free of any kind of ideology. Such critics simply imagined themselves to be doing scholarship; questions about their assumptions and methods were either inconceivable or considered to be intrusive.[7] Certain kinds of criticism were, however, considered to be methodologically deliberate and consequently suspect. Less than a decade ago, a department evaluating for tenure a candidate who wrote psychoanalytic criticism could wonder whether another psychoanalytic critic could possibly be unbiased in evaluating his work. The same doubts would never occur in choosing reviewers for conventional historical or textual criticism, although those methods have also been defended with enough intensity to suggest that their practitioners might well overvalue similar work. Now, however, the visibility of very different critical styles can make it virtuous to claim a rigorous, unitary procedure. Indeed, as with some structuralist critics, it is often the only defense against a reading of one's criticism as polysemous, contradictory, self-expressive, literary.

We can only pose the question of criticism from a vantage point that intensifies our awareness of these and other issues. The fact that there have been other periods when people wrote criticism that was self-consciously literary is less significant for approaching the question of criticism than the fact that we are beginning to think about those critical texts again. Our historical moment is shaped partly by the foregrounding of these elements of our literary and political past. As we reconsider both the history of criticism and our own critical practice, we have to consider seriously the possibility that our sense that criticism is becoming more like literature is as much a result of our increased sensitivity to the literary qualities of critical prose as it is to any actual increased literariness in the prose itself. It is perhaps less surprising that this shift is taking place than that it has taken so long. One of the remarkable features of the power of New Critical close reading during the past thirty years, particularly for those who inherited the method from their teachers, has been its success in avoiding overt self-reflection within its analytic practice, thereby preventing its procedures from being applied to its own discourse.[8]

The historicity of our moment, however, has an even more important component—the self-conscious, formally experimental heritage of modern literature. One might ask why it has taken this long for criticism, particularly academic criticism, to adopt that portion of the modernist perspective, but the delay may be understandable if we remember criticism's belated, secondary status. It is more appropriate to criticism's own secondary status that it reflect the conditions of contemporary literature, a body of literature itself often obsessed with its appearance after (and its possible inferiority to) a major period of imaginative synthesis. In many ways, the experimental aesthetics of contemporary literature are defined by its struggle to extricate itself from a paternity it experiences as an absolute origin: modernism. Too late for modernism, too late for the thing itself, contemporary literature worries that it may be merely an afterthought, an appendage, an unoriginal repetition. Criticism is less suited to structural innovation and self-reflexivity that is confidently visionary than to the same things rendered self-conscious, ironic, fatalistic, and uncertain of success. Although others, including Harold Bloom, have argued that these anxieties have dominated literature for some time, they have not always been so pervasive or so central to an entire historical context. It is this context of creative secondariness, combined with the sense of frustration and futility growing out of the sheer bulk of criticism written in the last thirty years, that makes critics more aware (excruciatingly or playfully) of their dependence on primary texts.

This ironic literary climate makes it more difficult simply to mimic the defensive—if generally understated—pose of scientism in so much humanistic scholarship. But because our recent past is so taken up with that goal of objectivity, the question of criticism for us tends to be not merely problematic but also partly argumentative and polemical. Even if one defines a subgroup within the larger community of critics and attempts to act as its spokesman, it will be impossible to write an innocently enthusiastic essay on the vocation of criticism. Any discussion of the nature of criticism is now unavoidably either reactive and defensive or, as may be the case with this discussion, designed to identify and master those very responses. The present atmosphere is pluralistic and competitive, qualities which color any attempt to describe critical writing.

Despite the necessity for recognizing the historical grounding of criticism's identity, we need not choose a completely open definition of criticism. Thus, while it is worthwhile to suggest that criticism is nothing more than what is sanctioned as criticism at any given time, just as what is considered literature is what is sanctioned as literature in a particular period, the concerns that structure the sanctioning process are recurrent ones. Secondary texts which are morally or politically corrective may seem superficially unrelated to secondary texts that aim to interpret a supposedly sacred or aesthetically transcendent essence, but they have structural similarities. Such apparently different interpretive stances can, for example, preserve comparable hierarchical or polar models of the relationship between primary and secondary texts. The relationship between primary and secondary texts may undergo continual and sometimes circular historical redefinition, but we can expect some notions of this relationship to be sanctioned at any given time. At the present, however, the sanctioning mechanisms are diverse, even contradictory; as the remarkable range of writing styles encouraged by different journals should make clear, there is no effective monolithic notion of what is acceptable within critical discourse. Nonetheless, if one combines a recognition of the recurring nature of critical concerns with an awareness of the variety of critical practices, it is possible to work toward a definition of criticism without actually turning the term into a transcendental signifier. That need not, however, prevent us from accounting for those moments in which critics have functioned as though an absolute notion of criticism existed, outside their writing, as an inviolable guarantor and center for their enterprise. The present climate puts such a notion under almost impossible stress. Yet it is partly the diversity of current practices that makes thought about the characteristics of criticism possible and necessary; whether this diversity is felt to be stimulating or threatening, it results in a need for theoretical generalization.

If we repeat the definitions of criticism offered above—an

institution designed to obtain and insure stability for literary texts, a special form of discourse simultaneously preoccupied with and distanced from its own literary status—we can now see how they can be used in analyzing critical texts. Applying these definitions will not result in static models of critical texts but rather in an analytic discourse itself structured, as this one is, by two mutually qualifying observations: first, that criticism exhibits all of the features we associate with literature, including metaphoricity, self-reflexive structuration, psychological expressiveness and deception, active engagement with historically and socially determining language; second, that criticism is not the same as literature, or rather that it is a special form of literature whose particular and often peculiar characteristics need to be described. For criticism, the boundary between criticism and literature, wholly unstable, finally unknowable, is nonetheless everywhere decisive. This boundary, as I have argued, is not only a boundary between different kinds of texts; it is also a boundary within critical texts. Constitutive but indeterminate, the boundary between criticism and literature can neither be fixed nor transcended; it is the subject matter, the informing anxiety, and the tantalizing object of critical discourse.

The body of texts that seem to call for this analysis is itself both historically determined and unstable. As the kinds of texts assigned primary status change, those texts included in the body of criticism change as well. Yet even when there is relative agreement on a particular group of primary texts, for example on that writing to be considered literature, the sanctioned body of secondary texts can be actively disputed. An inquiry into the nature of criticism, however, should be willing to consider a wide variety of texts, though it will be necessary at times to group these texts in different ways. Concern with the secondary status of interpretive discourse is, of course, manifested throughout the humanities, as is ambivalence about the metaphoric qualities of interpretive language. Our understanding of literary criticism would benefit from comparisons not only with interpretive acts in fields where aesthetic objects are the primary concern but also with, among others, the metaphoricity of texts by historians or the secondariness established in texts by specialists in the history of philosophy. We can even make useful comparisons with the sense of secondariness in sociological or anthropological writing that takes everyday life as its object of study. In addition, the whole long tradition of the essay can be reintegrated with our reading of recent academic and nonacademic criticism. Yet it is still worthwhile to look for the particular characteristics of literary criticism, at least in part because of the exemplary intensity of its simultaneous solicitation and avoidance of its own literariness. The most impossible and divided form of writing, literary criticism proceeds by bluff and self-deception, by adoration and independent vision, by an eloquence always ontologically awkward.

NOTES

1. My effort to answer this question is also an effort to identify and extend the implications of my previous publications in the area of critical theory: "The Paradox of Critical Language: A Polemical Speculation," *MLN* 89 (1974):1003–16; "Reading Criticism," *PMLA* 91 (1976): 801–15; "Letter to the Forum," *PMLA* 91 (1977):310–12; "Allusion and Authority: Hugh Kenner's Exemplary Critical Voice," *Denver Quarterly* 12, no. 1 (1977):282–95; "The Psychology of Criticism, Or What Can Be Said," in *Psychoanalysis and the Question of the Text: Selected Papers from the English Institute*, ed. Geoffrey H. Hartman (Baltimore: Johns Hopkins University Press, 1978), pp. 45–61; "Soliciting Self-Knowledge: The Rhetoric of Susan Sontag's Criticism," to be published in *Critical Inquiry*.

2. Perhaps the most careful presentation of the argument that criticism is becoming more like literature is to be found in Geoffrey Hartman's recent work. Although he observes that "literary commentary today is creating texts—a literature—of its own," he is also very much aware that "the uneasy coexistence, in essays, of their referential function as commentary with their ambition to be literature," a coexistence that "makes for a medley of insight and idiosyncratic self-assertion," has a long history. "Crossing Over: Literary Commentary as Literature," *Comparative Literature* 28 (1976):257–76. Even Hartman, however, tends to vacillate between assertions about the

special quality of contemporary criticism's literariness and cautions to remember the history of comparable literariness in critical essays.

3. For efforts to define the proper functions of criticism that are reactive to and often distressed at recent developments in criticism see Eugene Goodheart, *The Failure of Criticism* (Cambridge: Harvard University Press, 1978) and Gerald Graff, *Literature Against Itself: Literary Ideas in Modern Society* (Chicago: The University of Chicago Press, 1979).

4. Hayden White, *Tropics of Discourse: Essays in Cultural Criticism* (Baltimore: The Johns Hopkins University Press, 1978), p. 2. "This flight," White continues, "is futile; for tropics is the process by which all discourse *constitutes* the objects which it pretends only to describe realistically and to analyze objectively."

5. My use of the term "trace" echoes Jacques Derrida's use of the term. Elsewhere, my use of "supplement," "difference," "originary," and "center" are variations on Derridean suggestions.

6. No person, Frank Kermode has argued, "can go about the work of interpretation without some awareness of forces which limit, or try to limit, what he may say, and the ways in which he may say it. They may originate in the past, but will usually be felt as sanctions operated by one's contemporaries. . . . There is an organisation of opinion which may either facilitate or inhibit the individual's manner of doing interpretation . . . and determine whether a particular act of interpretation will be regarded as a success or a failure. . . . The medium of these pressures and interventions is the institution. In practice, the institution with which we have to deal is the professional community which interprets secular literature and teaches others to do so. There are better-defined and more despotic institutions, but their existence does not invalidate the present use of the expression." "Institutional Control of Interpretation," *Salmagundi*, no. 43 (1979):72–86.

7. For a discussion of reactions to identifying critical methods, see Herbert Lindenberger, "The Idea of a Critical Approach," in *Essays on European Literature in Honor of Liselotte Dieckmann*, ed. Peter Uwe Hohendahl et al. (St. Louis: Washington University Press, 1972), pp. 237–54.

8. Evan Watkins's comments on the tension between theory and practice in the work of the New Critics, *The Critical Act: Criticism and Community* (New Haven: Yale University Press, 1978).

Criticism is the (Dis)closure of Meaning

Michael McCanles

Literary criticism is discourse that presents itself as literal, about another kind of discourse that criticism treats as metaphorical. Criticism registers readers' desire to disambiguate the meanings of metaphorical discourse by showing what literal meanings metaphorical statements "really" have. By this self-conception criticism is literal discourse—nonmetaphorical, closed, codified according to a lexicon that renders a "natural" meaning of other lexicons—and consequently treats metaphorical discourse as incomplete without itself.[1]

The literal/metaphorical differential appears to be a constant in all semiotically sophisticated cultures (which is the same as saying that those cultures are semiotically sophisticated which distinguish between literal and metaphorical meanings). What changes from culture to culture, and from period to period within the same culture, is where the line is drawn between the two. Cultures and periods can in fact be defined by the lexicons and texts they privilege as official, natural, as naming

My thanks to the John Simon Guggenheim Foundation for a fellowship for the academic period 1978–79, and to Marquette University for a year's sabbatical in the same period, during which this essay was written.

reality "as it is." We also know that the history of Western thought can be segmented at those points where men for whatever reason have decided that texts that were official, natural, literal, and ultimate at one time are now "only metaphorical" and must be made equivalent to still other texts that claim the same status. Thus, for instance, medieval biblical exegesis declared that the text of the Jewish testament was "complete" only when transcoded into the text of the Christian "new testament." In the development of medieval Christian theology a similar set of equivalences and transcodages took place: from Greek philosophy into Christian theology, and still later from Christian theology back into Greek philosophy. The Renaissance gives us such transcodages growing in all directions like weeds: theology into Platonism, Platonism into alchemy (and much later with Jung, alchemy into psychology), cosmology into mathematics, natural magic into natural science, and so on. In this our post-Renaissance period natural science remains very much the repository of an official lexicon, although nuclear physics in the era of Einstein tends to retreat back into the metaphorical (an occurrence that will become significant later in this essay). The dominance of the human sciences by the lexicons of natural science has, however, partially given way to several competing lexicons at the present time, the most important of which are psychological (mainly Freudian), economic-political (mainly Marxist), and anthropological (mainly structuralist).

If interpreting a text is the same as disclosing its meaning, then interpretation asserts an equivalence: "the meanings of that text = the meanings of this text." To claim that a text requires interpreting, that it is not wholly intelligible by itself, is to say that its lexicon falls short of or deviates from some other lexicon granted a privileged place as "natural" in the hierarchy of codes.[2] Texts are discovered to be metaphorical and therefore in need of interpreting only from the perspective of official codes already granted this privilege. Interpretation then merely confirms redundantly and retroactively the claim of the official code to be natural and in that respect literal. Interpretation usurps whatever autonomy and authority the first text may claim, and displaces these onto itself the moment it brands that text as "metaphorical." In this respect interpretation claims for itself finality and closure on the meaning of the metaphorical text, and forecloses possible interpretations available through still other lexicons.

Criticism as interpretation becomes problematic because it must claim for itself such closures on meaning. In this respect criticism both dis-closes the meaning of another text, and closes down the possibility of further interpretation. And yet this closure is, it would seem, merely the occasion for still another dis-closure: the dismantling of the interpreting text, and the disclosure of its meaning in turn. In other words, the interpreting text is transformable into still another metaphorical text, one whose meaning requires still further literalization.

Interpretation is thus constituted as a three-stage relay sequence. We have, first, the text not written in an official lexicon, which is then translated into a second text that is. This text is in turn translated into a third text that claims the same finality asserted by the second. The crucial transformation in this set of relays is of course in the status of the second text, which is literal from one viewpoint and metaphorical from another. And if this seems a reasonable model of "what happens" once the human translation machine gets going, then the interplay between "literal" and "metaphorical" meanings, between fictional texts and critical texts turns into a kind of circular reciprocity: metaphorical texts demand interpretation by "literal" texts, and literal texts in turn invite still further interpretations that disclose their covert metaphoricalness.[3] If the disclosure of the meaning of a text requires the writing of still another text, then the meaning of the first text hangs decisively on the second text's closure of that meaning. But if such closure is dis-closed in still a third text, what happens to the meaning of the first one? Jacques Lacan's notion of discourse as the slide of the meaning under the metonymical chain of discursive segments suggests that the process of interpretation has become a demonic roller coaster, which we never chose to get on in the first place and from which in any case we can never escape.[4] The very notion of meaning turns out to be self-contradictory: meaning requires the interminable transcodage of texts, and meaning requires the closure of this transcodage.

For these reasons it is really no longer possible to view such transcodages as if they took place *sub specie aeternitatis*. In this respect what Jacques Derrida calls deconstruction—the discovery in a putatively literal text of its funding by a lexicon that is available to still further interpretation, further equivalences and transcodages—names in fact much of the evolution of Western thought.[5] The question that this history presents us is, knowing what we know about the fragility of any lexicon and texts that claim for themselves the status of the natural, whether criticism is still possible for us. It is in order to state some of the conditions under which criticism is still possible that I shall develop in the rest of this essay the consequences of the points I have just made.

Practically speaking, of course, criticism simply gets written all the time, each text issuing out of one natural lexicon or other, and at least implicitly indicting all other texts for unwarrantedly closing down the circulation of meaning, while proceeding to do the same thing itself. Any spectator of the current scene in literary criticism can see that interpretation has become a gigantic game of oneupmanship. Bastions of orthodoxy in America may not rise and fall as rapidly and predictably as they do in other parts of the world, but we have got the hang of it. The free-for-alls which are our national MLA conventions consist largely of discrete groups of speakers transcoding theological discourse into Marxist discourse, Marxist discourse into psychoanalytic discourse, psychoanalytic discourse into anthropological discourse, and anthopological discourse into theological discourse. The attempts of semiotics under the optimistic and buoyant sponsorship of Umberto Eco, Jurij Lotman, and their epigones to present us with a final code-of-codes have, as I suggest elsewhere, only sharpened the crisis for us.[6] It is little wonder that at this time interpretation should be in such bad odor. I am inclined to think that even without the prompting of Parisian upheavals and their belated transference across the Atlantic, American criticism would have sooner or later had to face this crisis. The paradoxes of Derridean deconstruction are in any case with us now, and they have only hurried the showdown. Reading through one leading periodical devoted to mediating and thrashing out current questions of critical theory will show that deconstruction has become almost the standard formula for discussing someone else's critical position.

I for one find the rampant relativism motivating the deconstructive approach a necessary and bracing thing. The problem with it, however, was already disclosed by Derrida some years before deconstruction became the way to do things in this country: deconstruction of meaning can never take place outside the systems of closure that it criticizes.[7] I take this caveat to mean something relatively simple, but nonetheless very troublesome: that deconstruction, in attempting to topple as unwarranted all naturalizations of meaning, all closures on the circulation of interpretive texts, has yet to confront the covert absolutizing that it yearns for, the failure of which it has transformed into discovering covert absolutizing everywhere else.

To put my point another way: the crisis of criticism that I described earlier is something it thrusts upon itself specifically because the critical act necessarily takes for granted that the literal/metaphorical differential signifies only a sharp mutual exclusiveness between the two kinds of texts. I have already suggested that this differential seems to be a constant throughout Western intellectual history, which in essence means the history of Western discursive practices. As long as this differential remains unquestioned, the literal text can only insist on its claim to be the site of "natural" meaning, and the other differentials that are versions of this one can only remain unquestioned as well. I am speaking, for instance, of the difference between the natural and the conventional, between the uncoded raw data of experience and the codes through which men give them meaning. I would include also the signifier/signified differential, by which we segregate the material substance of the sign and the text of rules that articulates it into meaningful segments.

Lying behind all these differentials is the assumption of a

noumenal reality that by definition is at once ultimate and yet unreachable, save through humanly constructed systems of meaning, which always remain suspect. If one were to reduce the multifarious complexity of current discoursing on discoursing to visceral war cries, such ejaculations would issue as a discordant combination of celebration: "All reality is only humanly constructed—Hurrah!" and despair: "All reality is only humanly constructed—Alas!"

I would suggest, in other words, that the circular transformation of metaphorical text into literal text, and (deconstructively) of literal text into metaphorical text becomes a nightmare from which we seem unable to awaken only as long as we continue to demand as necessary the very thing we insist is impossible: namely, a text that can be interpretive only by being literal, closed, and final. We need to deconstruct these texts only as long as we continue to be haunted by the dream of such a text; for it is nothing but the failure to be such a text that deconstruction features as its more or less indiscriminate *j'accuse* directed at all texts in general.

What would it mean to dismantle the literal/metaphorical differential that funds our notion of criticism? Would in fact anything like "criticism" or for that matter verbal discourse in general remain, if we "deconstructed" the signifier/signified differential, the distinction between the natural and the arbitrary, between the unmotivated sign and the "motivated sign," if such a thing exists? The most obvious thing we can say about these differentials is that we take them all for granted as "natural," as grounded in semiotic reality "as it is," that we treat them as the indispensable tools for constructing our sense of *vraisemblance* without which (is it not so?) all meaning and discussion of meaning would collapse. So far even deconstruction can take us, if we want to turn it back on itself.

But I think there is more that can be said of a constructive nature, and what I propose here can only be propaedeutic, a statement of a task to be carried out, and some suggestions for carrying it out.

If in fact doing away with these indestructible elements of

our interpretive enterprise appears to be literally inconceivable, which is the same as saying that we cannot conceive of them as anything else but "naatural," does this necessarily mean that we need be straitjacketed by the ideological, absolutizing component that seems inseparable from using them and, in a sense, believing in them? As I said elsewhere in another context when discussing the same problem in a different perspective, the problem is not how metaphorical fictions get written, but how literal texts get written.[8] Rephrasing this statement, I would ask now how it is possible to write critical texts without equivocating with our sense of their semiotic evanescence.

If we cannot do without the literal/metaphorical differential, and yet find ourselves unable to "do" with it either, then we must radicalize it, institutionalize its own inherent contradictions and turn them into positive components of the interpretive process itself. Differentiality, after all, whether semantic or any other kind, means not only mutual exclusion but also mutual implication. "Literal" and "metaphorical" texts seem always historically to spring into existence simultaneously, the designation of the one necessarily implying the designation of the other. One cannot call one text "metaphorical" without assuming still another text, actually written or not, that literalizes its metaphors. On the other hand, texts written in the official, literal lexicon of a societal group likewise claim the privilege of interpreting those texts which are written in some other lexicon, which they necessarily label "metaphorical." In such cases, the differential distinction between "literal" and "metaphorical" does not demarcate only a mutual exclusion between the two terms, but establishes mutual implication between them as well. Conceived in this way, the literal/metaphorical differential which interpretation assumes becomes a difference that implies its own transgression, the transformation of the differential slash into an equal sign, without at the same time yielding up the fact of difference. If as I said at the beginning the metaphorical text demands the literal text in order to state its own meanings, it might just as easily be said that the literal text cannot exist except as the extension of the metaphorical text, as that *of which* it is the meaning.

Yet we need not oscillate covertly between deifying the literal and deconstructing it if we are willing to challenge the naturalness of the literal/metaphorical differential. The literal and the metaphorical both exclude and imply each other, and this means in turn that what is literal from one perspective is always metaphorical from another perspective. Within metaphorical fictions (and what else are there?) metaphors are always treated as literal. And this is a statement that we must apply indifferently to "literature" as much as to "criticism."[9]

With these conclusions in mind we may discover that the demarcation between literature and literary criticism becomes rather fluid, a boundary that is honored only in the act of breacbing it. The interpretive text thus becomes the extension—one out of several possible—of the metaphorical text itself. Just as, through the interpretive strategies we presently use, the literary text becomes the extension of the interpretive text, reconstituted by being embedded literally in the site of its interpretation. The act of criticism is no less creatively metaphorizing than the act of creating, in pursuing the rigorous entailments of its own metaphors, is literalistically interpretive.

Every text then becomes literal not by attempting to dwell "at the top" in absolute Newtonian space, but rather by placing itself in Einsteinian space. By this I mean that the interpretive text can claim authority for its transcodages because it acknowledges its own metaphoricalness, its own motion, as it were, relative to the motion of the text it interprets. The exhortations of structuralism can help us by encouraging us to establish in the interpretive text not only the rules of the metaphorical text that is being interpreted, but also the rules of the metaphorical text that is doing the interpreting. These rules are always, vis-à-vis other models of meaning, arbitrary. But yet within themselves they owe allegiance to nothing but the rigors of their own self-appointed constraints on selection and combination. And according to these rules the text is absolute; it closes down the circulation of meaning, and its vulnerability to further transcodage does not undo or negate what it has articulated. It cannot, in this Einsteinian universe of expanding discursive space, expect to seize the privileges of still other texts. But on the other hand it need not yield the privileges of its own articulations to any other text that may interpret it in turn.

The prime condition of a text's capacity to interpret is that it be interpretable. In order to "construct" meaning it must pay the price of being deconstructible. The Derridean circulation of texts need not incarnate a despairing pursuit of a meaning that like the horizon beckons us ever onward by its own disappearance. If such a horizon of meaning is essentially an illusion of a Newtonian universe, the emblem both of meaning's necessity and of its own impossibility, then our dispelling its mystifications ought to dispel its contradictions and paradoxes as well.

Let me close with an observation that this essay forces on itself. To write it I have had perforce to assume the differential that I wanted to deconstruct. To talk about transgressing the literal/metaphorical differential I found it necessary to assume it. How else articulate something about these two terms without acquiescing in the constraints imposed by the plus/minus features that mark them? Does it now seem necessary to relegate "literal" and "metaphorical" to the limbo of quotation marks? Or to follow Derrida's desperate practice and write them *sous rature*: as in ~~LITERAL~~ and ~~METAPHORICAL~~? This essay has turned out to be a performance enacting the procedures of thought it has called for and explained. In a sense it has appeared to argue itself into its own cancellation. Possibly, but perhaps not quite. What I have written leads a provisional and temporary existence, like the kinds of texts it has discussed: making a brief gesture of closure before disappearing like a soul in Dante's *Inferno* back into the indistinguishable whirlwind of circulating meanings. Like the terms "literal" and "metaphorical" crossed out above, this essay appears only to disappear again. And the cost of its reappearance seems to be nothing less than this disappearance.

NOTES

1. I am exploiting in this essay the overlap among several meanings of "metaphorical": (1) Use of a word in a context where its prescribed dictionary meaning is inconsistent with its syntactical and semantic context, requiring the reader to recognize this deviance and the necessity of discovering another meaning that will recuperate its sense. (2) Related to this traditional meaning for the term is Jacques Lacan's notion of interpretation of dreams by analogy to the interpretation of rhetorical devices, such as those given in handbooks of tropes and figures, wherein "deviant" usages are explained by "normal" equivalents; see "The Function of Language in Psychoanalysis," *The Language of the Self: The Function of Language in Psychoanalysis*, trans. Anthony Wilden (New York: Delta Books, 1975), p. 31. (3) Related to this second meaning is Lacan's further notion (p. 113) of metaphor as the substitution of one word for a second when the latter is normally called for in the chain of discourse. (4) Finally, any lexicon is "metaphorical" that is different from the lexicons designated by a culture or a segment of a culture as official, natural, and literal. In my essay these last three terms are treated as equivalent.

2. See Jonathan Culler, *Structuralist Poetics: Structuralism, Linguistics and the Study of Literature* (Ithaca, N.Y.: Cornell University Press, 1975), pp. 137ff for the various meanings "naturalization" has accrued in the history of formalist and structuralist theory. In my essay lexicons are "natural" by a kind of collective, cultural fiat, which designates certain codes as motivated by a direct correspondence with the actual structure of the cosmos or some part of it.

3. Harold Bloom in "Poetic Crossing: Rhetoric and Psychology," *The Georgia Review* 30 (1976): 495–524 calls this interplay of perspectives on the same text an *aporia* that "is beyond resolution." Bloom's paradigm for this *aporia* is the Kabbalah which holds "that all distinction between proper and figurative meaning in language has been totally lost, since the catastrophe of creation" (513). Bloom says that he "verges . . . upon the true outrageousness of the Kabbalistic theory of rhetoric" when he argues that a reader of "strong poetry" finds it necessary to accept the text as literal while knowing that it is also metaphorical. I would suggest that this *aporia* does not result from abolishing the literal/metaphorical distinction. An *aporia* in medieval logic is the apparently equal claims to validity of two distinguishable and mutually exclusive propositions. And I would contend that the double awareness noted by Bloom does not lead to an *aporia* but rather to the recognition of two different perspectives on the text's claims, both of which while being opposed are yet complementary. As I argued in "The Literal and the Metaphorical: Dialectic or Inter-

change," *PMLA* 91 (1976): 279–90, the inability to distinguish between literal and metaphorical meanings is in fact a common sickness of metaphorical consciousness. What this means is that any text can be either literal or metaphorical in a completely random and uncontrolled fashion.

4. *The Language of the Self*, p. 212. Interpretation as indefinitely extended transcodage from text to text is implicit in the various versions of semiosis Umberto Eco synthesizes in *A Theory of Semiotics* (Bloomington: Indiana University Press, 1976), particularly Eco's development of C. S. Peirce's theory of interpretants, pp. 68ff. The literal/metaphorical differential as still another paradigm for the chain of meaning from signifier to signified has not, I think, been generally noticed. In terms of Jakobson's notion of discursive syntagms as metonymic displacement, it might be noted that the part-whole relation named by metonymy allows a literal text to brand a metaphorical text as a "part" of a whole which is the province of the literal text. Of course, wholes seem continually to transform themselves into parts of still other totalities; see Roman Jakobson and Morris Halle, *Fundamentals of Language* (The Hague: Mouton, 1956), and my article "'All Discourse Aspires to the Analytic Proposition,'" in *What is Literature?* ed. Paul Hernadi (Bloomington: Indiana University Press, 1978), pp. 190–210.

5. Jacques Derrida, *Of Grammatology*, trans. Gayatri Chakravorty Spivak (Baltimore: The Johns Hopkins University Press, 1976), pp. 233–35 and passim: also translator's introduction, pp. lxxvii–lxxviii.

6. See my article "Conventions of the Natural and the Naturalness of Conventions," *Diacritics* 7 (1977):54–63, on Umberto Eco's *A Theory of Semiotics*. Also Jurij Lotman, *The Structure of the Artistic Text*, trans. Ronald Vroon, (Ann Arbor: Michigan Slavic Contributions, 1977).

7. Jacques Derrida, "Structure, Sign, and Play in the Discourse of the Human Sciences," in *The Structuralist Controversy: The Languages of Criticism and the Sciences of Man*, ed. Richard Macksey and Eugenio Donato (Baltimore: The Johns Hopkins University Press, 1972), pp. 247–65.

8. "The Literal and the Metaphorical: Dialectic or Interchange."

9. The other semiotic tools we take as natural can likewise be made unproblematic once we recognize that there is no incompatibility between the unmotivated arbitrariness of codes vis-à-vis other codes, and the motivated constraints a given code imposes on the selections and combinations of its constituent signs. Within a Saussurian perspective we can grant the arbitrariness of the segmentations that a *langue* makes within the content- and meaning-substance available to it. But once these segmentations have been made, the signifier-signified relations within that *langue* are no longer arbitrary, but rather constrained regarding what signs can intelligibly be linked

with other signs. See Ferdinand de Saussure, *Course in General Linguistics*, ed. Charles Bally and Albert Sechehaye, trans. Wade Baskin (New York: Philosophical Library, 1959), pp. 133–34. More broadly, the conventional is just that in relation to other conventions, but establishes within itself a "naturalness" insofar as the units of the convention imply each other by the articulatory rules that constitute it. In short, transcodage from one lexicon to another is perfectly feasible without necessarily calling into question the "naturalness" of sign-combinations in texts funded by that code.

Criticism as a Secondary Art

Murray Krieger

Until a decade or so ago we would not seriously have doubted that the fundamental task of literary criticism was to interpret works of "imaginative literature," thereby making them available to their culture, and to subject them to the constant revaluations which, by arranging and rearranging the make-up of a literary canon, would supervise a culture's literary taste. In accordance with this historically sanctioned task, most literary critics have until recently taken for granted the commonplace that their verbal artifact finds its starting point where another verbal artifact has left off, and that the latter is prior both temporally and authoritatively to what they write *about* it. Whatever their feelings about the referentiality of the originally creative work of literature itself, they have seemed to accept the obvious fact of the intended referentiality of their own work of interpretation and judgment. Whatever their epistemology in aesthetics, they have appeared as naive realists in relating their own texts to the master text. For they mutely ac-

This essay is a condensed version of "Literary Criticism: A Primary or a Secondary Art?" in *Arts on the Level: The Fall of the Elite Object*, the author's John C. Hodges Lectures, copyright © 1981 by University of Tennessee Press. It is used here by permission.

knowledged that original work as the ground and the very reason for their own, thereby promising us some attempt at fidelity to their subject and inviting us to judge the work of criticism, at least in part, in accordance with the fidelity it achieves.

Since there are other critics writing on many of the same works, within a Western tradition that—with whatever changes become necessary from time to time—has established its restricted canon of original works deserving such critical treatment, the individual critic has likely proceeded in a way that recognizes not only the fixed and absolute priority of the original work, but also the subsequent—if conditional—priority of earlier critical works, which could have their authority challenged by the newer critic even if their temporal precedence were unquestioned. This critic can, in other words, argue with received interpretations and evaluations of individual works and the groups of works we call movements, beginning his own text where the others have left off in dealing with the original master text, but he begins—as presumably, did the others before him—by assuming that original authority against which his own work must be measured as it challenges its earlier (and later) rivals. But his work is not to challenge or threaten to supplant or supersede that original which, interpreted this way or that by this critic or others, will continue to stand and to authorize further critics. In this way the original is the ultimate judge of those whose work was intended to furnish a rationalization for our judgment of that original.

The critic is thus seen as the middleman between the original work and its culture, seeking to speak out for a work which, for all it says, must—like Keats's urn—be silent about its own meaning. That is, his is a twice-told tale: he tells a tale which, already told, can say no more in its own behalf. But his is a second telling, never a first. He tries to make manifest all that is potentially locked in the work, tries to allow it thoroughly to "perform"itself for the audience he seeks to create for it. So he interprets and—implicitly or explicitly—evaluates, helping to improve the taste of his culture by his arguments which can corroborate the place a work has in the elite canon of works or can claim a place in the canon for a work wrongly excluded or, more rarely, can seek to deflate a high received opinion of a work in order to remove it from the canon. For a work to be elevated into the canon is for it—almost literally—to be canonized.

Always, within such a conception of the nature and function of literary criticism, subsequent readers and critics judge the work of the critic and compare it to others by invoking that ultimate authority of the primary work, next to which all works are secondary. This is again to say that the critic's work of judgment is finally to be judged by the work he is presumably judging (or at least by our own version of that original work, a version which must, of course, itself come to be judged by it). The history of criticism may thus be seen as celebrating the sacred mystery which permeates the circle of both interpretation and judgment, a circle presumably made "just" by being made to end where it began.

I have deliberately overstated the case, using my rhetoric to urge the presence of a fetishizing motive for criticism as commentary on a sacred text, as allegory for an ultimately unspeakable symbol. In this way I point up my observation that, however sophisticated the critic has been about the nature of the discourse he seeks to unlock for us (however skeptical about its relation to *its* reality), he remains—at least hopefully—committed to a naive realism concerning the relation of his own discourse to its object. To the extent this is so, it may be no rhetorical exaggeration for my language to emphasize the fetishization of the original works and the sanctified canon made up of them.

These are the consequences to which the assumptions of the usual notion of criticism in our history can be shown to lead, although it is obvious that most critics who share them are hardly prepared to push them explicitly to such idolatrous extremes. Further, if such are the almost automatic assumptions made by critics as they have addressed their role as interpretive and judgmental mediators acting in behalf of literary works for their culture, it is also the case that individual critics have frequently acted in accordance with lines less cleanly demarcated between creative and critical functions. An obvious example is Matthew Arnold, who—in his central essay, "The Function of Criticism at the Present Time" (1864)—may have distinguished clearly enough between poetry and criticism, but largely in order to allow criticism to appropriate some of the creative power normally granted poetry.[1] In the course of his argument he further proceeds to free criticism from a referential obligation to poems by enlarging the domain of that word from strictly literary criticism (that is, the criticism of literary works) to the general criticism of human problems which constitutes the world of ideas. And it becomes clear here and in other of his writings that this general promulgation of "the best that has been thought and said in the world" by poetry and and criticism alike becomes, in the broadest sense, the indivisible realm of literature. As an early version of "*écriture*," such a notion clearly entails the loss of distinction between poetry (as self-conscious fiction-making) and its fellow discourses more directly concerned with communicating ideas, so that the door has been opened to putting the poem and the critical discourse about it at the same level of creativity, essentially blurring the distinction between them. Arnold hardly meant to dethrone poetry from its special role in culture (see, for example, his idolatrous claims in "The Study of Poetry" about poetry's "high destinies" and "immense" future as a surrogate religion), but implicit in the creative power he gave to criticism to generate ideas is a leveling of discourse which could serve to undermine the limited notion of criticism as a secondary art serving the primary art of poetry, held aloft as its proper subject and justification.

Or one may cite, as another example of critics who seem to blur the dividing line between poetic and critical discourse, the willed self-indulgence of critical impressionism. Whether we speak of the free subjective projections sponsored (late in the last century and early in this one) by the call to "creative criticism" or of the more recent merger of the critic's and the poet's subjectivities in the Geneva School "critics of consciousness," we seem to be licensing in the critic an independence of voice which may seem to challenge the priority of the poem as the critic's "object" which I have suggested our critical tradition has taken for granted. But even as liberating a suggestion as Poulet's that criticism is "literature about literature" acknowledges an about-ness in the critic's obligation, so that criticism, though literature, is clearly a second-order literature and hence derivative. However such criticism strays over the line toward poetry, it is hardly being granted an independent authority as an autonomous function.

Nevertheless, in contrast to occasional moods which have impelled some critics during the past century and a half toward usurpation of the poet's role, the more modest assumptions about the critic's role generally held sway until the revolutionary conceptions of criticism in the last decade or so. Indeed, during the days of the largely unquestioned supremacy of the New Criticism, the critic's role as faithful vassal to the poem achieved its strongest assertion: the poetic "object" was to be treated as the critic's idol, as the sole justification of his joyfully acknowledged subsidiary existence. Of course, the work was to be taken as totally interpretable, so that each critic was to have arrogance enough to offer the ultimate key to interpretation, but always—so the oath of fidelity went—in the service of each master text, from which it was his obligation to keep his own interests distinct. In the flurry of interpretations and reinterpretations—with the consequent evaluations and revaluations—all mystery was to be discursively exposed in a burst of hermeneutic hubris such as criticism had probably never known. And it may very well have been this excess which prepared the way for the inversion which the very concept of criticism as a serving art has undergone in recent years. I may in my turn have to suggest that the claim to critical autonomy—with its denial of priority to literature—is itself excessive.

Several varieties of criticism which are currently fashionable reveal an assumption which the critical tradition I have been describing must find shocking in its self-assertiveness, even if it has today become a commonplace: that the critical work and the poem which is its presumed object are of the same order of creativity; that, despite our intuitive sense of which comes first, both may claim an equal priority. In other words, criticism, no less than what we usually think of as "imaginative literature," is a primary art, and the writing of criticism a primary act. In speaking of "criticism" here, I am not using the word in the broad Arnoldian sense which would include all apparently nonfictional prose and could be applied to large groups of writers like Montaigne, Pascal, Rousseau, Marx, Nietzsche, or Arnold himself—writers whose work these days seems so attractively available for critical study. I shall not in this essay (though I do elsewhere[2]) argue whether or not that sort of criticism in the broad sense should be treated as imaginative literature of the same order of primacy as what we usually think of as poetry. The case here is more extreme in that I am speaking only of *literary* criticism—criticism which is, presumably, commentary *about* (and, consequently, commentary *after*) literary works, considered singly or in groups. The possible blurring between literature and criticism would, on the face of it, seem harder to justify when the case for criticism has been narrowed to cover only what appears to be literary commentary. Yet the revolutionary view of criticism which I am here introducing into the argument—though it might see itself free to dwell upon general nonpoetic discourse as well as poetry—would hardly settle for anything less than primacy even for itself as a work of explicitly literary criticism, though it appears to spring from the stimulus of other works. We can look, for example, at the complaint of Edward Said, who argues for this revolutionary concept of criticism, a criticism which for him shares the repetitive character of all literature:

> For in a very deep way, critical discourse is still ensnared by a simplistic opposition between originality and repetition, in which all literary texts worth studying are given the former classification, the latter being logically confined mainly to criticism and to what isn't worth studying. I believe such schemata to be hopelessly paralyzing. They mistake the regularity of most literary production for originality, while insisting that the relation between "literature" and criticism is one of original to secondary; moreover, they overlook, in both traditional and modern

literature, the profoundly constitutive use of repetition—as motif, device, epistemology, and ontology.[3]

Where repetition is everywhere, then all work is a coming-after, and originality—like the very notion of origins—is a myth. This notion reminds us that I may have put the matter wrongly by seeing recent criticism as fighting to claim poetry's primacy for itself; what I should rather have suggested is that criticism can accept a secondary status so long as it shares that status with literature. If there is no primacy in criticism, it is because there is no literal primacy in discourse at all; thus there is no *less* primacy in criticism than in "literature."

Let me suggest three related ways in which recent critical attitudes encourage such a notion of equal primacy (or non-primacy) for criticism to become an almost automatic presupposition in some quarters these days. To begin with, the notion may be seen as a consequence of the acknowledgment, produced by epistemological candor, that the critic's pretension to deal "objectively" with that thing out there which stands outside his discourse, having preexisted it, is belied by the reflexive nature of his activity. Critics have for some time been readier than they used to be to confront the radical subjectivity which underlies their sincerest efforts at disinterested analysis and appraisal.[4] Their desire to be responsive to controls in the object which they claim to discover—and which they seek to persuade others to discover with them—is no longer permitted to hide the fact that they have projected the controls out of their experience with the poem. So criticism is now confessed to be—and to have always been—a rewriting of the object in the critic's own terms, and thus in effect the creation of a new object, or rather of a projection which he then treats as if it were the discovered object. Whatever his hopes for fidelity, the poem he is faithful to is in the end his own. Once this element of narcissistic reduction is seen as paramount, the confessional nature of the critical act and product is itself confessed to. The poem itself, reduced to a minimal stimulus, becomes—in both senses of the word—a mere "pretext." And critical discourse can be elevated into the primary text itself.

A second justification of criticism as a primary art, perhaps another version of the first, is urged by those who put all forms of writing on the same footing as created fictions, refusing to make any distinction between those—like poems—which self-consciously intend to be fictions only and those—like criticism—which seem to intend to refer, with a claim to accuracy with which one can agree or disagree, to other discourse.[5] So viewed, criticism—plotted in accordance with the fiction that it depends on a prior fiction—is primary as both art and act in the sense that all acts, as art—that is, as texts—are equally primary. This concept can be pressed toward a third: that all writings, like their writers, are in rivalry with one another.[6] Poets are seen as competing with their predecessors no more than critics compete with their poet-subjects and with earlier critics of those poets: each work struggles against the fact of time to establish its own claim to primacy. All texts, poems and critical works alike, feed on one another, so that—from this perspective—no text is actually primary. The intertextuality all texts share is their ego-driven reason for being and assures the lack of hierarchy or priority among their claims, as these are given status by the theorist.

In view of the idiosyncratic freedoms—either of interpretation or of judgment—taken by critics throughout the history of their discipline, is it stubborn and naive to insist that such defenses of its primacy and independence are excessive? Is it, in other words, merely unrealistic to refuse to sanction in theory what in fact criticism is so often doing?

There is, however, this difference between the general failure of the critic to perform the "secondary" act which it has presumably been his function to perform and the particular commitment of critics under the aegis of this recent license to perform independently. For the first time, I believe, criticism has gone beyond rearranging the canon: in its recent revolutionary mode, criticism has undermined the very principle on which the canon—as a collection of primary works—exists, reconstructing it precisely in order to make a place for itself within it. Though in the past criticism has, intentionally or not, altered its object (or, to use a more precise epistemology, recreated it) to serve its needs, it now rejects the notion that it *has* an object, proclaiming itself as a free-ranging, arbitrary subject, an absolute subject which, in effect, can replace the object with itself. The critic thus becomes a true rival of the poet, filling his work with self-conscious reflexivity. He is dependent on prior texts, but no more so than the poet is, remaking them into the newness of his own work with the poet's abandon. He joins the parade of intertextuality as a totally unfettered participant. Freed from older criticism's myth of responsibility to an object, he can indulge the misreadings authorized by his irresponsibility and remake the body of discourse with his every contribution, fulfilling the task that Eliot had, decades ago, given to the talented traditional poet.

What, then, of the role criticism used to dedicate itself—however self-deceptively—to performing? Is it now to be dissolved, or will it not still exist, however unperformed or even unperformable? Because criticism, by its nature, must fail to perform it except by occasional indirection, should it no longer try, even if only with a self-conscious awareness of its necessary limits, at once epistemological and psychological? The only justification for obliterating the conventional notion of criticism's role is our acknowledgment that, in the new egalitarianizing of writing, there no longer are literary works—no longer a corpus of works to be served, a canon to be continaully created and sustained. But I am assuming that there *are* primary works—utterly primary despite their inevitably intertextual character—which deserve not to be abandoned, which historically have stimulated experiences we have found uniquely valuable, experiences which testify to the power of a self-consciously manipulated fiction in a self-consciously manipulated language.

Consequently, I am assuming also that the older and more conventional role of criticism still needs performing. Despite the seductions of critical self-inflation, I must still write in defense of the more modest—if less heroic—conception of criticism as a secondary art. It is an art, surely, and it may seem to share some of its secondary attributes with poetry in their commonly intertextual nature; but it is a second telling of the tale and should accept referential obligations to the poem's first telling. As a limited literary criticism, it must acknowledge the poem as its point of origin, whatever intertextual lines flow into and out of them both. Those readers for whom it is written retain the right to ask that it try to give readings rather than misreadings, however fated it may be—epistemologically and psychologically—to be trapped within the latter. And the reader, as a rival critic, may quarrel about how far the reading has missed.

What I am suggesting is that the new vogue in criticism, for all its revolutionary attractiveness, is, ultimately, another—though perhaps the most radical—of the many varieties of subjectivism we have seen in the last century. The standard answers given subjectivism by a critical tradition busy with its ongoing work can serve again here. We need the healthy skepticism which reminds us of our egocentric predicament, thereby demystifying the critic's authoritarian claims and their metaphysical ground; but the culture's need to have such claims made—and denied and remade—is not thereby eliminated. We are better off being aware of the pragmatic nature of our critical need, and thus alive to its shaky epistemological foundations, but not if we are led to surrender the referential responsibility of literary commentary and to license critical self-indulgence just because it plagues us even if we try to rein it in. The critic's instinct for arrogance is compelling enough without being encouraged by the suggestion that he need have no other motive, that his own work need never bow to the superior authority of a text proclaimed as primary by its every word. Critical humility is not a virtue in such oversupply that we should theoretically preclude it. On the contrary, the epistemological reality of the critic's relation to the original text is such that he must always be deluded about any pretense at humility: the subservience of his perspective to his own needs ensures a self-serving vision, whatever its guise. There can of course be no neutral object out there to serve as monitor, no matter how strait a jacket he would put on his predilections.

Yet there are times when fellow critics find one another talking about what seems to be the same work. Despite being trapped in our subjectivity, it is hard for us to ignore the partial agreement that dialogue occasionally makes possible among critical readers. If the extent of agreement in critical history seems slight next to the remaining disagreements, the fact that there is *any* agreement is another pragmatic justification for doing what critics ordinarily do and suggests grounds for the phenomenological assumption that there is a common object for critics to dispute about, or at least that the object is not altogether an idiosyncratic one invented to serve their needs. The history of taste can be made to exaggerate evidence about the subjectivity of judgments, despite the most pious professions of disinterestedness, but the disparities would be the more violent if critics began with the assumption that they owed fidelity to nothing but their own discourse and the misreadings it cultivates.

The conflict which the Anglo-American critical tradition still wages with the many dominant influences of continental poststructuralism has perhaps its most significant consequences (for literary study at least) in this question of the theoretical subservience of criticism to the elite literary text. Acknowledging the strength of the arguments which demystify all that criticism has commonly taken for granted about its operations, criticism yet must clear some ground on which to operate. Still willing to grant the special character of works it has canonized, it feels impelled to retain its function of playing middleman between these texts and their culture, both making their meaning available and judging them as being worthy of that mediating effort of interpretation.

The interpretive act assumes that the poem is of greater interest and is less self-explanatory as a marshaling of language than the criticism of it is; it assumes that the poem is reflexive and self-deconstructive, so that criticism about it must try—however vainly—to be the referential equivalent of that which cannot speak for itself. But the revolutionary critic who rejects such subservience sees his own work as possessing the attributes others would confine to poetry, matching or improving upon poetry's self-deconstructive powers. One might even argue that such a critic thrives the more as the fortunes of poetry decline. As poems, now denied elite status, dwindle into the common level of writing decreed for them by recent theory, the ambition of criticism can grow proportionately. The classless democracy of texts is encouraged when the nobility of poetry sheds its ennobling characteristics. But now the writer of criticism may try to pick those characteristics up, though without running the risk of becoming a poet himself: by seeking to deconstruct that which no longer is granted the capacity to deconstruct itself, the critic can hold his own ground while usurping the poet's. So the critic nowadays can be charged with having an interest in the leveling of poetry as discourse, since he sees himself in a stronger position when less distinguished poetry is produced. It is another version of my earlier charge that recent criticism seeks not just to rearrange the corpus, but to put itself into it as at least an equal—indeed, as a first among equals. If this is more than an empty charge, it may account for the fact that some of these critics are supportive of the antipoetic tendency in much recent poetry, that which would make each poem indistinguishable in kind from all writing, a text among indiscriminate texts. For the world thus becomes nothing but texts, postmodern texts served by—or rather manipulated by—a postmodern criticism. And only this criticism, providing the deconstructionist's interpretive key to all, turns out to serve as a master text.

This is to make culture pay a heavy price for the self-aggrandizing impulse of a criticism which would now collapse the world into its reduced vision. We can give full due to those factors in the critical process which inhibit a critic's capacity to close with his object on *its* terms, but in doing so we need not make his work as freely creative as—and no more referential than—a poem. It may thus be possible to profit from the theoretical skepticism which propels the self-conscious awareness of recent criticism, without depriving either criticism of its role as literary companion or culture of the interlocutor it requires to keep its most unique accomplishments in language continually functioning for it at their full performance potential.

About a dozen years ago, in the title essay of *The Play and Place of Criticism,* I tried to balance the needs of critical presumptuousness with those of critical modesty.[7] And although the theoretical issues seemed very different in those days, I believe the balance I tried to achieve between mutually constraining and even contradictory forces within the critic is not seriously different from what I would urge now. The critic must play, I said, but the critic must know his place; indeed, he must somehow make his peace with the injunction to play *within* his place. Although the notion of play would seem to presuppose freedom, somehow the critic's is an almost-but-not-quite-free play, at least according to this injunction. And in that slight qualification placed upon "free play" we find a lingering resistance to the revolutionary criticism of recent deconstructionists by even those who would be most flexible in accommodating older critical practice to what must now be acknowledged about the critic's egocentricity and logocentricity.

As play that is not altogether without referential responsibility, criticism becomes variations on a theme. Though those variations threaten to form a center of their own, an almost-rival center, that primary theme arising from criticism's perception *of the work* yet remains the original center which prevents any potential rival from being more than an almost-rival. Though the work must suffer the centrifugal motions which constitute the separate life of criticism, the work remains, ultimately, the origin and center for the critic's work.

The notion of a play that is not quite free, of independent variations that yet circle a theme, requires the positing of an origin and a center which persist to rivet the critic despite his arrogant and even jealous fondness for his own role. The setting forth of such paradoxical functions for the critic, must seem, in view of our recently most fashionable criticism, at once concessive and conservative. It must strike profound disagreement with the poststructuralist will to deconstruct the very claim to any origin or center. The insistence that the poem is the primary text and that criticism—for all its would-be independent flights—is secondary rests on just such a claim to an origin and a center. The contrary insistence on the exclusive and universal operation of intertextuality in discourse must preclude any primary text or such a hierarchy as I suggest and leave all texts leveled in a dynamic field of mutuality.[8]

In defense of our older critical habits, I can finally do little more than call attention to each critic's innate sense of the superiority of the work he has chosen, his sense of its difference as a mode of discourse from what he is writing. If his arrogance as the present writer (like all writers trying to free himself from his dependence on past texts) will in any case assert itself, he can be the better critic for using conservative theory to curb it. Even if there is futility in his attempt to get to the work (as if it were available to him objectively), there are slight—though crucial—differences in degree between what he can tell us when his criticism indulges in utterly free play and what he can tell us when he seeks to range his criticism around the poem. The critic may certainly wish his discursive freedom to be absolute, so that—though but a critic—he is telling his tale as if for the first time, but it is healthier for him to remember that—as I have suggested earlier—his is a second telling. Indeed, it is much more than the second as he joins the march of tellers behind the original teller (who *is* the original teller of this tale, if it is a good tale, no matter how rich his sources and how dependent upon them he may be). The parade of critics is a long one, and the critic is dependent upon them, as his secondary sources, in a way different from his dependence on his primary source and different from the latter's dependence on a tradition of similar primary sources.

The satellites that revolve about a major planet may persuade us of their independent brilliance, but satellites they remain. This is just about the relationship I am urging between criticism and its primary work. There is a different, but not totally unallied metaphor in the passage from Plato's *Ion* in which he speaks of the stone of Heraclea. Its wisdom still speaks to us. This passage furnished me with the epigraph for "The Play and Place of Criticism," and it seems especially appropriate as a closing metaphor for what the critic does and how he is related to the poet. Socrates is addressing the rhapsode and praising his excellent commentary about Homer:

> . . . there is a divinity moving you, like that contained in the stone which Euripides calls a magnet, but which is commonly

known as the stone of Heraclea. This stone not only attracts iron rings, but also imparts to them a similar power of attracting other rings; and sometimes you may see a number of pieces of iron and rings suspended from one another so as to form quite a long chain: and all of them derive their power of suspension from the original stone. In like manner the Muse first of all inspires men herself; and from these inspired persons a chain of other persons is suspended, who take the inspiration. . . . Do you know that the spectator is the last of the rings which, as I am saying, derive their power from the original magnet; and the rhapsode like yourself and the actors are intermediate links, and the poet himself is the first link of all?

NOTES

1. I treat Arnold's expansion of the domain of criticism beyond the criticism of literary works in my essay "The Critical Legacy of Matthew Arnold; or, the Strange Brotherhood of T. S. Eliot, I. A. Richards, and Northrop Frye," in *Poetic Presence and Illusion: Essays in Critical History and Theory* (Baltimore: Johns Hopkins University Press, 1979), pp. 92–107.

2. In "Literature vs. *Ecriture:* Constructions and Deconstructions in Recent Critical Theory," in *Poetic Presence and Illusion*, pp. 169–87.

3. Edward Said, "Roads Taken and Not Taken in Contemporary Criticism," in *Directions for Criticism: Structuralism and its Alternatives*, ed. Murray Krieger and L. S. Dembo (Madison: University of Wisconsin Press, 1977), p. 50.

4. See, as an example, my *Theory of Criticism: A Tradition and its System* (Baltimore: Johns Hopkins University Press, 1976), chap. 3 ("The Critic as Person and Persona").

5. For example, see Hayden White, "Introduction: Tropology, Discourse, and the Modes of Human Consciousness," *Tropics of Discourse: Essays in Cultural Criticism* (Baltimore: Johns Hopkins University Press, 1978).

6. The obvious example is Harold Bloom. Among his recent books, see especially *The Anxiety of Influence* (New York: Oxford University Press, 1973) and *The Map of Misreading* (New York: Oxford University Press, 1975).

7. *The Play and Place of Criticism* (Baltimore: Johns Hopkins University Press, 1967), pp. 2–16.

8. On the ubiquity of intertextuality and the lack of *origin*ality in any text, one may look almost any place in the recent work of J. Hillis Miller; for example, "Walter Pater: A Partial Portrait," *Daedalus* (Winter 1976), especially p. 105, and "Stevens' Rock and Criticism as Cure, II," *Georgia Review* 30 (1976), especially p. 334.

APPENDIX

A Historical Perspective

LITERARY CRITICISM

René Wellek

Literary criticism may be defined as "discourse about literature," and in this wide sense, usual in English, it includes description, analysis, interpretation as well as the evaluation of specific works of literature and discussion of the principles, the theory, and the aesthetics of literature, or whatever we may call the discipline formerly discussed as poetics and rhetoric. Frequently, however, literary criticism is contrasted with a descriptive, interpretative, and historical account of literature and restricted to evaluative, "judicial" criticism. In other languages the more narrow conception is preferred, particularly in German where *Kritik* usually means only "the reviewing of literary novelties and the judging of literary and musical performances in the daily press" (*Reallexikon der deutschen Literaturgeschichte*, Bern [1959], 2:63), though recently, probably under English and American influence, the wider use has again become common.

"Criticism" in English emerged early in the seventeenth century, apparently based on the analogy of such sixteenth-century terms as Platonism, Stoicism, skepticism, etc., devised to avoid the homonym which arose from the impossibility of distinguishing in English between "critic," the person, and "critique," the activity. Dryden, in the preface to the *State of Innocence* (1677), said that by "criticism, as it was first instituted by Aristotle, was meant a standard of judging

This essay is a considerably expanded and slightly revised version of the author's contribution, under the same title, to *The Dictionary of the History of Ideas*, ed. in chief Philip P. Wiener, 4 vols. (New York: Charles Scribner's Sons: 1968–73), 1:596–607. Reprinted by permission.

well," and in the same year in a letter (*Letters*, ed. C. E. Ward [1942]) he spoke of Thomas Rymer's *Tragedies of the Last Age* as "the best piece of criticism in the English language." Two years later, his play *Troilus and Cressida* was introduced by a preface on "The Grounds of Criticism in Tragedy." Pope's *Essay on Criticism* (1711) established the term for good, though for a time the term "critic," "critick," or "critique" was used in the eighteenth century where we would say "criticism."

Long forms, analogous to the English "criticism," are rare in other languages. *Criticismo* occurs in Spanish, in Baltasar Gracián's *El Heroe* (1637), and sporadically in eighteenth-century Italian, but disappeared as there was no problem of homonymy. In Germany, however, *Kritizismus* was used by Schelling, Friedrich Schlegel, Jacobi, and Hegel, for the philosophy of Kant. This nonliterary use penetrated then into French, Italian, and Spanish. In these languages *criticisme* or *criticismo* means today only Kantianism.

The term ultimately derives from the Greek *krínō* "to judge," and *krités, "a judge" or "juryman." Kritikós,* as "judge of literature," was used as early as the fourth century B.C. Philitas, who came to Alexandria in 305 B.C. from the island Kos as the tutor of the future king Ptolemy II, was called "a poet and also a critic." Crates was at the head of a school of "critics" at Pergamon which seemed to have argued for a distinction from the school of "grammarians" headed by Aristarchos in Alexandria. The word "critic" is used in contradistinction from "grammarian" in the pseudo-Platonic *Axiochos* (366E). Galen, in the second century A.D., wrote a lost treatise on the question of whether one could be a *kritikós* and a *grammatikós* at the same time. But the distinction seems to have become blurred in antiquity. The term is rare in classical Latin: Hieron in the *Epistolae* speaks of Longinus as *criticus*. *Criticus* was a higher term than *grammaticus*, but *criticus* was also concerned with the interpretation of texts and words. What today would be called literary criticism was, in antiquity, discussed by philosophers like Aristotle and by rhetoricians like Quintilian.

In the Middle Ages the word seems to occur only as a term in medicine: in the sense of "critical" illness. In the Renaissance the word was revived in its ancient meaning. Angelo Poliziano in 1492 exalted the critic and grammarian against the schoolman. Grammarian, critic, philologist became almost interchangeable terms for the men engaged in the great revival of classical learning. With Erasmus, "the art of criticism" (*ars critica*) was expanded to include the Bible. On the whole, however, among the humanists, the terms "critic" and "criticism" were limited to the editing and correcting of ancient texts. For example, Karl Schoppe (1576–1649) defined the "only aim and task of critics" as "taking pains to improve the works of writers in either Greek or Latin." Joseph Justus, the younger Scaliger (1540–1605), made criticism even a subdivision of grammar, confined to distinguishing the spurious lines of ancient poets from the genuine, to correcting corrupt readings, in short to what today is called "textual criticism."

The elder Julius Caesar Scaliger (1484–1558) was the most influential propounder of a wider conception. In his posthumous *Poetics* (1561) the entire sixth book, entitled *Criticus*, is devoted to a survey and comparison of the Greek and Roman poets with the emphasis on weighing and ranking. The penetration of the term into the vernacular was, however, very slow. Modern books entitled "Literary Criticism in the Renaissance" obscure the fact that these questions were discussed in the sixteenth century only as rhetoric or poetics. In Italy the term *critica* seems to have occurred first as late as 1595 in the *Proginnasmi Poetici* of Benedetto Fioretti (published under the pseudonym Udeno Nisiely), while it was in France that the term caught on and spread rapidly early in the seventeenth century, probably under the influence of Scaliger and his Dutch disciples, Heinsius and Vossius. Chapelain called Scaliger *le grand critique* in 1623. In 1687 La Bruyère could complain that the "critics and censurers" appear now in swarms and form factions which retard the progress of the arts (*Les Caractères*).

In France, in the seventeenth century, criticism emancipated itself from its subordination to grammar and rhetoric and absorbed or replaced "poetics," at least in part. This movement is connected with the growth and spread of the critical spirit in general, in the sense of increased skepticism, distrust of authority and rules, and later with the appeal to taste, sentiment, feeling, *je ne sais quoi*. The few writers who expressly reflected on the concept of criticism or the role of the critic, Father Bouhours in France and Alexander Pope in England, defended their ideal against pedants, censurers, and mere verbal quibblers, and described and exalted the true critic as a man of taste, a wit, a *bel esprit*. Pope, in particular, deplored the false divorce between wit and judgment and advocated a respect for antiquity, and even of the rules, while admitting "a grace beyond the reach of art" and praising the invention and imagination of Homer and Shakespeare. Fontenelle in *Discours sur la Nature de l'Eclogue* (1688) states expressly that he will devote himself to a "criticism of authors which is an examination and not a satire."

During the eighteenth century, a term which had become confined to the verbal criticism of classical writers was slowly widened to include the whole problem of understanding and judging and even the theory of knowledge and knowing. Lord Kames, a Scottish judge, attempted in his *Elements of Criticism* (1762) to give criticism an elaborate groundwork in association psychology, and proudly claimed that he was founding a new science: "To reduce the science of criticism to any regular form, has never once been attempted." In practice, he defends neoclassical taste based on universal human nature which, he recognizes, is, however, upheld only by a small group of people who enjoy leisure, live in an enlightened age, and escape corruption. Dr. Johnson's ideal is also to "establish principles of judgment," but he does not rely on any psychology theoretically formulated and always finds "an appeal open from criticism to nature" (*Preface* to Johnson's edition of Shakespeare, 1765). He is both a classicist, who believes in "fundamental laws of criticism dictated by reason and antiquity" (*Rambler* no. 156), and an empiricist, who admits that many rules are temporal and local, defensible only as custom or fashion. He is already touched by the new revolutionary force in the history of criticism: the historical spirit.

It was in Germany that the most radical consequences of the historical approach affected criticism. Johann Gottfried Herder was the first critic who completely broke with the ideal of the (fundamentally) Aristotelian tradition aiming at a rational theory of literature and permanent standards of judgment. He conceived of criticism as a process of empathy, of identification, of something intuitive and even subrational. He constantly rejected theories, systems, faultfinding. We find Herder quoting Leibniz with approval to the effect that "he likes most things he reads" (*Sämtliche Werke*, ed B. Suphan, 17:338). The correct method "in order to understand and interpret a piece of literature is to put oneself in the spirit of the piece itself" (ibid., 6:34). It is "the natural method, which leaves each flower in its place, and contemplates it there just as it is, according to time and kind, from the root to the crown. The most humble genius hates ranking and comparison. Lichen, moss, fern, and the richest scented flower: each blooms in its place in God's order" (ibid., 18:138). Each work of art is seen as part and parcel of its milieu, fulfilling its function and thus needing no criticism. Literary study became a kind of botany.

Goethe, Herder's pupil, has the same gospel of tolerance. Criticism should be only criticism of beauties. He distinguishes between destructive and productive criticism. The first is easy as it is simply the application of a yardstick. Productive criticism is much harder. "It asks: What did the author set out to do? Was his plan reasonable and sensible, and how far did he succeed in carrying it out?" (Review of Manzoni's *Conte di Carmagnola*, *Werke*, Jubiläums-Ausgabe, 37, 180). Goethe hopes that such criticism may be of assistance to an author and admits that his own criticism describes largely the influence which books have had on himself. "At bottom this is the way all readers criticize" (ibid., 37, 280). Herder and Goethe with all their historical relativism and subjectivism have not yet broken their ties to the classical tradition: but by the nineteenth century their theories had led to complete critical relativism or to the subjective criticism memorably characterized by Anatole France's definition of criticism as "the adventures of a soul among masterpieces."

Actually, about the same time, Immanuel Kant, in his *Critique of Judgment* (1790) had offered a solution to the central problem of criticism which recognized the subjectivity of aesthetic judgment but still allowed for its universality. Kant rejects any view of criticism by *a priori* principles, by laws or rules. Taste is subjective, yet aesthetic judgments differ from a taste, say, for olives or oysters by claiming universality. Aesthetic judgment, although subjective, appeals to a general judgment, to a common sense of mankind, to an ideal totality of judges. It is thus neither relative nor absolute, neither completely individual, which would mean anarchy and the end of criticism, nor absolute in the sense of an application of eternal norms. While Kant stresses the role of personal feeling he recognizes something like an aesthetic duty. We should respond to great art if we are to be fully human. It is a contemplative, problematical imperative—not a categorical imperative as in ethics. Kant's view of criticism rejects principles and doctrines. Criticism works always by examples, from the concrete. Criticism is historical, in the sense of being individual and thus different from generalizing science; it is comparative, in the sense of being a confrontation with other men, and hence is introspection, self-criticism, an examination of one's feelings.

Kant had, however, little interest in concrete works of art. Still, the speculative movement inaugurated by him gave rise to a flowering of aesthetics in the philosophies of Schelling and Hegel and to the elaborate literary theories of Schiller, Wilhelm von Humboldt, and many others. The two brothers Schlegel (closely connected with Fichte and Schelling) formulated the most complex and coherent theory of criticism at that time. The younger, Friedrich (1772–1829), was the more original mind, but August Wilhelm, the elder (1767–1845), found the most influential formulas for the romantic-classical contrast, for the organic-mechanical dichotomy which through Coleridge became part of the history of English criticism. Friedrich Schlegel decisively rejected Herder's universal tolerance which would lead to an abdication of criticism. He knew that the critical view could not be susperseded by the historical as books are not "original creatures." Criticism must "ascertain the value and non-value of poetic works of art" (*Prosaische Jugendschriften*, ed. Minor, 2:11). It can be done by close attention to the text, which must begin with an intuition of the whole. This whole is not only the individual work of art but the whole of art history. Every artist illuminates every other artist: together they form an order. The critic must "reconstruct, perceive, and characterize the subtle peculiarities of a whole" (1:40–41). This "characterization" is the business of criticism. But Schlegel also recognizes another function of criticism; polemics, incitory, anticipatory criticism, a criticism which would be not merely explanatory and conservative but productive, by guidance and instigation stimulating an emergent literature.

August Wilhelm, while in general agreement with his brother, emphasizes in his Berlin Lectures the role of history: "Even though a work of art ought to be enclosed within itself, we must consider it as belonging to a series" (*Berlin Lectures*, 3:9). Criticism, in relation to theory and history, is the mediating middle link. The critic is subjective but can strive for objectivity by a knowledge of history and by reference to theory: "critical reflection is a constant experimentation to discover theoretical statements" (ibid., 1:27). Disagreement does not necessarily result in general skepticism. "Different people may very well have their eyes on the same center, but since each of them starts from a different point of the circumference, they inscribe also different radii" (ibid., 1:28). A "perspectivism" mediating between historicism and absolutism is thus envisaged.

This mediating function of criticism was exalted by Adam Müller (1779–1829), who arrived at a completely historistic point of view. In his Lectures of 1806 (*Vorlesungen über Wissenschaft und Literatur*) he conceives of the totality of literature as developing like an organism. Friedrich Schlegel is criticized for not seeing the complete continuity of literary tradition and for exalting one kind of art: romantic art. This reconciling, mediating criticism does not, however, imply a complete abdication of judgment; every work of art is to be judged by its place and weight in the whole of literature. Each work contributes to the whole and in so doing modifies the whole. Its goal is to achieve the reconciliation of judgment and history.

Compared to the attention given to the theory of criticism in Germany, England and France contributed little at that time. Samuel Taylor Coleridge, who was the one Englishman thoroughly familiar with German critical thought, said surprisingly little about his concept of criticism. Coleridge did formulate an ambitious program of aiming "at fixed canons of criticism, previously established and deduced from the nature of man," and, in retrospect, said of himself, referring to the 1790s, that "according to the faculty or source, from which the pleasure given by any poem or passage was derived, I estimated the merit of such a poem or passage" (*Biographia Literaria*, ed. Shawcross, 1:14, 44). The theory of criticism implied is a psychological one: a ranking of the faculties with the imagination higher than fancy, reason higher than the senses. But Coleridge never developed this as a theory of criticism.

Among the English critics of the time, William Hazlitt made a conscious attempt to formulate what would later be called "impressionistic criticism." "I say what I think: I think what I feel. I cannot help receiving certain impressions from things; and I have sufficient courage to declare (somewhat abruptly) what they are" (*Complete Works*, ed. Howe, 5:175). The task of criticism is the communication of feelings. He uses the new methods—elaborate evocative metaphors, personal reminiscences, a feeling of intimacy—like an enthusiastic guide in a gallery or a host in a library. Hazlitt faces a new middle-class audience; he wants to win it over, to cajole it to the enjoyment of literature. The critic becomes neither a judge nor a theorist, but a middleman between author and public.

Thomas Carlyle, in his early essays, adopted the idea of sympathetic criticism, drawing apparently on Herder and the Schlegels. The critic's aim, he says, is "transposition into the author's point of vision"; he must work his way into the poet's "manner of thought, till he sees the world with his eyes, feels as he felt and judges as he judged" (*Essays*, Centenary ed., 1:39). In the act of enjoying a work of art "we partially and for the time become the very Painter and the very Singer" (ibid., 3:46). The older view survives, however, in Macaulay when he called the critic "a king at arms versed in the laws of literary precedence, who must marshall his author to the exact seat to which he is entitled" (*Critical and Historical Essays*, Boston [1900], 6:50). Judging and ranking of authors was Macaulay's passion.

Criticism in the United States echoes these views. Edgar Allan Poe exalted the function of criticism and hesitated whether to consider criticism a science or an art. Criticism requires art in the sense that each essay should be a work of art, but it is also a science based on principles. Ralph Waldo Emerson like Carlyle knows only a criticism of empathy and identification. He calls the old saw that "every scripture is to be interpreted by the same spirit which gave it forth," "the fundamental law of criticism," and he boldy asserts that "the reader of Shakespeare is also a Shakespeare" (*Complete Works*, Centenary ed., 1:35). Surprisingly, among Americans Margaret Fuller reflected most concretely on the nature and office of criticism. She distinguishes three kinds of critics: "subjective" critics who indulge in a personal caprice, "apprehensive" critics who can enter fully into a foreign existence, and finally "comprehensive" critics who also must enter into the nature of another being but must, besides, judge the work by its own law. The critic "must examine, compare, sift and winnow." Saying that "I cannot pass on till I know what I feel and why" (*Art, Literature and the Drama*, Boston [1841], pp. 23–24) is not a bad expression of a critic's conscience.

In France, prescriptive criticism survived longer than elsewhere. In Julien-Louis Geoffroy (1743–1814) it found a theorist who thought of it as serving the government, "good taste, sound morals and the eternal foundations of the social order" (*Journal des débats*, Feb. 16, 1805). He would call in the police to punish bad authors. Désiré Nisard attempted to establish criticism as an "exact science," by which he meant a setting up of ideal norms—of the universal human spirit, of the genius of France, and of the perfection of the French language—which would allow him to judge every work of French literature correctly. He expressly condemned criticism of "each according to his taste" and criticism which would reduce literature to a mirror of history and social change (*Histoire de la littérature française,* 4:540). François-René de Chateaubriand, in a famous essay on Dussault (1819), advised us "to abandon the petty and easy criticism of faults in favor of the great and difficult criticism of beauties." With Victor Hugo, particularly in his late book on *Shakespeare* (1864), the repudiation of judicial criticism is complete. The complete negation of criticism as judgment is proclaimed complacently. "Genius is an entity like nature and must, like her, be accepted purely and simply. We must take or leave a mountain." Hugo admires everything *comme une bête.*

Charles Augustin Sainte-Beuve, however, was the French critic of the nineteenth century who most consistently reflected on the concept of criticism. His attitude shifted in the course of a long career from an early, more subjective concept of criticism as personal expression to one of greater objectivity, detachment, and tolerance, and at the same time from a rather uncritical, sympathetic acceptance of the role of "secretary of the public" (*Causeries du lundi,* 1:373) to an increasing emphasis on the role of judgment, to a definition of taste and tradition. These two trends are often at cross-purposes in Sainte-Beuve. His early romantic historicism goes with tolerance and relativism, but it is often contradicted by his partisanship in the literary battles of the time. He became, for a time, the "herald" of Victor Hugo. The objectivity and the detachment of Sainte-Beuve's later stage appeals rather to natural science as the model. The late Sainte-Beuve aimed at a theory of psychological types of men (see the essay on Chateaubriand, 1862). Still, his return to classical taste brought about a reassertion of the judicial function of criticism, a tone of authority and even of dogmatic certainty. "The true critic precedes the public, directs and guides it" (*Chateaubriand et son groupe littéraire* [1949], 2:95). The critic "maintains tradition and preserves taste" (*Causeries,* 15:356).

In the later nineteenth century, the divergence between concepts of criticism aiming at scientific objectivity and views that considered criticism an act of personal appreciation became more accentuated. The concept of criticism as judicial, as an upholder of the tradition, receded into the background, though in England it found an influential spokesman in Matthew Arnold. Arnold was an important apologist for criticism, for "disinterestedness," for a free circulation in England of ideas from Europe. At times he believes in a purely descriptive criticism, informative, liberating, preparatory to creation.

But later Arnold stressed the judicial function of criticism, and defended the "real estimate" against the "historical" and "personal" estimates, both of which seemed to him fallacious. By personal estimate he meant an estimate in terms of "our personal affinities, likings and circumstances," which made it inevitably subjective; the historical estimate would in turn distort values, overestimating works useful in a certain stage of the development of literature. The "real estimate" is the only critical one—it appeals to permanent standards, to "the very best" that has been thought and said in the world. (See "The Study of Poetry" in *Essays in Criticism*, 2nd Series [1888], pp. 6–7, 11.) Arnold's own criticism, appealing to impressionistic "touchstones" or to a historical concept of the "adequacy" of a literature to its time, may be riddled by contradictions but consistently upholds judgment as an ideal of criticism.

In Italy, the greatest critic and historian of the nineteenth century, Francesco De Sanctis, came to similar conclusions independently. He distinguishes three stages in the critical act: first, an act of submission, a surrender to first impressions, then re-creation, and finally, judgment. "Criticism cannot take the place of taste, and taste is the genius of the critic. Just as one says that poets are born, so also are critics born" (*Saggi critici*, ed. Russo, 1:307). The critic should "remake what the poet has done in his own manner and by other means" (ibid., 2:90), by translating into consciousness what is created in a work of art. Still, the proper critical act is deciding the intrinsic value of work and "not what it has in common with the times, or with its predecessors, but what it has that is peculiar and untransferable" (*Saggio critico sul Petrarca* [1869], ed. Bonora, Bari [1954], p. 10). In Germany, Wilhelm Dilthey, who wrote a psychological poetics (*Die Einbildungskraft des Dichters, Bausteine für eine Poetik*, 1887) which aimed at scientific rigor, came late in his life to recognized the need for criticism. "Criticism," he argued, "is inevitably linked with the hermeneutic process. There is no understanding without a feeling of value, but only by comparison can the value be ascertained to be objective and universal" (*Gesammelte Schriften*, 5:536).

Hippolyte Taine, with his theory of *la race, le milieu, le moment* ("race, environment, moment") was the outstanding figure who tried to model criticism on the pattern of deterministic science. Taine upholds the view that criticism is "analogous to botany, which studies the orange, the laurel, the pine, and the birch, with equal interest" (*Philosophie de l'art* [1865], p. 22). The historicism of this conception seems (as in Herder) to lead to universal tolerance and hence to complete relativism. But actually Taine does not consider all works of art to be of equal value. He tries to overcome relativism by the criterion of representativeness. He asks whether a work represents a transient fashion, or a historical moment, or the spirit of a nation, or humanity in general, and ranks works according to such a scale. The work of art is always considered a sign or symbol of humanity, nation, or age. It is a mistake to consider Taine as a sociologist who thinks of works of art as social documents. They are, rather, in his scheme the essence or summary of history, in terms which are ultimately Hegelian.

Among Taine's followers Émile Hennequin tried in *La Critique scientifique* (1888) to give a different scientific basis to criticism than Taine. He criticized Taine's triad of *milieu-moment-race* and preferred a psychology of the author and the audience. The emphasis on the audience as a mental analogue of the work was particularly new though it remained only a suggestive proposal. Still, Hennequin offered a way out from purely causal thinking into a "synthetic" literary criticism which would include an aesthetic, a psychology, and a sociology in a discipline he called "anthropology."

Ferdinand Brunetière, who followed Taine in his adherence to a scientific ideal (in his case, biological evolution), reflected more systematically on the theory of criticism. He believed that criticism must focus on the work of literature itself and must distinguish the study of literature from biography, psychology, sociology, and other disciplines. He defended the final aim of criticism as that of judging and even ranking, and distinguished this act of judgment from any purely personal preference, impression, or enjoyment. Brunetière saw clearly that the work of literature itself and not the soul of the author or the social background is the object of criticism. "If criticism," he argued, "forgets that a poem is a poem, when it claims to refrain from judgment, it is no longer criticism but history and psychology" (*Études critiques,* 9:50). Taine's and Hennequin's attempt to make criticism scientific in the sense of abstaining from praise or blame is inevitably a failure. Brunetière also argued passionately against the impressionist creed, which at that time was wittily stated by Anatole France when he declared the ideal of objective criticism an illusion: "The truth is that one never gets outside oneself. What would we not give to see for a minute the sky and the earth with the faceted eye of a fly, or to understand nature with the crude, simple brain of an orangutan? . . . The critic should say, if he is candid: Gentlemen, I am going to speak about myself in connection with Shakespeare, Racine, Pascal, or Goethe" (*La Vie littéraire,* 1:5–6). Brunetière answers that we are neither flies nor orangutans but men, and that the whole of life consists in a going out of oneself. "Otherwise there would be no society, no language, no literature, no art" (*Essais sur la littérature contemporaine* [1892], pp. 7–9). He proves that even the most extreme impressionists make judgments all the time and that they themselves cannot obscure the fact that "there are differences in rank between Racine and Campistron, or that one cannot put Victor Hugo below Madame Debordes-Valmore, or Balzac below Charles Bernard" (ibid.). Brunetière sees in criticism "a common effort" (*Études critiques,* 4:28) and finds a wide agreement about the classics. Mere enjoyment is not a criterion of value. We laugh more at a farce than at Molière's *Misanthrope.* Still "we can raise ourselves above our tastes" (*L'Évolution de la poésie lyrique* [1894], 1:25). Sympathy and judgment, sensibility and reason, in this case are dangerously divorced.

An English writer equally preoccupied with the scientific ideal, John Addington Symonds, also saw, like Brunetière, that the evolutionary scheme with its fatalistic assumption of a necessary rise and decline raises the problem of criticism in its most acute form. The analogy with the life of a plant or animal must lead to universal tolerance, to an abdication of criticism. It is impossible to criticize youth for being young, or old age for being close to death. But he sees the need for overcoming such relativism. The critic cannot be confined by history. "He must divert his mind from what is transient and ephemeral, must fasten upon abiding relations, *'bleibende Verhältnisse'" (Renaissance in Italy: the Catholic Reaction* [1886], 2:396). There are three types of critics: the judge, the showman, and the natural historian of art and literature. The judge is the classical critic who judges by principles and the decisions of his predecessors. The showman is the romantic critic who exhibits his own sensibilities. The scientific analyst is the morphological historian who sees literature in terms of evolution. But even this scientific analyst does not satisfy Symonds, who demands that the true critic must combine all three types. "He cannot abnegate the right to judge" but ". . . it is his supreme duty to train his faculty of judgment and to temper his subjectivity by the study of things in their historical connections" (*Essays, Speculative and Suggestive* [1890], 1:98–99). Ultimately, Symonds admits that criticism is not a science but can be exercised in a scientific spirit.

In many variations the importance of sympathy, even of identification, is stressed by many writers. Charles Baudelaire formulates this ideal well: "You must enter into the skin of the created being, become deeply imbued with the feelings which he expressed, and feel them so thoroughly, that it seems to you as if it were your own work" (*L'Art romantique,* ed. Conard, p. 198). But often Baudelaire thought of criticism as self-expression and self-criticism. It should "be partial, passionate, and political, that is to say, written from an exclusive point of view, but a point of view that opens up the widest horizon" (*Curiosités esthétiques,* ed. Conard, p. 87).

For Jules Lemaître, criticism is nothing but "the art of enjoying books and of enriching and refining one's impression of them." The divorce between admiration and liking accepted by Brunetière is not only deplorable but false. "One calls good what one loves." The critic is not a judge but only a reader. He needs "sympathetic imagination"

(*Les Contemporains*, 3:342; 2:85; 1:164). The same was said in the United States by Henry James, who greatly admired Sainte-Beuve. As early as 1868 he wrote that "the critic is simply a reader like all the others—a reader who prints his impressions" (in *The Nation*, 1:330–31), and repeated that "Nothing will ever take the place of the good old fashion of 'liking' a work of art or not liking it" (*Partial Portraits* [1888], pp. 395–96). Criticism is "the only gate of appreciation" (*Future of the Novel*, p. 97). The true method of criticism is always that of sympathy, of identification with the work of art.

The English aesthetic movement presents arguments along the same lines. But Walter Pater is wrongly called a mere impressionist. He stresses the duty of the critic to grasp the individuality, the uniqueness of a work of art. He considers the question, Does this book give one pleasure? as no more than a first step in criticism. The critic must go beyond it: penetrate "through the given literary or artistic product, into the mental and inner constitution of the producer, shaping his work" (*Guardian* [1901], p. 29). He must, moreover, know how to communicate this insight by finding what Pater calls the "formula," the "active principle" or the "motive" of a work. Oscar Wilde, among English writers, is the one who went furthest in advocating subjectivity. In "The Critic as Artist" (1893) he argues for criticism as a creative art. Criticism is a form of autobiography. The work of art is only a starting point for a new creation, which need not bear any obvious relation to the thing it criticizes. Objectivity is an absurd ideal: "Only an auctioneer can equally and impartially admire all schools of Art." Wilde sees the dialectics of subjectivity and objectivity: "It is only by intensifying his own personality that the critic can interpret the personality and work of others." Wilde's position thus fluctuates between an advocacy of criticism as empathy and historical imagination, as an exercise in cosmopolitanism, and as a paradoxical plea for sheer wilfulness and caprice. His concept of criticism represents the other extreme at which nineteenth-century thinking had arrived.

The twentieth century brought a new sharpening of the conflicts between the main concepts of criticism—judicial, scientific, historical, impressionist, and "creative"—and added some new motives and refinements. In England, an empiricist and antitheoretical point of view prevailed even in such a critic as T. S. Eliot. Eliot is suspicious of aesthetics and thinks of criticism for the most part as that of a poet "always trying to defend the kind of poetry he is writing" (*The Music of Poetry*, 1942). In distinguishing three types of criticism—the so-called creative criticism, really "etiolated creation" for which Pater serves as a horrifying example; "historical" and moralistic criticism represented by Sainte-Beuve; and "criticism proper" or the criticism of the poet—Eliot forgets or ignores theory completely. The only exception Eliot allows is Aristotle, whose influence as a critic seems quite inexplicable in Eliot's scheme (*Chapbook*, no. 2, 1920). Criticism is left with little to do. Occasionally Eliot described the function of criticism as "the elucidation of works of art and the correction of taste" or even as "the common pursuit of true judgment" (*Selected Essays*, pp. 24–25). But he rejects both interpretative and judicial criticism in any case. "Interpretation" seems to him only a necessary evil productive of fictions, and judgment is expressly forbidden to the critic. "The critic must not coerce, and he must not make judgments of worse and better." The critic "must simply elucidate" (an activity which differs obscurely from interpretation); "the reader will form the correct judgment for himself" (ibid., p. 10). In practice, Eliot judges, however, on almost every page, and conceives his own role as that of an upholder of the tradition or even as "the creator of values" (*Criterion*, 4 [1926], 751). Eliot's concept of criticism thus seems quite inadequate in the light of his practice.

Eliot's rival I. A. Richards belongs to the upholders of a scientific ideal. Criticism should become a new science, or at least "a cooperative technique of enquiry that may become entitled to be named a science" (*Coleridge on Imagination* [1934], p. xii). Richards hopes for an ultimate total victory of science: "We have," he said in 1952, "to seek a way by which Value must unrestrictedly come into the care of Science" (*Speculative Instruments*, p. 145). The science on which he leans is psychology and, in his early books, neurology. But in his *Practical Criticism* (1928) he uses no scientific experimentation, no analysis in quantitative terms, nor any controlled method of formulating the questionnaire. Richards's work is rather an attempt to analyze the sources of misreadings made by students when confronted with anonymous poetic texts. A theory of emotive language obscures Richards's successful manner of looking at texts and judging them sensitively.

Both Eliot and Richards deeply influenced F. R. Leavis. His concept of criticism is equally tentative and empirical, but he is more deliberately moralistic and pedagogical. Criticism trains "intelligence and sensibility together, cultivating a sensitiveness and precision of response and a delicate integrity of intelligence." "Everything must start from and be associated with the training of sensibility" (*Education and the University*, pp. 34, 120). Criticism begins with the texture of texts in front of us. Hence literary history and scholarship are useless, though on occasion Leavis recognizes the necessity of a "critique of criticism." The central ethos of criticism is the preserving of the tradition, but tradition, in Leavis, is very different from Eliot's view. Leavis's view is nonreligious, Arnoldian, and appeals to the basic values of the old English organic society, though in recent decades this Arnoldian concept has been modified or subverted by Leavis's unbounded admiration for D. H. Lawrence and his worship of "Life." Life, with Leavis, is a vague and shifting term. Ultimately he has to appeal to intuitive certitude. "A judgment," he tells us, "is a real judgment, or it is nothing. It must, that is, be a sincere personal judgment; but it aspires to be more than personal" (*Scrutiny*, 18 [1951], 22).

English criticism has not extricated itself from these antinomies, though very diverse formulas can be found for alternatives. Herbert Read, in a piece on "The Nature of Criticism," advocates simply Jungian psychology as the solution. William Righter, in *Logic and Criticism* (1963), argues for the "irrelevance of precise intellectual machinery to the general criteria of critical success," while John Casey, in *The Language of Criticism* (1966), which is indebted to Wittgenstein's critique of language, comes rather to rejecting the whole English tradition of a theory of emotion and to stressing the need of history. Historical criticism was also defended by Helen Gardner in her *The Business of Criticism* (1959), while George Watson in *The Literary Critics* (1962) distinguishes "legislative" (i.e., judicial) and "theoretical" criticism, and judges that "descriptive" criticism is "the only one which today possesses any life and vigour of its own." The history of criticism appears to Watson as "a record of chaos marked by a sudden revolution." "The great critics do not contribute: they interrupt." Against these excesses of empiricism in England one can quote, at least, one book, Harold Osborne's *Aesthetics and Criticism* (1955), which makes a reasoned defense of the dependence of criticism on aesthetics and expounds a theory of "organic configuration" which appeals to the main tradition of aesthetics. Criticism is, for Osborne, applied aesthetics. Also Graham Hough, in *An Essay on Criticism* (1966), sees criticism as rational discussion and as leading to judgments of value. The principles of literary criticism are not "just matters of taste." In principle, literary judgments are objective: some things are really better than others. The Toronto philosoher F. E. Sparshott's *Concept of Criticism* (1967), although scholastically elaborate in its distinctions, comes to the conclusion that there is "no general theory of evaluative discourse," though criticism is, in his definition, a "discourse apt to ground evaluations" (p. 39). A recent English book, Philip Hobsbaum's *Theory of Criticism* (1970) is misnamed. It is rather a collection of discussions, in the manner of F. R. Leavis, of individual poems, plays and novels, culminating in a plea for a "group approach to criticism." A communication theory of language is assumed, but the conclusion amounts to a purely empirical appeal: "At best the theorist is saying something like this: 'Here are my findings—relate them back to the work, are they right, do you think?'"

In the United States, early in the twentieth century, criticism became largely social, and generalized to embrace a criticism of American society. H. L. Mencken showed, however, a surprising sympathy for the view of Joel E. Spingarn, the propounder of a somewhat diluted version of Croceanism. What appealed to Mencken in aestheticism was the rejection of the old didactic view of criticism: the critic as constable or "birchman." Mencken saw only another version of the old kind in the criticism of the New Humanists: of Paul Elmer More and Irving Babbitt, who defended judicial criticism, a criticism with standards which were basically classical and ultimately moral. Norman Foerster argued most clearly for the view that an aesthetic judgment is equally an ethical judgment in *The Intent of the Critic* (1941).

With the advent of the New Criticism, closer definitions of the nature of criticism were attempted. They all reflect the deep divisions even in the movement misleadingly called the "New Criticism," a name derived from a book (1941) by John Crowe Ransom which was actually extremely critical of T. S. Eliot, I. A. Richards, and Yvor Winters. Ransom has most consistently advocated the necessity of grounding criticism in theory and aesthetics. He has focused on the central object of criticism: the work itself, the "criticism of the structural properties of poetry." His philosophic alignment with Croce and Bergson is obvious.

Ransom's followers and disciples differ from him widely. Allen Tate asked skeptically whether literary criticism is possible and came to the conclusion that criticism is "perpetually obsolescent and replaceable," a parasitic growth on creation. He hands over philosophical and stylistic criticism to other disciplines and asks for a criticism which would "expound the knowledge of life contained in a work"—surely something that has been done for centuries—and finally queries whether criticism is possible without a criterion of absolute truth. Criticism is paradoxically both "perpetually necessary" and "perpetually impossible" (*The Forlorn Demon*, 1952).

No such antiintellectualism pervades the critical writings of either Cleanth Brooks or William K. Wimsatt. Brooks has argued against critical relativism and for standards, and Wimsatt has defined the "domain of literary criticism" as "the verbal object and its analysis." Wimsatt sees the critical act largely as an act of explication out of which a judgment of value grows almost spontaneously. "The main critical problem is always how to push both understanding and value as far as possible in union, or how to make our understanding evaluative" (*The Verbal Icon*, p. 251). Brooks and Wimsatt's *Literary Criticism: A Short History* (1957) and Wimsatt's classifications of critics allow a combination of methods, a pluralism which belies the reputed charge of dogmatism or formalism often made against the New Critics.

Dogmatism can be ascribed rather to Yvor Winters, who has most strongly urged the need for ranking and has practiced it. "Unless criticism succeeds in providing a usable system of evaluation it is worth very little," he says, and he proceeds to supply such a system which, in practice, amounts to the application of a criterion of rational coherence and moral soundness.

Two twentieth-century critics, R. P. Blackmur and Kenneth Burke, have expanded the field of criticism far beyond the boundaries of literature. Burke has become a philosopher aiming at a system which combines psychoanalysis, Marxism, semantics, and "whatnot" with literary criticism. He tries to absorb literary criticism into a philosophy of motives which he calls "dramatism." The critic, for Burke, is a prophet who is to remake society and life. Blackmur, who diagnosed the pathologies of our culture, speculated more modestly also on the concept of criticism. Oddly enough he defines it at first as "the formal discourse of an amateur" but then argues that "any rational approach is valid to literature and may be properly called critical which fastens at any point upon the work itself" ("A Critic's Job of Work," 1935, in *Language as Gesture*, 1952). He recognizes that aesthetics is at least implicit in any criticism. Still it is no science because "science cannot explain the feeling or existence of a poem." In these pronouncements Blackmur is near the New Critics, but later he felt that they provide methods only for the early stages of criticism—analysis and elucidation—but fail to compare and judge. He advocates a rational judgment, but neither his practice nor his later theory lives up to this ideal. The critical act becomes with him the creative act, the product of the tension of the writer's lifetime, a self-definition which, in many later essays, seems hardly related to any literary text.

Other American New Critics upheld concepts of criticism which can be described as broadly social. F. O. Matthiessen pleaded in 1949 for the social "responsibilities of the critic" in *The Responsibilities of the Critic* (1952). Lionel Trilling is mainly concerned with the moral and political issues in modern literature. Harry Levin also conceives of literary criticism in broadly cultural terms, viewing literature "as an institution," but is relativistic and historistic in his orientation. The relativity of all critical judgments has been argued in many contexts; e.g., in George Boas's *Primer for Critics* (1937, new edition *Wingless Pegasus*, 1950), in Bernard Heyl's *New Bearings in Esthetics and Art Criticism* (1943), and in Wayne Shumaker's *Elements of Critical Theory* (1952). A pluralistic and instrumentalist view of criticism is also defended by Ronald S. Crane, the main spokesman of the so-called Chicago Aristotelianism. Criticism is defined as "reasoned discourse, an organization of terms, propositions and arguments," which is subject to the critic's choice and hence necessarily relative. Still, in practice, the group has been committed to a rigid application of a doctrine of genres and ranking within the elements of a work of art, appealing to Aristotle as its ultimate source. In contrast to the New Critics, language and symbol are slighted in favor of plot and character. The Chicago Aristotelians consider criticism "a department of philosophy" and claim for their doctrines an immense certainty.

These pretensions have been questioned insistently in the twentieth century by poets such as Karl Shapiro, who shies away from anything that has to do with philosophy. He recommends "creative criticism, as a work of art about another work of art" (*In Defense of Ignorance*, 1960), while Randall Jarrell has pleaded for the strict subordination of criticism "to help us with works of art." "Principles and standards of excellence are either specifically harmful or generally useless; the critic has nothing to go by except his experience . . . and is the personification of empiricism" (*Poetry and the Age*, 1955). No theory, no history.

There is only room for theory in Northrop Frye's *Anatomy of Criticism* (1956). In a "Polemical Introduction" Frye excludes all value judgment from criticism, as criticism "should show a steady advance toward undiscriminating catholicity." The book tries to construe an all-inclusive scheme where literature is conceived as "existing in its own universe, no longer a commentary on life and reality, but containing life and reality in a system of verbal relationships." Criticism in Frye's sense clarifies this order and should succeed in "reforging the links between creation and knowledge, art and science, myth and concept." Criticism in Frye becomes not only a theory of literature but a form of theology, an all-inclusive system, a world hypothesis. R. W. B. Lewis formulated this well when he said that "criticism, ceasing to be one of the several intellectual arts, is becoming the entire intellectual act itself," and the critic has become a "prophet announcing to the ungodly the communication of men with ultimate reality." This is meant as serious praise; it shows that this concept has broken completely loose from the traditional concern with literature. It has ceased to be *literary* criticism, and has become a version of philosophy.

In recent years several attempts have been made to completely abolish the traditional concept of criticism as characterization, interpretation, and evaluation. They come from two different directions, and are differently motivated but lead to similar or identical conclusions. There are, first, those critics who are dissatisfied with the idea that criticism is serving literature and try to exalt the critic to the level of a creator who has no obligation to a given text, its prescriptive and challenging power, and thus allow themselves to batter it in any way which would enhance the display of their personality. Harold Bloom, in several books, has argued that "there are no interpretations, only misinterpretations and so all criticism is prose poetry" (*The Anxiety of Influence*, 1973). Susan Sontag demands "an erotics of art" and rejects interpretation (*Against Interpretation*, 1964).

Ihab Hassan propagates a "paracriticism," an indulgence in all kinds of speculations on a great variety of subjects. Traditional criticism is to be replaced by a "theory of playful discontinuity," leading to a new "gnosticism" (*Paracriticisms*, 1975). The basic assumption is an apocalyptic irrationalism and a personal ambition to become a prophet or at least a kind of poet freed from the restraints imposed by an order of literature, past and present.

The other attempt to abolish criticism comes rather from the theorists who learned from linguists and semioticians that man lives in a prison-house of language, that there is no relation between sign and referent, language and reality, word and thing. They claim that we import meaning into a text which has no meaning in itself. Thus a complete liberty of interpretation is vindicated. Sometimes, interpretation is simply rejected as impossible and undesirable. Some, under the influence of Jacques Derrida, openly confess the inevitable consequences: skepticism, relativism, and nihilism; the end of scholarship and criticism. To quote the formulation of Robert Scholes ("The Fictional Criticism of the Future," *Tri-Quarterly*, 34, 1975): "Criticism has taken the very idea of 'aboutness' from us." Language is only about itself. "Poetry is about poetry, and criticism is about the impossibility of its own existence." Some of the adherents of this point of view have not gone so far in "deconstruction": they have rather tried to devise a new poetics and rhetoric completely divorced from any reference to external reality, a new extreme formalism which rejects interpretation and evaluation as unscientific in favor of some general scheme of literature ultimately absorbed into a theory of signs. In practice these two motifs achieve the same result: license is given to fancy and fiction in criticism, as the very existence of a determinate object, the work of art, is denied.

The older views do not lack defenders, however. Thus Gerald Graff in *Literature Against Itself* (1979) argues for the referential function of literature, its propositional truths, and, implicitly, for realism; and Murray Krieger, in many writings, particularly in *The Theory of Criticism* (1976), upholds the representational power of literature and the evaluative function of criticism while making many concessions to new views. E. D. Hirsch, in *Validity in Interpretation* (1967) and *Aims of Interpretation* (1976), is the most coherent defender of objective criticism based on a recognition of the intention of the author. A return to the age-old concept of criticism seems overdue. But it will have to learn from the doubters to examine its own assumptions more carefully if it is to reconstitute its authority and influence.

In France, despite the great differences in the ideologies and concrete tastes of the critics, the same variety of concepts of criticism was stated and restated. There is the rationalist tradition of the new classicists who upheld an ideal of judicial criticism, eloquently put, for example, by Charles Maurras. Ramon Fernandez, who had his affinities with T. S. Eliot, formulated an ideal of a rather philosophic criticism, whose aim would be an "imaginative ontology," a definition of the problem of being. Fernandez believes that there is a "philosophic substructure" of a work, a body of ideas which the critic has to relate to the problems of general philosophy. But Fernandez knows well that critical consciousness is not the task of the author: it is reserved for the critic (*Messages*, 1926).

Generally, however, in the France of the early twentieth century irrationalistic tendencies were victorious: Bergson became the philosopher inspiring, for example, the theory of criticism in Albert Thibaudet (1874–1936), who among the French reflected most fruitfully on the concept of criticism. Still, while pursuing an intuitive and metaphorical method of criticism, Thibaudet understands that the critic translates what is conceived in poetic terms into intellectual terms, changes the concrete into the abstract. At the same time, he is aware of the perils involved with such a translation substituting "for the profound clarity of an image the semi-obscurity or the shadow of an idea" (*Paul Valéry* [1923], p. 160). Besides translation, Thibaudet recognizes two other kinds of criticism: "pure" criticism which is theory of literature, thinking about genres and principles, and historical criticism. He sees also that "there is no criticism without a criticism of criticism" and has written sketches of the history of French criticism (*Physiologie de la critique*, 1930) in which he attacks the *certitudiens*, the dogmatists of the Right. He wanted mobility, flexibility, or what he called "literary pantheism." What in Thibaudet is phrased as a defense of tolerance, became in some contemporaries an emphasis on complete submission, on a lack of critical personality, on identification which, at times, sounds like mystical union. Jacques Rivière laments his "frightening plasticity" while Charles Du Bos made much of his "liquidity," of the central virtue of the critic as a "pure receptacle" of the life of another. Also Marcel Proust, in many scattered pronouncements, sees the critic as entering the mind of others and complains of Sainte-Beuve's detachment and irony as well as of his confusion of life with art. Imitation, the *pastiche*, is the proper form of criticism for Proust.

The Second World War brought a reaction against all theories of pure art and pure criticism. Jean-Paul Sartre's watchword *"la littérature engagée,"* propounded in *Qu'est-ce que la littérature?* (1947), implies a concept of committed criticism, criticism committed to a social and political cause. Sartre chides academic critics for "having chosen to have relations only with the defunct." Pure art and empty art are the same thing. But Sartre reserves a nook for pure poetry and in his actual criticism uses largely psychoanalytical methods to criticize Baudelaire as a man or to exalt Genet for the identity of man and work.

Surprisingly enough, the finest, most intellectual critic of the first half of the century, the poet Paul Valéry, held a theory of criticism which opens the way to a total divorce between the work of art and the reader or critic. Valéry believed that a work of art is so ambiguous that it has no proper meaning and that it is open to what he calls "creative misunderstanding." "There is no true sense of a text. The author has no authority." The critic is completely free to read into a work his own mind. The solution seems to be "creative criticism" which sounds like Oscar Wilde's defense of caprice or Anatole France's "adventures among masterpieces," but is in Valéry rather motivated by a deep conviction of the unbridgeable gulfs between author and work and work and reader.

This liberty of interpretation is then preached and practiced by the "new critics" in France. Their concerns may be very different: psychoanalytical, mythographical, structuralist, or what is called *la critique de conscience*; in all cases, the new French critics argue that the work of art is not something out there which has a proper meaning for the critic to discover and to formulate, but that the work itself is a mental construct realized only in collaboration with the subject. The conflict of concepts of criticism came out most clearly in the recent debate between Raymond Picard and Roland Barthes. Picard attacked Barthes's interpretation of Racine from a historistic and philological point of view. Barthes, in replying (*Critique et vérité*, 1966), criticized cogently the limitations of conventional historical criticism, its ignoring of the changing "life" of a work through history, its obtuseness toward ambiguity and symbolism, but he goes far beyond this in asserting the right of criticism to "duplicate" a work of art. The term *écriture* is used to assimilate the critic to the poet, the critic transforming the work of art into his image.

The other new critics seem to take the opposite position: Georges Poulet, for example, advocates participation or better "identification" with an author, the "integral transposition of a mental universe into the interior of another mind." This is an old idea known to the Schlegels or Croce, proclaimed as great novelty. The declaration, "The basis and substance of all criticism is the grasping of a consciousness by the consciousness of another" (*Les chemins actuels de la critique*, 1968), gives it a new twist: the "identification" is not with a text but with the "consciousness" of a writer, which is not identical with his biographical psyche but is a construct accessible through the totality of his writings. His attitudes toward time or space (Poulet), or toward the life of the senses (J.-P. Richard) are to be reconstructed without regard to the individual works or their form. It follows even for a critic such as Jean Rousset who does pay attention to the form of individual works that the aim of criticism is "to participate in the existence of another spiritual being" by "an act of adhesion so total that it excludes, at least provisionally, all judgment" (*Forme et signification* [1962], p. xiv). The older concepts of criticism, judicial and aesthetic in the sense of an analysis and interpretation of a single work as an entity, are dismissed or minimized.

In recent years the most radical rejection of traditional criticism comes from Jacques Derrida, to whom I alluded before as the progenitor of a new trend in American theorizing. Derrida is mainly a philosopher of language (*De la Grammatologie*, 1967) who denies that a text has any stable identity, any stable origin or end. Word and thing and thought can never come together. Knowledge is only a freeplay with words and their etymologies. Motifs from Nietzsche, Freud, and Heidegger, together with a strain from Dadaism combine to result in a complete skepticism and even self-proclaimed nihilism. Criticism in the traditional sense has ceased to exist.

In Italy, Benedetto Croce had come to deceptively similar conclusions long before. One of Croce's earliest publications was a book, *La Critica letteraria* (1894), which simply denied that the various operations and approaches which are called "literary criticism" make a unified and meaningful subject. But later Croce defended a view of criticism as identification. He went so far as to say that "if I penetrate the innermost sense of a canto of Dante, I become Dante" (*Problemi di estetica* [1909], p. 155). But at an even later stage of his thinking he considered imaginative re-creation only a presupposition of criticism and concluded that criticism is a translation from the realm of feeling into the realm of reason and thought. He found that critics should be reminded of the prohibition posted in some German concert halls in his youth: *Das Mitsingen ist verboten*. In practice Croce asked of criticism nothing else than that it "know the true sentiment of the poet in the representative form in which he has translated it" (Letter to R. W., June 5, 1952). Besides confronting the task of characterization, the critic must also judge; there is, however, no other criterion than the distinction between art and non-art, poetry and non-poetry, as in Croce there can be no intermediary between the individual and the universal. No classification of the arts, no genres, no styles or technical devices matter, because "what is external is no longer a work of art."

After the death of Croce, two different concepts of criticism have become more vocal: Marxism and stylistics. An adherent of Croce, Mario Fubini, advocates a broadening of criticism to include the study of style and genres (*Critica e poesia*, 1956), and a whole group of Italian scholars has returned to a concept of criticism as a study of the aesthetic surface, of language and style. In recent years French existentialism and structuralism have made their impact in Italy.

The peculiarity of the German situation is the sharp divorce between criticism as carried on in the daily press and the *Literaturwissenschaft* of the academy, which was traditionally philological but early in the twentieth century became largely speculative, philosophical (under the influence of *Geistesgeschichte*). Concepts of criticism were not widely examined, though the trends prevailing in the West were also reflected in German discussions. Alfred Kerr, for example, argued (in *Vorwort zum neueren Drama*, 1904) for the superiority of criticism over creation, for criticism as a kind of poetry, thus going even beyond Oscar Wilde. The scholars went the other way, arguing for criticism as a science, though Ernst Robert Curtius, for instance, sees criticism "as the form of literature whose subject is literature" (*Kritische Essays über europäische Literatur*, 1958). The creed of most German scholars was relativism and historicism: it is formulated by Erich Auerbach, for example, in a review of my *History of Modern Criticism* in *Gesammelte Aufsätze zur romanischen Philologie* (Bern, 1956).

Still, there were many critics interested in judging and ranking. Hugo von Hofmannsthal, who usually defends empathy and understanding, recognizes also the need for ranking, as does, in practice, the whole circle around Stefan George, who thinks of its master as prophet and judge laying down the law. Among more recent German critics Hans Egon Holthusen shows a concern for ethical judgments, and commitments also in political matters, arguing that there is no such thing as "pure" literary criticism. He is one of the few Germans who have written on critical understanding (*Kritisches Verstehen*, 1961) and have thought about the concept of criticism, whereas there is, of course, a proliferation of theories of poetry and much that could be called close reading or interpretation. Emil Staiger's preface to *Die Zeit als Einbildungskraft des Dichters* (1939) formulated the rejection of *Geistesgeschichte* and signaled the new focus on the text.

Walter Benjamin (1892–1940), who during his lifetime was little known but became famous following the republication of his writings in 1952, had a concept of criticism which is related to phenomenology or even to Heidegger's thought. Criticism, he tells us in his long article on Goethe's *Elective Affinities* (1925), searches for the truth-content of a work of art, or, phrased differently, "looks for the sisters of a work of art which must be found in the realm of philosophy." Works of art have a deep affinity with the ideal of a philosophical problem. All beauty is related to truth. But Benjamin insists that this relationship must not be thought of as truth being somehow concealed within a work of art. Beauty is not a cloak, not a wrapper, not appearance, but essence (*Wesen*). Criticism must respect this veil: it must not attempt to lift it. The critic can only define an analogon of a work of art.

Few Germans meditate on the nature of criticism as such, but there has been an impressive movement for the revival of "hermeneutics," the art of interpretation, in the wake of Dilthey, stimulated by

Heidegger's philosophy. Hans Georg Gadamer's *Truth and Method* (1960) provides the philosophical and historical basis. Peter Szondi has focused these ideas on literary texts, particularly in posthumous lectures (*Einführung in die literarische Hermeneutik*, 1975).

In recent years "the aesthetics and history of reception" propounded by Hans Robert Jauss and Wolfgang Iser has attracted much attention. They have focused on the role of the reader and on the implied reader in the works themselves: the assumed audience, which can be reconstructed with some certainty. They have promoted the history of taste and criticism but, in theory, have not guarded against extreme relativism: the view that any standpoint is as good as any other, that there is an undiscriminated multiplicity of reader's reactions, including the critic's himself. (See Hans Robert Jauss, *Literaturgeschichte als Provokation*, 1970; Wolfgang Iser, *Der implizite Lesser*, 1972).

Russian criticism has great interest because in Russia radically opposed conceptions were formulated most sharply. As late as 1825 Alexander Pushkin could complain that "we have no criticism . . . we have not a single commentary, not a single book of criticism." But this changed soon with the advent of Vissarion Belinsky (1811–48), who dominated Russian criticism for the rest of the century. Belinsky's concept of criticism is expounded in a "Speech on Criticism" (1842) in which he rejects arbitrary pronouncements of taste or judgment by rules and defines "criticizing as seeking and discovering the general laws of reason in particulars." Criticism is philosophical knowledge while art is immediate knowledge. In practice, criticism in nineteenth-century Russia was ideological and social. Apollon Grigoriev seems to be an exception. He advocated an "organic criticism" which is intuitive, immediate. The aim of the critic is to grasp the individuality and tone of an author or of an age, its particular atmosphere or "drift." Grigoriev rejected historical relativism but in practice was, like his radical rivals, mainly concerned with social types. Impressionistic and aesthetic concepts emerge only late in the nineteenth century. A symbolist poet like Alexander Blok, in an article on criticism (1907), complains rather of a lack of philosophy, of a "soil under one's feet." The Russian Formalists on the whole dismissed criticism in favor of a technical science of literature, while Soviet criticism constitutes a return to nineteenth-century demands for ideological clarity, for the "social mandate" of both writer and critic.

Today in Russia and generally behind the Curtain, the Marxist concept of criticism prevails. In its official version it is simply didacticism: criticism serves the inculcation of Communism and writers are judged according to whether they do so or not. This didacticism is combined with sociologism: a study of the society which assumes that the writer is completely determined by his class origins and reflects and should reflect the society he describes. In subtler versions of Marxism, mainly in the writings of the Hungarian György Lukács and his follower Lucien Goldmann in France, this simple version is rejected; rather, the critic's task is to analyze the structure of his society and that of former ages and to interpret and judge authors in their historical place, dividing them into reactionary and progressive without regard, however, to their overt intentions and allegiances. Goldmann draws a distinction between comprehension and explication. Explication is the insertion of a work into the context of a social structure. In the dialectical thinking of Lukács no contradiction is felt between asserting that the relative truth of Marxism is absolutely valid (*Beiträge zur Geschichte der Ästhetik*, Berlin [1954], p. 102) and that the party spirit demanded of the critic is not in contradiction to the other duties of an author: the objective reproduction of reality. In practice, the exact rules for criticism are laid down by solemn deliberations of the party congresses. Marxist criticism has returned to prescriptive criticism, to the imposition of specific themes, views, and even styles imposed by the immense power of the state, the party, and the literary organizations, which enforce the edicts in ways undreamt of even in the days of Richelieu.

Such a survey of the diverse concepts of criticism in history leads to the inevitable conclusion that "criticism" is an "essentially contested concept," that in the last two hundred years the possible positions were formulated and reformulated in different contexts, for different purposes, in different countries, but that the issues are reducible to a strictly limited number. The conflict between objective and subjective standards is basic and overlaps somewhat the debate between absolutism and relativism, which may be historical. Subjectivism may be absolute in its claims. The methods of criticism also divide easily into intuitive and objective. Objective may mean an appeal to absolute standards of beauty or an appeal to the model of science with an implied indifference to criteria of quality. Intuitive (misnamed impressionistic) criticism can be judicial. Judicial criticism is usually absolutist, at least by implication. Scientific criticism can abdicate all judgment but may try to arrive at it by new criteria. All kinds of crossbreedings and compromises between these positions are possible and have been actually formulated. While the dominance of judicial criticism, until the latter part of the eighteenth century, is incontestable, the development of criticism since about 1760 cannot be described in terms of a simple succession of concepts which can be clearly related to social, political, or even literary contexts. There appears to be a tug of war between the main trends—judicial, personal, scientific, historical—a tension which was still continuing unabated in the 1970s.

BIBLIOGRAPHY

There is no extensive history of the concept of criticism. See, however, "The Term and Concept of Literary Criticism" in René Wellek, *Concepts of Criticism* (New Haven, 1963); and most histories of criticism, e.g., George Saintsbury, *A History of Criticism and Literary Taste in Europe*, 3 vols. (Edinburgh and New York, 1900–04); J. W. Atkins, *Literary Criticism in Antiquity*, 2 vols. (London, 1934; reprint New York), and three sequels on English Criticism up to the end of the eighteenth century; René Wellek, *A History of Modern Criticism, 1750–1950*, 4 vols. (New Haven, 1955–65); up to 1900; and Cleanth Brooks and William K. Wimsatt, *Literary Criticism; A Short History* (New York, 1957). There is no large history of French criticism. In German: G. Gudemann, "Kritikos," in Pauly-Wissowa-Kroll, *Real-Encyclopädie der Classischen Altertumswissenschaft* (Stuttgart, 1921), vol. 2, 1912–15; "Kritik," "Kritik, Literaturkritik" (by C. v. Bormann, G. Tonelli, H. Holzhey, F. Schalk, H.-D. Weber) in *Historisches Wörterbuch der Philosophie* (ed. Joachim Ritter and Karlfried Gründer), vol. 4 (Basel, 1976); Bruno Markwardt, *Geschichte der deutschen Poetik*, 5 vols. (Berlin, 1937–67). In Russian: B. P. Gorodetsky, A. Lavretsky, and B. S. Meilash, eds. *Istoriya russkoi kritiki*, 2 vols. (Moscow, 1958). In Italian: Luigi Russo, *La Critica letteraria contemporanea*, 3 vols. (Bari, 1946–47). G. Marzot, "La Critica letteraria dal De Sanctis ad oggi," in *Letteratura italiana: Le Correnti*, vol. 2 (1956). On English criticism: George Watson, *The Literary Critics* (Harmondsworth, 1962). On American criticism: Norman Foerster, *American Criticism* (Boston, 1928); Bernard Smith, *Forces in American Criticism* (New York, 1939); Stanley Edgar Hyman, *The Armed Vision* (New York, 1948); William Van O'Connor, *An Age of Criticism: 1900–1950* (Chicago, 1952); Floyd Stovall, ed., *The Development of American Literary Criticism* (Chapel Hill, 1955); Walter Sutton, *Modern American Criticism* (Englewood Cliffs, N.J., 1963).

SUGGESTIONS FOR FURTHER READING

Almost any instance of critical theory and practice can shed needed light (or contrasting shadow) on the question raised in the title of this book. Yet limitations of space even preclude the complete listing of the nearly two hundred books published by the authors of the present volume. The following references represent the most pertinent items by each of the contributors. Many of the books listed are available in revised and/or paperback editions; the dates in parentheses indicate the year of the original publication.

Beardsley, Monroe C. *Aesthetics: Problems in the Philosophy of Criticism* (1958); *Aesthetics from Classical Greece to the Present: A Short History* (1966); *Literature and Aesthetics* (editor, 1968); *The Possibility of Criticism* (1970).

Booth, Wayne C. *The Rhetoric of Fiction* (1961); *Modern Dogma and the Rhetoric of Assent* (1974); *A Rhetoric of Irony* (1974); *Critical Understanding: The Powers and Limits of Pluralism* (1979).

Ellis, John M. *Schiller's "Kalliasbriefe" and the Study of His Aesthetic Theory* (1969); *Narration in the German Novelle: Theory and Interpretation* (1974); *The Theory of Literary Criticism: A Logical Analysis* (1974); *Heinrich von Kleist: Studies in the Character and Meaning of His Writings* (1979).

Esslin, Martin. *Brecht: A Choice of Evils* (1959); *The Theatre of the Absurd* (1961); *The Peopled Wound: The Plays of Harold Pinter* (1970); *Artaud* (1976).

Fish, Stanley E. *Surprised by Sin: The Reader in Paradise Lost* (1967); *Self-Consuming Artifacts: The Experience of Seventeenth-Century Literature* (1972); *The Living Temple: George Herbert and Catechizing* (1978); *Is There a Text in This Class? Interpretive Communities and The Sources of Authority* (1980).

Hartman, Geoffrey. *The Unmediated Vision: An Interpretation of Wordsworth, Hopkins, Rilke and Valéry* (1954); *Beyond Formalism: Selected Essays* (1970); *The Fate of Reading: Literary Essays 1970–75* (1975); *Criticism in the Wilderness: The Study of Literature Today* (1980).

Hernadi, Paul. *Beyond Genre: New Directions in Literary Classification* (1972); *What Is Literature?* (editor, 1978).

Holland, Norman N. *The Shakespearean Imagination* (1964); *The Dynamics of Literary Response* (1968); *Poems in Persons: An Introduction to the Psychoanalysis of Literature* (1973); *5 Readers Reading* (1975).

Jauss, Hans Robert. *Zeit und Erinnerung in Marcel Proust 'A la re-*

cherche du temps perdu': Ein Beitrag zur Theorie des Romans (1955); *Untersuchungen zur mittelalterlichen Tierdichtung* (1959); *Literaturgeschichte als Provokation* (1970); *Ästhetische Erfahrung und literarische Hermeneutik. Vol. 1: Versuche im Feld der ästhetischen Erfahrung* (1977).

Krieger, Murray. *The Tragic Vision: Variations on a Theme in Literary Interpretation* (1960); *The Classic Vision: The Retreat from Extremity in Modern Literature* (1971); *Theory of Criticism: A Tradition and Its System* (1976); *Poetic Presence and Illusion: Essays in Critical History and Theory* (1979).

Lindenberger, Herbert. *On Wordsworth's 'Prelude'* (1963); *Georg Büchner* (1964); *Historical Drama: The Relation of Literature and Reality* (1975); *Saul's Fall: A Critical Fiction* (1979).

Martin, Wallace. *"The New Age" under Orage: Chapters in English Cultural History* (1967).

McCanles, Michael. *Dialectical Criticism and Renaissance Literature* (1975).

Nelson, Cary. *The Incarnate Word: Literature as Verbal Space* (1973).

Ohmann, Richard. *Shaw: The Style and the Man* (1962); *English in America: A Radical View of the Profession* (1976).

Peckham, Morse. *Beyond the Tragic Vision: The Quest for Identity in the Nineteenth Century* (1962); *Man's Rage for Chaos: Biology, Behavior, and the Arts* (1965); *Art and Pornography: An Experiment in Explanation* (1969); *Explanation and Power: The Control of Human Behavior* (1979).

Pratt, Mary. *Toward a Speech Act Theory of Literary Discourse* (1977); *Linguistics for Students of Literature* (with Elizabeth Closs Traugott, 1980).

Ryan, Marie-Laure. *Rituel et poésie: une lecture de Saint-John Perse* (1977).

Shattuck, Roger. *The Banquet Years* (1958); *Selected Works of Alfred Jarry* (co-editor and translator, 1965); *Marcel Proust* (1974); *The Forbidden Experiment* (1980).

Sparshott, Francis. *The Structure of Aesthetics* (1963); *The Concept of Criticism* (1967).

Stimpson, Catharine R. *Signs: Journal of Women in Culture and Society* (founding editor, 1975–80).

Suleiman, Susan Rubin. *The Reader in the Text: Essays on Audience and Interpretation* (co-editor, 1980).

Valdés, Mario J. *Death in the Literature of Unamuno* (1964); *Interpretation of Narrative* (editor, 1978); *Shadows in the Cave: A Phenomenological Approach to Literary Criticism* (1980).

Wellek, René. *Theory of Literature* (with Austin Warren, 1948); *A History of Modern Criticism*, 4 volumes (1955, 1965); *Concepts of Criticism* (1963); *Discriminations: Further Concepts of Criticism* (1970).

Index

Abrams, Meyer Howard, 84, 85
Achebe, Chinua, 169
Adorno, Theodor W., 121, 122, 123
Althusser, Louis, 68
Apollinaire, Guillaume, 103, 104, 144, 147n
Aristarchos, 298
Aristotle, 57, 106, 201, 224, 244, 297, 298, 300, 309, 313
Arnheim, Rudolph, 104
Arnold, Matthew, 164, 169, 216, 235, 283, 304, 305, 309
Ashby, William Ross, 91, 92
Auerbach, Erich, 223, 318
Austin, John Langshaw, 99

Babbitt, Irving, 311
Bachelard, Gaston, 94
Bacon, Francis, 93
Balzac, Honoré de, 40, 41, 306
Barthelme, Donald, 107
Barthes, Roland, 12, 67, 68, 69, 70, 72, 77, 78, 93, 99, 101, 140, 143, 144, 257, 260, 316
Battestin, Martin C., 168
Baudelaire, Charles, 102, 144, 307, 315
Belinsky, Vissarion Grigorevich, 217, 319
Benjamin, Walter, 122, 123, 318
Bergson, Henri, 311, 315
Bernard, Charles, 306
Blackmur, R. P., 312
Blake, William, 30, 31, 32
Bleich, David, 78
Blok, Alexander, 319
Bloom, Harold, 263, 313
Boas, Charles, 312
Booth, Wayne C., 78, 184, 224
Bouhours, Dominique, 299
Bradbury, Malcolm, 29
Bradley, A. C., 249
Bremond, Henri, 68, 69
Brontë, Charlotte, 236, 237
Brooks, Cleanth, 120, 311
Browning, Elizabeth Barrett, 55
Browning, Robert, 41
Brunetière, Ferdinand, 306, 307
Bultmann, Rudolph Karl, 136
Burke, Kenneth, 114, 244, 312

Campbell, Joseph, 60
Campistron, Jean Galbert de, 306
Capote, Truman, 54
Carlyle, Thomas, 303
Carr, Edward Hallett, 15
Casey, John, 310
Céline, Louis Ferdinand, 169
Cervantes de Saavedra, Miguel de, 97, 108
Chapelain, Jean, 299
Chateaubriand, François-René de, 304
Chaucer, Geoffrey, 88
Chladenius, Johann Martin, 136
Choudhury, Serajul Islam, 168
Cohen, Philip K., 168
Coleridge, Samuel Taylor, 57, 59, 60, 61, 117, 164, 225, 244, 301, 302
Conrad, Joseph, 168, 169
Crane, Ronald Salmon, 162, 312
Croce, Benedetto, 311, 316, 317
Culler, Jonathan, 33, 71, 79, 257
Cummings, E.E., 107
Curtius, Ernst Robert, 318

Dante, Alighieri, 317
De Man, Paul, 69, 89, 90, 255

Derrida, Jacques, xiii, 12, 68, 69, 70, 219, 220, 225, 271, 272, 276, 314, 317
DeSanctis, Francesco, 305
Dickens, Charles, 42, 44, 168
Dickinson, Emily, 108, 110
Diderot, Denis, 100
Didion, Joan, 172
Dilthey, Wilhelm, 79, 115, 305, 318
Dostoevsky, Fyodor, 100
Dryden, John, 218, 297
Du Bos, Charles, 315
Dussault, Jean Joseph François, 304

Eco, Umberto, 271
Eichenbaum, Boris, 76
Einstein, Albert, 269, 275, 276
Eliot, T. S., 115, 216, 218, 259, 308, 309, 311
Emerson, Ralph Waldo, 303
Erasmus, Desiderius, 298
Erikson, Erik, 250
Euripides, 106, 293
Even-Zohar, Itaman, 75

Fast, Howard, 178
Faulkner, William, 154, 156, 157, 158, 160
Fernández, Ramón, 314, 315
Fichte, Johann Gottlieb, 301
Fiedler, Leslie, 260
Fielding, Henry, 168, 169
Fioretti, Benedetto, 299
Fish, Stanley Eugene, 78, 117, 244
Fisher, Philip, 184, 185, 188
Flaubert, Gustave, 56, 100, 107
Foerster, Norman, 311
Fontenelle, Bernard Le Bovier de, 299
Foucault, Michel, 68, 69, 74
France, Anatole, 301, 306, 316
Frechtman, Bernard, 198
French, Marilyn, 172
Freud, Sigmund, 59, 102, 121, 246, 250, 317
Frye, Northrop, 12, 88, 101, 244, 313
Fubini, Mario, 317
Fuller, Margaret, 303

Gadamer, Hans-Georg, xii, 118, 121, 137, 139, 319
Galan, F. W., 75
Gardner, John, 168, 169, 170, 310
Genet, Jean, 315
Genette, Gérard, 68, 69, 73
Geoffroy, Julien-Louis, 303
George, Stefan, 222, 318
Gobineau, Joseph Arthur, comte de, 190
Goethe, Johann Wolfgang von, 100, 129, 225, 300, 306, 318
Goldmann, Lucien, 320
Gracián, Baltasar, 298
Graff, Gerald, 26, 314
Gramsci, Antonio, 192
Gray, Thomas, 242, 243
Greimas, A. Julien, 68, 69, 73, 257
Grigoriev, Apollon, 319

Hardy, Barbara, 168
Hardy, Thomas, 168
Hartman, Geoffrey H., 77, 84, 184
Hartshorne, Charles, 154
Hassan, Ihab, 314
Hawthorne, Nathaniel B., 231
Hazlitt, William, 302, 303
Hegel, Georg Wilhelm Friedrich, 121, 220, 223, 298, 301, 306
Heidegger, Martin, 70, 121, 220, 225, 317, 318, 319
Heinsius, Daniel, 299
Hellingrath, Norbert von, 222
Hennequin, Émile, 306
Herder, Johann Gottfried, 300, 301, 303, 305
Heyl, Bernard, 312
Hirsch, David Harry, 26
Hirsch, Eric Donald, 12, 31, 77, 116, 117, 118, 314
Hobsbaum, Philip, 310
Hofmannsthal, Hugo von, 115, 318
Hölderlin, Friedrich, 222
Holland, Norman Norwood, 116, 117
Hollander, John, 104
Holthusen, Hans Egon, 318
Homer, 6, 134, 293, 299
Horace, 204
Hough, Graham, 310
Howe, Irving, 154, 155, 157
Hugo, Victor, 304, 306
Hume, David, 154
Husserl, Edmund, 70, 139

Hyman, Stanley Edgar, 321
Hyman, Virginia R., 168

Ingarden, Roman, 10, 12
Iser, Wolfgang, 118, 140, 141, 319

Jacobi, Friedrich Heinrich, 298
Jakobson, Roman, 55, 99
James, Henry, 308
Jameson, Fredric, 73, 74
Jarrell, Randall, 313
Jauss, Hans Robert, 118, 319
Johnson, Samuel, 164, 243, 244, 249, 300
Joyce, James, 100, 107
Jung, Carl Gustav, 269

Kames, Henry Home, Lord, 299
Kant, Immanuel, 117, 122, 225, 298, 301
Kaye, Mary Margaret, 178
Keats, John, 117, 281
Kenner, Hugh, 255
Kermode, Frank, 220, 221
Kerr, Alfred, 318
Khlebnikov, Velemir, 217
Kierkegaard, Søren, 120, 121, 123
Krantz, Judith, 178
Krieger, Murray, 89, 90, 92, 314
Kristeva, Julia, 68

La Bruyère, Jean de, 299
Lacan, Jacques, 102, 270
Langbaum, Robert, 83
Langer, Susanne K., 108, 109
Laurencin, Marie, 104
Lawrence, David Herbert, 260, 310
Leavis, F. R., 191, 309, 310
Leibniz, Gottfried Wilhelm, 300
Lemaître, Jules, 307
Lenneberg, Eric, 107
Lerner, Laurence, 107
Lévi-Strauss, Claude, 68, 69, 77, 79, 84, 99, 102
Levin, Harry, 312
Lewis, David, 57, 58
Lewis, R. W. B., 313
Lichtenstein, Heinz, 247
Locke, Richard, 26
Longinus, 298
Lotman, Jurij, 271
Lukács, György, 170, 223, 320

Macaulay, Thomas Babington, 303
McLuhan, Marshall, 104
Mallarmé, Stephane, 115
Manzoni, Alessandro, 300
Marx, Karl, 101, 121, 285
Matthews, R. J., 56, 59
Matthiessen, F. O., 312
Maurras, Charles, 314
Mayakovsky, Vladimir, 217
Melville, Herman, 154
Mencken, H. L., 311
Mendeleev, Dmitry Ivanovich, 100
Michener, James, 178
Miller, Henry, 170
Miller, J. Hillis, 85, 91
Molière (Jean-Baptiste Poquelin), 307
Montaigne, Michel de, 285
More, Paul Elmer, 311
Morris, Wright, 172
Müller, Adam, 302
Murdoch, Iris, 115
M'Uzan, Michel de, 244

Newton, Isaac, 275, 276
Nietzsche, Friedrich, 70, 86, 220, 285, 317
Nisard, Désiré, 303

Ong, Walter J., 104
Ortega y Gasset, José, 121
Orwell, George, 59
Osborne, Harold, 310
Ozick, Cynthia, 172

Pascal, Blaise, 285, 306
Pater, Walter, 255, 260, 308
Phillips, Jayne Anne, 172
Piaget, Jean, 104
Picard, Raymond, 316
Picasso, Pablo, 216, 217
Plato, 8, 122, 220, 293
Poe, Edgar Allan, 143, 303
Polanyi, Michael, 114
Poliziano, Angelo, 298
Pope, Alexander, 298, 299
Popper, Karl, 94
Poulet, Georges, 259, 284, 316

Proust, Marcel, 41, 100, 107, 223, 315
Pushkin, Alexander, 319

Quintilian, 298

Racine, Jean, 129, 306, 316
Raine, Kathleen, 30, 31
Ransom, John Crowe, 311
Read, Herbert, 310
Richard, Jean-Pierre, 316
Richards, I. A., 98, 114, 115, 121, 202, 226, 309, 310
Richelieu, Louis François Armand du Plessis, duc de, 320
Ricoeur, Paul, 77, 79, 121
Riffaterre, Michael, 140, 141
Righter, William, 310
Rilke, Rainer Maria, 119, 243
Rimbaud, Arthur, 115
Rivière, Jacques, 315
Rochefort, Christiane, 238
Rousseau, Jean-Jacques, 190, 219, 285
Rousset, Jean, 316
Rymer, Thomas, 298

Said, Edward W., 285
Sainte-Beuve, Charles Augustin, 304, 308, 315
Sardou, Victorien, 202
Sartre, Jean-Paul, 121, 189, 190, 315
Saussure, Ferdinand de, 68, 72, 73, 76, 78, 100, 101, 105, 115, 118
Scaliger, Joseph Justus, 299
Scaliger, Julius Caesar, 299
Schelling, Friedrich Wilhelm Joseph, 298, 301
Schiller, Friedrich, 301
Schlegel, August Wilhelm, 301, 302, 303, 316
Schlegel, Friedrich, 121, 298, 301, 302, 303, 316
Scholes, Robert, 71, 314
Schutz, Alfred, 140
Schwartz, Murray M., 245, 246
Scribe, Augustin Eugène, 202
Searle, John R., 99
Shakespeare, William, 34, 44, 114, 117, 129, 169, 172, 202, 207, 218, 220, 247, 248, 249, 299, 300, 303, 306
Shapiro, Karl, 313
Shelley, Percy Bysshe, 218
Shklovsky, Viktor, 75, 216, 217, 218, 219, 225
Shoppe, Karl, 298
Shumaker, Wayne, 312
Smith, Bernard, 321
Socrates, 107, 120, 234, 293
Sollers, Philippe, 220
Sontag, Susan, 135, 313
Sparrow, John, 40
Sparshott, Francis E., 153, 310
Spatz, Jonas, 57, 60, 62
Spillane, Frank Morris (Mickey), 169
Spingarn, Joel E., 311
Spitzer, Leo, 135
Staiger, Emil, 318
Starobinski, Jean, 83, 146
Stein, Gertrude, 107
Steiner, George, 129
Stendhal (Henri Beyle), 210
Sterne, Laurence, 217
Suetonius, 226
Swift, Jonathan, 100
Swinburne, Algernon Charles, 41
Symonds, John Addington, 307
Szondi, Peter, 136, 319

Taine, Hippolyte Adolphe, 100, 305, 306
Tate, Allen, 311
Tennyson, Alfred, 49, 218
Thibaudet, Albert, 315
Todorov, Tzvetan, 68, 69, 70, 78
Tolstoy, Leo, 107
Toporov, Vladimir Nikolaevich, 226
Trevanian, 178
Trilling, Lionel, 312
Tynjanov, Yuri Nikolaevich, 224

Valéry, Paul, 114, 115, 316
Vico, Giambattista, 115
Virgil, 129
Vossius, Gerhard Johann, 299

Warren, Robert Penn, 218, 219, 220
Watson, George, 310
Wellek, René, 6, 16, 259
White, Hayden, 85, 257
Whitman, Walt, 107
Wiener, Philip P., 297

Wilde, Oscar, 98, 102, 168, 260, 308, 316, 318
Williams, Raymond, 170, 186, 187, 190, 196
Williams, William Carlos, 260
Wilson, Edmund, 96, 172
Wimsatt, William Kurtz, 311
Winnicott, D. W., 245
Winters, Yvor, 191, 224, 259, 311
Wittgenstein, Ludwig, 163, 310, 311
Woolf, Virginia, 223, 231
Wordsworth, William, 222, 223
Wright, Austin McGiffert, 172

Yeats, William Butler, 115, 120

Zeno, 249